"Finally—a book that can serve as a blueprint for anyone trying to get the most from everyone in their organization. Les McKeown's fresh perspective on the persistent problem of bringing together people with different work styles is a must-read for anyone who works with groups or teams."

—JJ Ramberg, host of MSNBC's *Your Business*
and CEO of Goodsearch.com

"*The Synergist* is a brilliant look at people and styles and how to synthesize them for huge personal and company success. Les McKeown's books and teachings show businesses how to get past those natural hindrances and, instead, thrive. In this book, he's done it again!!"

—Bob Burg, coauthor of *The Go-Giver* and
It's Not About You

"Some business books take a few chapters to get into, while others never quite deliver. Not so with *The Synergist*. Les McKeown's astute observations leap off the page from the get-go. Throughout the book I laughed, I nodded, I cringed—and I couldn't wait to turn to the next page.

I've seen the personality types Les chronicles do unintentional damage within myriad companies, all too often with no one even understanding what's going on. This book presents a necessary exposition of what happens in the real world of business, and I'm going to use its ideas to make my company perform at a much higher level."

—Steve McKee, president of McKee Wallwork Cleveland
and author of *When Growth Stalls*

"Les has done it again; a brilliantly written, insightful guide both to identifying your leadership style and learning how to keep team members working toward a common goal. Whether you have a one-person or a 1,000-person organization, you will want every employee to read this book and learn how to become a 'Synergist.'"

—Carol Roth, business strategist and *New York Times*
bestselling author of *The Entrepreneur Equation*

"This book is a must-read for anyone on a team, leading a team, or aspiring to do so. In his usual witty and refreshingly candid style, Les provides laser-focused clarity around why teams fail and offers simple yet powerful tools that will turn any group of individuals into high-performing teams. Reading this book will give you the skills to engage in rich dialogue, build meaningful relationships, and contribute to a specific goal all while playing to your strengths. The days of hiding out in your office are over!"

—Halley Bock, president and CEO of Fierce, Inc.

"The challenge for members of groups of people, such as in a work department, is to create alignment and to function as a team instead of going in separate directions. Les McKeown offers a practical explanation of the reasons for the failure of teams, even well-intentioned ones, and what they can do to elevate their game. He offers a practical model to engage the strengths of each team member in activities that enable them to work together more effectively and efficiently. Whether your group is newly formed or unhappily struggling, *The Synergist* is a blueprint for personal and team success."

—Andrew Marshall, founder and principal of
Primed Associates, LLC

"We all know an ineffective team when we see one, but it's often hard to figure out why the team is ineffective. *The Synergist* shows us that it's the particular way the people in the groups work—and then shows us the one role within a team that brings it all together. If you're serious about harnessing the power of your team, this is a must-read."

—Charlie Gilkey, founder and CEO of Productive Flourishing

"*Finally!* We all know that most teams and groups are excruciatingly ineffective at best, mainly because no one knows what to do to make group dynamics actually work. With *The Synergist* in hand, gone are the days of teams and groups plagued by frustration, mistrust, and uncertainty. Les McKeown lays out one very simple and incredibly powerful way to take the reins of any group and lead them out of the typical group quagmire and into unprecedented success. A must-read for anyone who leads a group of any kind!"

—Sarah Robinson, leader of the hooligan tribe,
www.escaping-mediocrity.com

"Reading Les McKeown's work is like having an honest conversation with your own private guide to dysfunctional organizations and how to fix them.... *The Synergist* is a deeply insightful take on what needs to happen in teams for them to realize their potential. Armed with the suggestions in the book, you will be ready to follow, ready to lead, and ready to galvanize others."

—**Rita Gunther McGrath, associate professor**
at Columbia Business School and author of
Discovery-Driven Growth

PRAISE FOR *PREDICTABLE SUCCESS*

"He's got it right. Les McKeown has uncovered the core dynamics of organizational growth, and mapped it to the best (and worst!) practices to achieve and maintain optimal, in-your-zone conditions—no matter where a group is in its evolution. This is real-world expertise, with simple but subtle and sophisticated prescriptions for all of us involved in getting things done with other people. And, oh yeah, he nailed how to address some key opportunities in my own company... should be required reading for every management team."

—**David Allen, bestselling author of**
Getting Things Done* and *Making It All Work

"Les McKeown is absolutely on top of his game. Les not only knows—and shows—how your businesses can grow and succeed, he explains it in a way that is intuitive, entertaining, and immediately actionable."

—**Darryl Hutson, CEO of American Express Incentive Services**

"Les McKeown has for over seven years assisted us in the growth and development of our distributorship network. He has an understanding of what makes a business succeed—and a passionate commitment to teaching others how to achieve it. *Predictable Success* has been our secret weapon and can be yours, too."

—**Mel Haught, CEO of Pella Corporation**

THE SYNERGIST

THE SYNERGIST

How to Lead Your Team
to Predictable Success

LES McKEOWN

palgrave
macmillan

THE SYNERGIST
Copyright © Les McKeown, 2012.

All rights reserved.

First published in 2012 by
PALGRAVE MACMILLAN®
in the United States—a division of St. Martin's Press LLC,
175 Fifth Avenue, New York, NY 10010.

Where this book is distributed in the UK, Europe, and the rest of the world,
this is by Palgrave Macmillan, a division of Macmillan Publishers Limited,
registered in England, company number 785998, of Houndmills,
Basingstoke, Hampshire RG21 6XS.

Palgrave Macmillan is the global academic imprint of the above companies
and has companies and representatives throughout the world.

Palgrave® and Macmillan® are registered trademarks in the United States, the
United Kingdom, Europe, and other countries.

ISBN: 978–0–230–12055–6

Library of Congress Cataloging-in-Publication Data

McKeown, Les (John Leslie), 1956–
    The synergist : how to lead your team to predictable success / by
    Les McKeown.
        p. cm.
    ISBN 978–0–230–12055–6 (hardcover)
    1. Teams in the workplace. 2. Leadership. I. Title.

HD66.M3947 2012
658.4′092—dc23   2011030804

A catalogue record of the book is available from the British Library.

Design by Newgen Imaging Systems (P) Ltd., Chennai, India

First edition: January 2012

10 9 8 7 6 5 4 3 2 1

Printed in the United States of America.

To Rebekah, David, and Hannah—my very own V, O, and P—and to LBJ, who arrived during the writing of this book, and who is proof that Synergists come in all sizes.

CONTENTS

PART III   Becoming a Leader of Leaders

FOREWORD
Why You Should Read This Book

IN THIS BOOK I SHOW HOW any individual (that's you) can lead any group of people to achieve success—whether or not you're the formal leader of that group.

You'll learn to do this by performing a key role, usually unseen and unrecognized, that exists in every successful group, a role that I've come to call the Synergist.

As you will discover, being the Synergist in any group is a natural, uncomplicated process. It doesn't require you to unlearn anything, or to become someone you are not. There are no lengthy rules to memorize, no complicated exercises to master, and nothing artificial to engage in. Because of this, the learning curve to becoming an effective Synergist is minimal, and most people can grasp the underlying principles and begin applying them immediately.

The secret to being an effective Synergist is simplicity itself: it lies in recognizing a small number of key interactions that every team or group experiences, and in making unobtrusive but essential interventions at those pivotal moments on your group's path to success. This book will teach you what those key interactions are, how to recognize them, and when and how to intervene appropriately.

If you work regularly with a team or group, you will discover that you have almost certainly been subconsciously practicing many of the principles of the Synergist already. For you, this book will pull those subconscious insights together into a simple but comprehensive methodology, and will equip you with a powerful toolkit to consciously guide your team, group, or organization to success—faster and with less stress—by using a structured, accelerated process.

The fundamentals of the Synergist are universal: they apply to any group of two or more people who are trying to achieve common goals. While for the sake of clarity I have chosen to write in the primary context of business, the principles of the Synergist will work for any group, in any situation. So whether you lead or are part of a Fortune 100 company, a division or department, a project team, a not-for-profit, a government agency, a nongovernmental organization, a charity, a soccer league, a church committee, or a family—in short, any group of people who are trying to achieve something together—then *The Synergist* is for you, and you will benefit from reading this book.

Note: The case histories found in this book are composites created from the hundreds of businesses and people I've worked with and learned from over the years. Any resemblance to a particular living or deceased individual or specific business situation is unintended and is purely coincidental.

INTRODUCTION

WHAT A SYNERGIST IS AND WHY YOU SHOULD CARE

IF YOU'RE INVOLVED WITH ANY GROUP OF PEOPLE who are trying to achieve common goals, whether by leading a Fortune 500 company or volunteering part-time at a kid's soccer league, you soon become acutely aware that those goals will be achieved *only through the work of the people in the group.*

Put simply, organizations don't succeed in and of themselves. They succeed only through *individuals* working in groups and teams.

Groups and teams lie at the heart of every successful enterprise—in fact, they *are* the heart of a successful enterprise. Walk the halls of any organization, large or small, and you'll see huddles of two or more people everywhere, interacting formally and informally, face to face and virtually, meeting in conference rooms and hallways, communicating by email, phone, web conference, social media, and text messages, even occasionally by pen and paper.

In the best—and most successful—organizations, it's these interactions among individuals that together form a vital bridge between the organization's overarching vision and the day-to-day actions required to realize that vision. From these multifaceted human interactions spring the ideas, decisions, plans, strategies, and tactics necessary to move the organization forward to success.

In the worst—and least successful—organizations, these same interactions between individuals produce stress, indecision, confusion, uncertainty, and distrust, frustrate the organization's goal of realizing its vision, and drain the enthusiasm, commitment, and direction of everyone involved.

For many organizations, perhaps even the one you work with, each day brings a mix of each. Some interactions gel and produce a profitable, positive result, while others gridlock or stall, producing little or nothing of actionable value.

Yet for every organization, the difference between the two is by far the single most important factor in determining whether the enterprise succeeds or fails. If you can ensure that when your people interact they are effective and deliver the goods, you win. Watch them stutter or fail in those same interactions, you lose.

PASS ME A PAPER CLIP

This simple fact—that the quality of people interaction is a fundamental requirement for organizational success—seems self-evident. Yet every day in organizations large and small, untold thousands—quite probably millions—of group interactions take place, most of which fail to take the organization any closer to its goals. In many cases groups meet, interact, then part, no closer to achieving their objectives than when they started.

This tide of unproductive and ineffective group interactions has a massive cost: it drains the global economy of billions of dollars a year, strangles creativity and initiative, and results in many businesses, divisions, departments, projects, groups, and teams stalling out long before they've even begun to realize their full potential.

On an individual level, the cost of group dysfunction is just as high: it generates inordinate levels of stress, demoralizes entire workforces, and demotivates otherwise high-performing people who would rather take a paper clip, straighten it out, and stab it in their eye than sit through another interminable, ineffectual meeting.

And it's not only formal meetings that are caught in this seeping maw of interpersonal dysfunction. Every type of interaction—one-on-one discussions, phone calls, emails, water-cooler chats, performance reviews, brainstorming sessions, even the annual picnic—can become blighted by misperceptions, misunderstandings, and outright manipulation.

Most frustratingly of all for CEOs, senior vice presidents, leaders, managers, and millions of individuals working in organizations around the globe, all of this—the expense, the personal pain, the lack of progress—repeats over and over again, every single day.

BREAKING THE CYCLE

Not surprisingly this frustrating, repeating cycle of dysfunction has produced an avalanche of resources purportedly designed to help groups and teams be more effective. Books, workshops, conferences, assessments, quizzes, coaching—you name it, there's a tool of some sort designed to make group interactions work harmoniously and effectively.

Here's a news flash: they almost never work. You'll know this if you've ever been part of a group which has worked through a "team-improvement" process. The pattern is predictable. A group or team isn't firing on all cylinders, so everyone gets packed off to a workshop or conference, or is given a book and study guide and told to work through it together. Some do so excitedly and with engagement while others comply grimly and in silent (or not-so-silent) protest. The process can be painful and disruptive. The result? After everyone completes the program, the team enjoys a short period of brittle improvement before everyone reverts to their previous positions and attitudes.

The reason why most group- and team-improvement programs fail to produce permanent long-term change is simple: it's because they address the *symptoms* of group dysfunction (distrust, poor communication, fear of change, to name just a few) rather than the root cause. In fact, in many cases symptoms are incorrectly labeled as root causes. Take distrust as an example, a factor that many team-improvement programs concentrate on. Distrust doesn't appear out of nowhere; it always has a root cause. There's always a reason (valid or not) why one team member distrusts another. Trying to eliminate distrust without dealing with the underlying root cause of that distrust is like filling up your gas tank when the car's tires are punctured—it might be worth doing, but it isn't going to fix your problem.

MAKING AN END RUN AROUND THE SYMPTOMS

As I'll show in this book, the basic difference between an ineffective group interaction and a highly productive one lies in the existence of a single component—a natural, uncomplicated, and easily introduced component at that—the role of the Synergist.

Introducing the Synergist role to your people interactions can produce a dramatic, profound, and lasting effect precisely because it blows past the lengthy and complex list of all possible symptoms of team and group dysfunction, and instead concentrates on just one thing: the single root cause of team and group dysfunction.

I'll show you clearly what that single root cause is, how and why the role of the Synergist fixes this debilitating dysfunction, and how to incorporate the Synergist role as an integral part of every interaction you're involved in.

THE STRUCTURE OF THIS BOOK

I've set out the path to Synergist-driven success for any group or team in three parts:

Part I describes the three natural styles that occur in every group or team, and shows how, if left alone, those three styles lead to unavoidable gridlock.

Part II describes the fourth, all-important Synergist style, shows how every effective group subconsciously develops its own Synergistic mindset, and explains how doing so unblocks the group's path to success.

Part III provides a simple, easy-to-learn, yet highly effective process that you can use to ensure that every group or team you manage or work with adopts this model right from the start, thus avoiding gridlock and accelerating your path to success.

Put another way, in Part I you'll see the root cause as to why most groups and teams are ineffective and fail to produce their best results; Part II will show you how highly effective groups and teams subconsciously and intuitively address that root cause; and Part III will give you the tools and techniques to do so consciously and in an accelerated and structured way.

Addendum: *Recently it has become common to encourage readers of business books to dip into the text wherever they fancy, to cherry-pick those parts that take their interest and leave the others. This is not such a book. You will be rewarded by reading sequentially through the three sections in turn.*

Part I

THE UNSTABLE TRIANGLE

1

OVERVIEW

The Failure Gene That's Baked into the DNA of Every Group and How to Escape It

"HE'S OFF AGAIN."

I glanced up from the multitabbed workbook I'd just been handed and looked across to the doorway. It was true—he *was* off again. He was Andy, the wiry, late-thirties founder-owner of the components manufacturer whose offices I was sitting in. And by "off" my co-observer meant "off to anywhere that isn't here."

We'd been working in this windowless room for just over ninety minutes, the start of what was intended to be a two-day strategic planning session, and we'd already lost Andy three times. Well, twice, in the wandering-out-of-the-room sense. The other time was when he'd simply failed to turn up at 8 A.M. when the meeting was supposed to start—a meeting *he* had planned, convened, and insisted everyone else clear their schedules to attend.

While his high-powered team of C-level executives cooled their heels, Andy had wandered in at 8:10 talking casually on his cell phone, finished up the call in his own good time, and eventually called the meeting to order a full twenty minutes late.

Late or not, the meeting had begun well enough. Andy delivered a superb off-the-cuff tour d'horizon, recapping the company's recent history (its precipitous 5-year growth, 3-year stagnation, and now, this year, a return to growth, if modest), summarized the business's strengths (brand awareness, perceived quality, superb management talent) and weaknesses (spotty distribution, no middle-market product), and finished with a genuinely inspiring call for openness, creativity, and full engagement during the next two days.

At that point Andy handed off to the company's CFO, Joanne, for a review of the current year's financial performance. Seven minutes into her presentation, as Joanne was explaining why inventories had risen in the first quarter, Andy stood, stretched, and quietly moved to stand by the side wall of the room. Two minutes later, he'd slipped wordlessly through the door into the corridor outside, off to do who knows what.

I watched as Joanne continued with her presentation despite Andy's absence, but it was clear that she was doing so with less energy and less enthusiasm than before. The degree of engagement by everyone else in the room had slipped as well. Ten minutes later, her presentation finished, Joanne simply ground to a halt. I was surprised that no one had any questions for her; instead, with a barely subdued sense of frustration, the rest of the executive team took restroom breaks and checked email as we all simply waited for Andy to return and for the meeting to restart.

OOPS, HE DID IT AGAIN

When he did return 15 minutes later, Andy did so with no explanation or apology, just his usual firm but affable demeanor. Sitting back down at the head of the table, he simply picked up his copy of the agenda for the day and, with a "Right then, what's next?" moved on to the next item.

For the hour since then Andy had stayed (mostly) focused on the matters at hand, albeit on his own terms. High-level, 30,000-feet topics got his attention, as did anything "big"—new ideas, innovative approaches, creative thinking. But when the discussion moved into detail, it was clear that Andy had a strictly limited tolerance for minutiae, and it usually wasn't long before he shut that part of the discussion down, often to the obvious dismay of the person most responsible for the matter at hand.

Now, however, there was no avoiding detail. This part of the session involved us critiquing each department's 12-month operating plan: seven reporting departments, each with a 15- to 20-page document and supporting spreadsheets. Plans that everyone around the room had spent massive amounts of time and energy putting together. Plans they depended on for success in the year ahead. Plans that they very much wanted to discuss—in detail. This time, Andy hadn't lasted even five minutes before slipping out of the room.

I looked slowly at the other 11 people seated around the large conference table. We were supposed to be working in teams of three, each group examining a different color-coded section of the workbook we'd all been handed, but most of the participants had disengaged in frustration at Andy's latest absence. They talked desultorily about last night's game, scrolled through emails on their cell phones, some worked through paperwork they had brought with them to the session. It was as if the energy of the group, their sense of focus, even the very purpose of the session itself had departed the room with Andy.

I looked over at Joanne, who, with Andy, I'd known since they'd started the business almost a decade previously. She had a wry grimace on her face. "This isn't funny anymore," she said. "It used to be amusing, watching Andy squirm when we try to get the detailed stuff done, but now…"—she looked around the room and dropped her voice a little—"now we have a business to run. A big business. And we have top-class folks here who just aren't going to put up with this."

"I know," I said. "I can see you're at a breaking point here." I looked around one more time. All that talent around the table, all that preparatory work. All that frustration. I could see why Joanne was deeply worried. I looked at her reassuringly. "You have a true visionary in Andy. Remember that tiny workshop where you both started out? Back there, back then, being a visionary worked…you wouldn't, and couldn't, have made it without him. We just need to help Andy understand how a visionary works." I spread my arms, taking in the whole of the room, "here, and now."

INTRODUCING THE VISIONARY

The Visionary is one of three natural "styles" or roles that all of us default to when we are in a group or team situation (we'll meet the other two, the Processor and the Operator, shortly).

Andy may be an extreme case, but most Visionaries possess similar traits. Big-thinkers turned on by ideas, they're easily bored with minutiae and are consumed instead by the need to create and to achieve. Visionaries are often charismatic, engaging communicators, able to motivate people to bring their best to every endeavor. They inspire deep loyalty in others, and frequently a small tight team or posse will develop around them, a group of committed individuals who share the Visionary's ... well ... vision, and want to help realize it.

If you're not a Visionary yourself, you certainly know a few and meet them at work. They're the folks who are always having more bright ideas than they can implement, the glass-half-full types who believe there's always a way through every problem. You can always recognize a Visionary through a few behavioral traits:

They abhor routine. A Visionary will do anything to avoid having to clock in and out at the same time, in the same place, to do the same things every day. They find ways to make every day different, and much prefer improvising solutions to problems on the spot, rather than getting locked into lengthy diagnostic and problem-solving processes.

They adore discussion and debate. Visionaries love to talk. In fact, it's how they think. Rather than mull an issue at length and come up with a measured response, a Visionary is much more likely to find someone to debate it with, and to use that discussion to work out an opinion on the fly. And as we'll see in a later chapter, the way in which they engage in that discussion can often leave the other person confused and frustrated.

They're comfortable with ambiguity. Unique to all three of the natural styles, the Visionaries are not only comfortable with ambiguity, they relish it. Along with uncertainty, the Visionary finds ambiguity a great place to linger while working out a problem or issue. Capable of carrying at least two, if not three or four competing views on the exact same issue, Visionaries will often not settle on a final resolution, or firm up their opinion, until they absolutely have to—not because they're fearful or indecisive (they are resolutely neither of those things)—but simply because they feel no pressure to do so.

They like risk. At the extreme, Visionaries can be risk junkies, actively and persistently seeking ways to push to the very edge of the envelope whenever possible. At a minimum, a Visionary will always be inclined to take a risk rather than avoid it.

They trust their own judgment—and use it often. Most Visionaries have a high degree of self-confidence in their own intuition and judgment, and draw on both a lot when making decisions. Although they will often listen to others and seek counsel and advice, in the end, their final decisions on most matters will be highly visceral and guided by their own instincts.

They aren't wedded to past decisions. Visionaries can—and do—change direction easily and frequently. Pulled by the need to create and build for the future, a Visionary refuses to be trapped by the past. They will only rarely allow past decisions to constrain their future options, even where there's a large sunk cost in those decisions.

As we'll see, Visionaries are an essential element in any high-performing group or team, but they can be immensely disruptive if not managed correctly—and, of course, Visionaries dislike being managed. In later chapters we'll see how they are best integrated into any group or team, and how to make the most of their undoubted skills without disrupting the group as a whole.

RIYA HITS A WALL

Three weeks later, as I stepped out of a cab in midtown Manhattan, I was still pondering our problem with Andy. He was the epitome of what I had come to call a Visionary—with a big V—someone so defined by that aspect of their personality that it adversely affects their interactions with everyone else.

Coincidentally, I'd been summoned to the sleek, 37-story office block now looming high above me by another Visionary: Riya, the CMO (chief marketing officer) at a global media company. Riya possessed the same Visionary traits as Andy: love of the big picture, frustration with detail, an ability to motivate and inspire, and an almost inextinguishable need to create, to make a difference in the world.

Although Riya had chosen a career in marketing precisely because it gave her the opportunity to utilize her Visionary talents on a daily basis, because of the constraints of her job (not being a company owner, she didn't have the close-to-absolute freedom Andy had), she learned intuitively over the years how to control the less-helpful extremes of her Visionary characteristics. As a result she'd quickly risen to the CMO position, a job she adored, one where she got to come in every day and inspire her team to think big, to be creative, and to design innovative, even risk-taking ways to expand her company's already ubiquitous brand.

Now, Riya had hit a problem that neither her prodigious work ethic, intellect, or considerable charm had managed to overcome. Two years earlier, in a considerable expansion of her role, she'd been given the additional responsibility of managing the small but politically powerful investor relations (IR) department at her company. At first, this was something she had enthusiastically embraced, and the transition of the 9-person IR unit into her marketing division was accomplished pretty much seamlessly.

After just a few months, however, things had begun to sour in her relationship with the head of the IR team—a clash of personalities, Riya had explained to me, which had led, regrettably, to his leaving. Riya had personally supervised the search for a replacement, and brought in a bright, successful up-and-comer who was creating quite a stir in the industry. To her utter astonishment, after just six months the new guy, citing buyer's remorse, handed in his resignation and returned to his old job.

For Riya, this was both a personal and a professional blow. She'd never before had two people quit on her from the same position, and with the investor relations team occupying such a prominent position in her firm's internal radar, she was attracting the wrong sort of attention from her colleagues in senior management. This time, she delegated most of her other priorities for the three months it took to find a replacement, hired a prominent search firm to advise her (for a six-figure fee), and felt relieved when she landed Brianna, a top-notch player from a competing firm. Riya had known Brianna for years, liked her a lot, and knew how highly she was regarded, not just in her own company, but throughout the entire industry.

THE THIRD SHOE DROPS

Relieved, that is, until one morning two weeks ago—eight months after Brianna's appointment—when, as she told me on the phone later the same day, she was forced to admit something about which she knew she'd been in denial: Brianna wasn't working out either. Their relationship had become frayed, even icy, and Riya confessed that she'd got to the point where she recoiled at the thought of interacting with Brianna—which, of course, their jobs required them to do.

As I traveled up in the elevator to Riya's department on the fourteenth floor, I recalled the strain in her voice when we had spoken, a combination of tiredness and apprehension: "Les, I don't have the luxury of this not working," she'd said. "Three people in the same key post in less than two years? It's barely acceptable in itself. But four? That would kill me." From the long pause that followed, I knew she wasn't just referring to her career prospects; it would be a shattering blow to her ego, her self-confidence, her self-belief. "I need a fresh pair of eyes on this. I need you to help me understand what's happening here."

And so here I was, standing at the reception area leading to Brianna's office. I'd told Riya that I wanted to meet with Brianna first, to come to my own conclusions about her without prejudice, without hearing Riya's side before-hand. Brianna and I had agreed to meet at 11 A.M., and as it was now four min-utes to the hour, her assistant asked me to take a seat.

Precisely at 11 Brianna appeared at her office door and beckoned me in, guiding me to a small circular table with three seats arranged neatly around it. I noticed immediately that the office was spotless—not a thing was out of place. Two massive filing cabinets, each drawer precisely labeled, stood to one side of a credenza, on the surface of which were four impeccably squared-off stacks of what I assumed were current project files awaiting their return to the filing cabinets, once completed. Brianna's own desk was similarly regimented, with precisely positioned tools of her trade laid out for maximum ergonomic effect: a keyboard, two monitors, a phone with the direct-dial numbers neatly labeled, and a universally recognizable printout—her schedule for the day, with four or five boxes indicating meetings including this one, each color-coded and annotated with neat handwriting. The boxes indicating the two meetings before mine each had a perfectly straight diagonal line drawn through them, indicat-ing, I assumed, that they had been concluded satisfactorily.

As I asked about her role and responsibilities, Brianna responded by slid-ing across the table a thin three-ring binder she had obviously prepared in advance of our meeting. At the front was a photocopy of our introductory email exchange, the questions I'd posed highlighted in yellow. Behind were labeled tabs with supporting material answering each of those questions in turn: an organization chart of her team, her job specification, current operating plan, and goals for the next six months.

As we spoke, Brianna made precise, lengthy, impeccably neat notes in a lab book, numbering and dating each new page as she wrote. Over her shoulder, in the bookshelves behind her, I could see a row of identical lab books, each spine labeled with the dates they covered. I felt sure that if I looked, I'd find a stock of those self-same lab books in one of the drawers in her desk, quietly stacked, awaiting future use.

At precisely 11:40—we'd agreed to meet for 45 minutes—Brianna reminded me that she needed to finish our meeting in the next five minutes, to give her adequate time to prepare for her next meeting at noon. Did I have anything else I wanted to ask of her? No? Then did I mind if she briefly summarized what we had discussed so that we could both ensure that nothing important had been missed? At 11:45 precisely I was on my way with a firm, courteous handshake from Brianna and a free gift: a squeaky toy version of the company's allegedly cute animal mascot.

A TWO-COFFEE PROBLEM

Later, over lunch, I gave Riya the good news. "You haven't turned into an ogre, Riya. You're not scaring people away. And I don't think, insofar as I can tell, that Brianna is incompetent, or in any way wrong for the job." Riya frowned as she picked at her garden salad and took a minute to mull what I'd said. "Then explain to me what's going on," she said. "If it isn't me that's at fault, and it isn't Brianna, why isn't this working? Why has our relationship broken down? And why am I looking at the third failure in the same position in two years?"

I beckoned our waiter over and ordered a couple of espressos. I knew what I was about to say would raise more questions than it answered, and I wanted a clear head. "It's pretty simple. You're a Visionary." I looked at Riya, and got a nod back that confirmed, yes, she remembered the work we'd done together on her management style when she first got the CMO position, and yes, she agreed with that assessment—"Well, Brianna is something very different. At her core, she's what I call a Processor. She works by bringing order—systems and processes, if you will—to all that she does. You can see it in her precision, her attention to detail, her commitment to consistency." Riya snorted and rolled her eyes. "You saw the lab books, then?" she asked.

"Yes, I did. And the files, and the cabinets, and the three-ring binders. It's part of who she is, an important part. In fact, it's why you hired her." I paused for a moment to make sure Riya didn't skim past what I'd just said. She thought for a moment, then nodded: "I guess that's right—that *is* why I hired her. Her job in investor relations requires precisely that sort of—what did you call it?—processor mentality."

"Well, here's the thing." The coffees arrived and I took a sip. "Brianna isn't just a processor. She's a Processor, with a capital P. It's an integral part of her personality. And so will it be for anyone you hire for that position—anyone competent at it, anyway." I stopped. I wanted Riya to figure out the next bit for herself.

We each drank our coffee for a while in silence, then Riya looked at me skeptically. "I think I see where you're headed," she said. "You're going to tell me that Vs and Ps don't get on well together. One of those oil and water things, right? That this is a systemic issue, not a personal one, and if I want the relationship to work, I need to find a way to work with a P."

"Not quite." I said. "You'd be right to be skeptical if I suggested something that simplistic. The relationship between Vs and Ps is more nuanced than that. For example, I'm prepared to bet that you like Brianna personally and get on well with her in social situations." Riya raised her eyebrows and nodded assent. "But at certain times, in certain specific interactions, the Visionary and Processor do indeed clash in predictable ways. Painful ways, too, as you've found out."

"Fair point," Riya said. "We *do* get on well when we're not actually working on stuff together. And I've often thought that if only we could get that same type of relationship—I don't know...maybe 'flow' is a better word—if we could get that flow going at work then a lot of this stuff would sort itself out."

"Right on the button," I said. "A V and a P who can get their relationship to work well is a powerful combination. And the good news is, now that you've seen the problem so clearly, fixing it is relatively easy."

"Okay," said Riya. "I'll buy that, but now that I see it, I have questions. Lots of them. I'll get us another coffee."

INTRODUCING THE PROCESSOR

The second natural style that people in group or team situations default to is that of the Processor.

Processors have an innate desire to bring order to any situation. They focus not only on what they've been asked to do, but also on the underlying systems and processes that will make doing it more consistent and repeatable. And if those systems and processes don't yet exist, they'll begin by designing and implementing them.

Most at home in what are popularly referred to as left-brain activities, Processors are highly rational and analytical by nature, and they think in a logical, sequential way, preferring to arrive at an objective assessment of the facts rather than trusting to emotion and judgment.

Most medium- to large-sized organizations have many Processors dotted around (which, as we'll see in a later chapter, brings its own problems), and if you've ever had dealings with a government agency, then you almost certainly have interacted with a Processor or two. As with the Visionary, you can recognize a Processor by certain behavioral traits:

They value routine. For a Processor, routine is one of the fundamental building blocks of getting things done. With their emphasis on systems and processes, they find that a predictable rhythm provides a more effective environment in which to work than one which is constantly changing and varied.

They trust data and collect a lot of it. Data is the currency of the Processor. They collect it, analyze it, trade it, and, most of all, they present it. Called upon to explain something, particularly in a group or team environment, Processors are rarely comfortable doing so without considerable amounts of backup data, most of which they'd prefer to explain at copious length.

They dislike risk. Processors start from the premise that if the underlying systems and processes are correctly designed, risk can be reduced to minimal levels. To Processors, the idea of untrammeled or unexpected risk is abhorrent, and they will go to great lengths to extinguish it as far as possible.

They are wary of intuition and hunches. Unlike the Visionary, Processors have great reservations about using experiential factors such as intuition and judgment when making decisions. And they're not only skeptical about the judgment of others; they equally doubt their own, much preferring the more solid ground of proven data and detailed analysis.

They prefer not to be rushed. It's very hard to get Processors to short-circuit their preferred way of doing things. Tell a Processor that you need a list of accounts payable over 90 days old, and whether you need it pronto or by next week, he'll prepare the list exactly the same way. Hovering over Processors in an attempt to speed things up is usually an exercise in futility: they'll complete whatever you've asked them to do just as if you weren't there in the first place.

They tend toward the status quo. The basic rule of thumb for a Processor is "if it ain't broke, don't fix it." They often need a lot of convincing that something is in fact broken enough to require fixing. As a result, once Processors make a decision—particularly a tough decision, with painful consequences—they find it hard to reverse that decision later, even if the evidence shows that it was wrong.

Processors bring a crucial skill set to any group or team. They manage risk, provide consistency, and ensure that all the details so cavalierly dismissed by the Visionary are hunted down and recorded appropriately. At times, however, their reluctance to embrace change, their steady unvarying pace, and their dogged attachment to data can frustrate their colleagues. In later chapters we'll see how to work with Processors to reap the very best from their detailed, analytical approach while ensuring the other team members don't become frustrated or impatient.

BRAD GETS WHIPLASH

"Uh, okay. I understand. I can be there in about twenty minutes, I guess."

I was on the phone with Brad, an old colleague and one of the funnest guys I know to hang out with—if you could ever catch him. As vice president of sales for a highly successful carpet manufacturer, Brad traveled constantly, finding and consummating deals, building relationships with potential clients, and seemingly on call 24/7 for his key customers. Perennially upbeat and naturally gregarious, Brad loved his work, and his hard-charging just-do-it attitude endeared him to his customers. Not surprisingly, Brad was not only a v-p of sales (one of three in the company); he was also consistently the company's highest sales performer.

On this call—the third I'd had from him that afternoon—he seemed intent on proving once more just how hard he could make it for us to meet. A perpetual motion machine, Brad seemed to accomplish more in one day than most people got through in a week, but he did so by burning through meetings, people, and places at a dizzying pace. Perpetually arriving late for meetings, then staying longer than he'd intended, Brad was constantly recalibrating his plans as the day wore on. If his schedule was a GPS device, it would be forever muttering "Recalculating, recalculating…

Consummating a planned meeting with Brad was an exercise in patience and persistence. Ideally, you'd grab a breakfast slot on the grounds that his day, at that point, wouldn't yet have collapsed into improvised chaos—but that could still be foiled by his early morning gym visit coupled with the ten to twenty phone calls he would fire off every morning.

Today, Brad had already shifted the time for our meeting twice and its venue once. Now I was driving to what he'd assured me was the final location, a Mexican restaurant we both liked all the way across town.

When I arrived, Brad was already in our favorite booth, guacamole and chips to hand (and shirt, I noticed), briefcase open, papers out, phone at his ear, iPad on the table. As I sat down, signaling to the waiter with a circular bring-me-some-too gesture around the guacamole and chips, two things stood out from the usual cyclone of activity surrounding Brad: a large margarita (unusual for Brad on a weekday) and his résumé, printed sharp and crisp on a heavy piece of vellum, and positioned front and center at my place in the booth.

"I'm done," Brad said, slapping his cell phone closed and tossing it into the open briefcase. "I'm finished." Immediately, his phone started to vibrate, as if complaining at the rough treatment. Ignoring the phone and sullenly dragging a chip through the guacamole, Brad looked up at me, and I could see his eyes were red and dull. For the first time I could recall in years, Brad looked less than happy. In fact, he looked like a whipped puppy, if you can imagine a 6' 2", 220-pound puppy.

"I'm finished," he repeated. "There's my résumé—" Brad gestured with his chip, and green spots rained on the previously pristine document. "Damn. I'll get you another copy. I'd really appreciate it if you'd keep an eye out for anything you think might suit me."

"Hold up there, Brad. Let's back up a bit." I needed a little time to process what I was hearing: I'd rarely seen Brad this deflated. "What's the problem?" I asked. "Isn't this a little out of the blue? Last time we talked everything seemed fine. Great, in fact. You've been there 13 years, and I've never known you to be anything but successful—and happy. We both know you'll be COO this time next year, so why this . . . ?" I gestured down at Brad's résumé, as if the white page with the green dots could finish the sentence.

"The pair of them have me exhausted," Brad said. "You want one?" He motioned for two more margaritas. "Tony and Carla, I mean. They've beaten me into the ground. I just can't do it anymore."

"Can't do what, Brad? Your job? You've got to be kidding me. You're a force of nature. You could do my job and his job"—I stuck a thumb in the direction of the barkeep—"before lunch and still make time to fit in a full day's work. I've never known you to be worn down by hard work, ever."

"Barkeeps don't work before lunch," said Brad, with a faint shadow of his usual grin. "But that isn't the point. It isn't the work that's beaten me. It's this." I waited while Brad fiddled with his iPad. I assumed he'd intended to dramatically reveal something to me, but it took him three or four minutes of finger sliding and dabbing before he finally slipped the screen round so I could see it.

"There's just one month's emails from Carla, my beloved CEO. Take a look."

"Well, yes, I see the item count. Two hundred and twenty-nine emails." I paused to do the math. "About ten a day. That's a lot, I agree, but you've never let administrative stuff stand in the way of your success. You've always found a way to. . . ."

"Read a few—go on, pick a few and read 'em. You're an approved consultant to the firm; you've signed the confidentiality agreement. Just read some at random."

I looked at Brad, trying to convey that I felt like a kid being taught how to tie my shoelaces, but the expression coming back at me from across the table didn't leave a lot of room for debate. I stabbed at one of the emails from Carla and read it. Then another. And another. I couldn't help but smile.

"You think what you're reading is funny?"

"Yes, I do." I looked up and grimaced sheepishly at Brad. "But I can definitely see how you wouldn't find it funny at all." I punched open four or five more of Carla's emails just to make sure I understood what was infuriating Brad so deeply, then swiveled the iPad back to its owner.

"So Carla's gone a bit over the top with expansion plans. And new initiatives. And she's definitely read a bunch too many fad management books in the last while. I can see she's fire-hosing you with all these bright ideas. Nobody in their right mind could possibly keep track of all that stuff, let alone implement them. I get it. Where does Tony come in?"

"Well, you know how our CFO works. Brad was pulling a fat manila folder out of his briefcase as he spoke. "Paper is his preferred method of communication. Something to do with his auditor background I guess. Anyway, take a look." He slid the folder my way, and a dozen or so documents fanned out into my lap. Gathering them up, I guessed there were maybe another hundred pages or so still in the folder.

"So . . . these appear to be statements of policy . . . procedural guides . . . systems flowcharts." I was flicking through what were mostly printed memos, reading the titles. " . . . and a lot of memos with 'NOI' in the subject line." I looked up at Brad. "What does 'NOI' mean?"

"Notice of Infraction," said Brad, making air quotes. "It's Tony's favorite acronym. He uses it to tell us when we've done something wrong." Brad feigned disgust by looking at the menu.

"It's been steadily getting worse. Couple of months ago, Carla would have tossed one or two new ideas at us in a month, worst case. Tony had maybe two or three new policies or processes each quarter. Now it's like an arms race. Carla sends out more and more bright ideas she wants us to implement. Tony responds with twenty systems and processes we all have to adhere to."

Brad paused, absently stirring his drink. "That just seems to goad Carla into finding even more clever things to keep us occupied, then Tony—well, you get it—the spiral escalates. And now, I've had it."

Brad paused, but I could tell he wanted to say more. I waited silently while he collected his thoughts.

"Look, I love this company. I love my job—and I'm good at it. Three-time President's Award winner for highest sales. It doesn't—didn't—get any better than that. But this pair...." Brad motioned vaguely at Tony's files and the iPad, still displaying Carla's emails—"They've pretty much made it impossible for me to *do* my job. I can't take any more of it, and I'm going to resign as soon as I get my head around what I'm going to do next."

A TWO-MARGARITA PROBLEM

We both sat back on the padded banquette at either side of the booth. I slid the manila folder back to Brad and signaled to the waiter. He didn't come over—just mouthed "The usual?" I nodded.

After a long silence, I said gingerly, "So, what if I said that you didn't need to resign?"

"I'd say I agree with you. It doesn't have to be like this and I shouldn't have to resign. But it is what it is, and I'm not going to put up with it any longer."

"That's not what I meant. What I mean is, I think this can be fixed. I can't guarantee it, but knowing all three of you as well as I do, I think I see what's happening here, and I believe I know how you—all three of you—can change it."

Brad shot me his best "I don't think so" expression. "I don't think so," he said. "But let's hear it anyway."

"Well, it's not complicated," I began. "Carla, we know, is a big V—a Visionary who loves to spitball new ideas and think big. Everything she's doing here is right in keeping with that—she's just got a little out of control lately." I could see Brad reacting to my use of the word "little," but I held my hand up so I could finish. "And Tony's as strong a P as they come. He loves systems and processes, as this"—I pointed at the manila folder—"demonstrates. Getting those two—a V and a P—to work together smoothly is difficult enough, and right now, it's clearly not working."

I looked at Brad to make sure he was with me so far. "I get it," he said. "I remember you giving us a heads-up about that when we hired Tony a couple of years ago."

"Good, I'm glad you remember. Well, the issue has now become more acute for a simple reason: you're an O, an Operator. And a highly successful one at that. For you, happiness is going home at night feeling you've accomplished something definite, that you've taken the items in your to-do list and checked them off, that you've actually got some real work done as you would see it. In your world, that means signing deals. Lots of them.

"You're not by nature interested in Tony's policies and memos. I'd say that on good days you'd be happy to let him work on his systems and processes, and on a bad day—when all this is getting between you and your customers—you couldn't see him far enough away. As for Carla, well, you know as well as I do that if you hadn't had each other for the past few years—her setting the vision, you making it happen—then the business would have gone nowhere. As it is, together you've built a powerhouse in your industry. It's just that now, the interaction between her as a V and Tony as a P is breaking down. And you're the bystander, out there just trying to do your job and suffering the consequences."

Brad looked at me, still skeptical, but interested enough in what I'd said to ask the question I was hoping for. "Okay, smart guy. I get that as far as it goes. How do we fix it?"

"Well, it isn't necessarily going to be pain-free—for any of you—but it is relatively simple. You're in an unstable triangle—a V, O, and P will always end up gridlocking like this. We just have to show you how to break that gridlock, and that means introducing you to some new ways of interacting. You won't get everything you want—you'll still need to deal with some of Carla's V and Tony's P, but I think we can get you back to doing what you love most—out there selling."

Brad looked at me, and I saw a trace of the old just-do-it glint return to his eyes.

"Let's eat," I said, "and I'll tell you some more."

INTRODUCING THE OPERATOR

The third and last natural style that people default to in group or team situations is that of the Operator.

Operators are the *doers* in any enterprise—they're the practical-minded folks that get stuff done. Operators work best alongside Visionaries, and in a sense, they're mutually dependent: a Visionary needs an Operator to translate his or her vision into day-to-day tasks, and then to get those tasks completed. An Operator, on the other hand, looks to the Visionary for the big picture, for motivation and inspiration in the tough times, and for the flexibility and lateral thinking to change the enterprise's direction if things aren't working out.

Because of their task-oriented disposition, Operators are often hard to tie down in an office environment. Easily bored by meetings and unimpressed with simply putting in face time, Operators don't like to sit around in offices and can usually be found in jobs, like sales, that keep them on the move.

As with the Visionary and the Processor, you can recognize an Operator by certain behavioral traits:

They're action oriented. Sharks and Operators live by the same principle: they need to keep moving to stay alive. For Operators to feel fulfilled, it's important that they get the endorphin rush of ticking a task off as complete. For this reason, Operators often have a short fuse when anyone—or anything, such as an IT breakdown or a shortage of needed resources—gets between them and finishing a task.

They improvise—and move on. Because of this strong need to keep moving, to complete one task and move on to another, an Operator, when faced with a last-minute hiccup or problem, will often do whatever is necessary to improvise a solution there and then, rather than have to come back and address the matter later. (Going back over old ground is extremely painful for an Operator—it feels like wasted effort.)

They ask forgiveness rather than permission. As a direct result of this tendency to improvise hot-wired solutions, Operators often find themselves working outside their organization's recommended policies. As a result, most Operators learn to report back *after* the event and take their lumps rather than subject themselves to what they would view as a tortuous approval process.

They work prodigious hours. Operators are rather like blinkered racehorses—their eyes are on the prize of getting things done, and until they've passed the finish line they're going to run like crazy. Of course, the problem is that in business, the line never gets crossed—there are always more things to get done. As a result, most Operators work all the hours God sends, plus some for good luck.

They often work alone. Most Operators have a give-it-here approach—when they see that something needs doing, their natural reaction is to just do it. As a result, they can sometimes appear brusque and uncaring, and people working for Operators often complain of not receiving much in the way of direction and few assignments of real value, with little or no mentoring or coaching.

They don't like being micromanaged. Try to impose on an Operator what a Processor would view as a mild adherence to nonintrusive systems and procedures, and the result can look like an enraged bull in an extremely small china shop. Operators value independence of action above all else, and requiring from them even the most basic of consistent systems compliance can often be a prolonged, ongoing battle.

It's obvious that unless you're working for a full-blown bureaucracy, no group or team, no organization or enterprise can ever achieve its goals without one or more Operators in the mix. The problem is, as we'll see in chapter 3, Operators are the least naturally inclined of our three types to play well in teams—they'd much rather be out on their own getting stuff done.

The trick is to find a way to involve them positively in the group or team's activities, without them feeling overmanaged or being pulled off the front line for too long.

HOW TEAMS WORK

Now that you've met—through Andy, Brianna, and Brad—the three natural personality styles that apply to us all, we can now begin to examine how the three styles interact, and the impact they have on the success (or otherwise) of groups and teams.

The rest of Part I will expand in detail how each style, and each combination of styles (Visionary—Operator, Visionary—Processor, and Operator—Processor), interacts, but for now there are just three key principles to bear in mind.

The first key principle is that all of us have a bias toward acting as a Visionary, an Operator, or a Processor. We may not exhibit tendencies quite as extreme as Andy, Brianna, or Brad, but we all have a definite leaning toward one primary style.

Most people will also have a secondary tendency. In other words, very few people are *just* a Visionary, or *just* an Operator, or *just* a Processor—if you were, you'd be a caricature or a monster (I've met some in my time, but mercifully few). Most of us are a combination of two styles—one strong suit and one secondary. I, for example, am a strong V and a secondary P (a rare combination, but not uncommon among consultants).

You can find out exactly what your style is—both primary and secondary—right now, by taking the free online Predictable Success Management Styles Quiz. Just click on the resources link at the end of this chapter and follow the instructions there. (Tip: Based on what you've read in this chapter, first jot down what you instinctively think your primary and secondary styles are before taking the quiz, then compare the results with your initial guess.)

The second key principle is that the V-O-P triangle is an innately unstable one. This is because Visionaries, Operators, and Processors each achieve a sense of fulfillment or satisfaction in very different, often competing ways.

A Visionary can feel fulfilled by just the very act of creation—a fresh idea, a new insight, or an innovative concept can be the trigger for them to move on to something new. The Processor, meanwhile, needs to document and categorize the new idea or fresh insight—they need to collect data on it, analyze it, test it, and they think the Visionary is flaky for jumping from idea to idea without doing this due diligence.

Finally, the Operators, frustrated at being coopted onto this team in the first place when all they want to do is go outside and get stuff done, quickly lose patience with both the Visionary and the Processor—the Visionary for not sticking to one game plan that the Operator can see through to completion, and the Processor for slowing everything with their interminable systems and procedures.

The unavoidable outcome of this V-O-P instability is that, left to itself, every group or team will eventually implode, gridlock, or underperform—it's just a question of when. (*Note:* When it does happen, the blame will usually be placed on whatever is the most prominent *symptom* of the V-O-P instability: poor communications, distrust, lack of clarity—choose your reason. The reality is that all of these are just symptoms—the V-O-P instability is the root cause.)

The third key principle is that to avoid this fate, and to produce a high-performing group or team, a fourth, learned style—that of the Synergist—must be added to the mix. In Part II we'll see how many high-performing teams do this intuitively and subconsciously, and in Part III, you'll learn how you can do it naturally, consciously, and effectively.

CHAPTER SUMMARY

Organizations do not achieve success—people achieve success through working individually and in groups and teams.

Everyone who participates in group or team work tends to act primarily in one of three naturally occurring styles: as a Visionary, an Operator, or a Processor.

Visionaries think big, generate creative ideas, and take risks. They also become irritated by detail and can disengage easily when bored.

Operators get stuff done. They take the Visionary's big idea and translate it into actionable tasks. They like to be left to work alone and will do whatever is necessary to complete the task they're given, even if it means breaking a few rules.

Processors devise and monitor the systems and procedures necessary to enable an organization or enterprise to deliver consistent results in a complex environment. They think linearly and objectively, and are averse to undue risk.

The V-O-P relationship is not a naturally stable one. The tensions and conflicts caused by often competing desires are the root cause of most group and team dysfunction.

To make the V-O-P relationship stable, a fourth, learned style needs to be introduced. The Synergist style acts as a buffer between the V-O-P styles, taking the best from each and enabling them to work effectively together.

 Scan this QR code to be taken to a web page containing case studies and examples specific to this chapter, or point your web browser to http://PredictableSuccess.com/syn-ch01.

2

THE VISIONARY

Hold on Tight, We're Going to Mars

AT LEAST I HAD BROUGHT MY LAPTOP WITH ME.

I was perched at the edge of a desk in Andy's office, stealing power from the one remaining outlet not already attached to one or another of Andy's computers, waiting for him to return. We'd been scheduled for a 10 A.M. coaching meeting, but when I'd arrived, Lori, one of his three direct reports, had apologized—Andy had forgotten he was on a team looking at new sourcing options for key components, and they were due to meet from 9:30 until 11. Lori had shown me into this room and brought me coffee, then returned to her desk right outside where I could now see her and her two colleagues working intently—even a little feverishly.

Looking around the room, I could see Andy's character reflected in the surroundings: multiple gizmos (he seemed to have one of every new piece of electronica that had come out that year), a small but impressive business library containing many recent bestsellers, and framed photographs on every surface, each showing a different aspect of the growth of his components business over the years. The only thing missing was any evidence of actual work—no files, no folders strewn around. Not even a legal pad. It looked and felt like Andy did any "real" work elsewhere, outside of this office.

By now it was 11:10, and I sensed from the activity outside that Andy was on his way. Sure enough, Lori stuck her head around the door: "Andy'll be here in 10 minutes or so," she said. "Is there anything I can get you while you're waiting?"

"No," I said, "but you could answer a question." I smiled, hoping Lori would take a moment or two from the frenetic work she'd been doing. She looked momentarily back at her desk as if taking a silent inventory of its contents. "Sure," she said, sliding past the door and taking a seat at the desk opposite me. "What can I help you with?"

"Well, I was just wondering what you and your two colleagues do when Andy isn't around. He seems to have a lot of things that take him out of the office, and I've noticed that you're all incredibly busy even though he's not here right now. Is it always like that when Andy's not around?"

"Pretty much, yes," said Lori, after a brief reflection. "Andy has a lot going on, and he delegates a large part of it to us. He's very trusting that way, and it's one of the fun parts of the job. We also each have our own projects, which are a full-time job on their own. So we do have a lot to do, yes." She paused. I could tell she was wondering whether or not to say something else, so I stayed quiet, waiting for her to make her own mind up.

"Also...I don't know if it's talking out of school, but you'll see it yourself shortly...it's next to impossible to get anything done when Andy *is* here. It's hard to explain, but when he's physically around, it's almost like getting caught up in a mini-whirlwind, and we have to wait until he's next out of the office to get back to..." Lori gestured to the files and folders stacked on her desk outside, "this."

Lori returned to her desk, and a few minutes later Andy appeared at the other side of the large open plan office that housed his 50 or so administrative staff. He threaded his way slowly toward his office, stopping to speak every now and again to someone, handing each of them a book from a pile he had under his arm, gesticulating to it and talking for a minute or so to each person. As he approached Lori and me, he had only one copy left of the book, which he extended toward me. It was the recently released autobiography of a celebrity CEO who was currently receiving a lot of press.

"This is great!" said Andy, pointing toward the book, now in my hands. "There's some game-changing stuff in there we absolutely have to adopt in our marketing department." He looked over at Lori and shot her a beaming smile. "Hey Lori. Sorry I'm late. There's a box of these," he pointed at the book again, "in my trunk—can you go get 'em? I want a copy given to all the sales v-p's and everyone in marketing. If we haven't enough, order some more. Also, schedule it as the featured book in Andy's Book Club. I'll share from it at next week's meeting."

"Sure," said Lori. "Do you want me to reschedule the last two Book Club meetings on the current book we're studying? We haven't finished it." There was a pause while Andy collected his thoughts. I could tell he had moved on from the topic. "Naw, I think we've got all we can out of that one. Les, walk with me. I've already overrun our time. I'm sorry." Lori was headed out the door—presumably to get the books from Andy's car—and I was...well, I didn't know where I was going, but it seemed Andy did.

"Let's go see Joanne," said Andy, over his shoulder. He was already three paces ahead of me. "I had some thoughts over the weekend about this 'Visionary coaching' we talked about, and I think you'll like them." As we rounded a block of cubicles on the way to Joanne's office, Andy made a brief detour—Brendan, his senior v-p of marketing had emerged from a doorway. I watched as Andy threw his arm over Brendan's shoulder and gestured toward Lori, now struggling back to her desk carrying a large box. Andy was talking about the book, no doubt. Even from here I could see the contrast—a look of eager enthusiasm on Andy's face and one of weary resignation on Brendan's.

While I waited, I looked over at Joanne's office, now visible through the sheer glass curtain at the other side of the room. As Andy's cofounder and the business's CFO, she was, as almost always, in a meeting with someone. I could see her well-organized desktop from here, the neat file in front of her, the ubiquitous legal pad she used for notes. Her computer screen was angled so that she and her visitor could both see it, and they were staring intently at the spreadsheet it was displaying, Joanne pointing at a specific cell with a pen. Just at that point Andy returned to my side, carrying a copy of the book—obviously, Lori had restocked him. "Let's go," he said, pointing at Joanne's office. "She'll love this!" Andy strode off, his energy and enthusiasm palpable. "Um, does she know we're coming?" I said. I was pretty sure I knew the answer.

INSIDE THE HEAD OF A VISIONARY

Visionaries operate in creative spurts, which means you will usually encounter them in one of two primary modes: active or idle.

ACTIVE MODE

The Visionary's active mode occurs when they're in a creative phase, which can last for an hour or two, or for days on end, depending on the object of their attention (or, as we'll see, more likely the objects—plural—of their attention). During this time they contribute generously with ideas, direction, and problem-solving, display great energy, and are usually gregarious and fun to work with.

Because they don't like to be involved with anything they would view as trivial, a Visionary in active mode will automatically assume that whatever they're engaged in at that point is of vital importance: vital for them, vital for the organization, and vital for anyone else who happens to be passing. As a result, being around Visionaries in active mode can feel like being close to a whirlwind—everything not bolted down is in danger of getting sucked into their orbit at any time.

IDLE MODE

Between bouts of creative energy, Visionaries will move into idle mode—which doesn't mean that they aren't doing anything, just that they aren't in the whirlwind-like creative mode we just witnessed. When in idle mode, a Visionary becomes gregarious—they will walk around a lot, stopping in on folks unexpectedly to talk about whatever comes to mind; they'll go to conferences or workshops, play golf, or go skiing—anything to meet other people and get new ideas.

And therein lies the danger of idle mode. When the Visionary gets recharged, it's rarely done in a vacuum—usually, getting recharged for a Visionary means glomming on to a new idea or concept to bring back to the office as the "next new thing." At which point the Visionary goes into active mode once more, with that new thing as the starting point.

HYPERLINKING

And it usually is just that—only a starting point. One of the most prominent characteristics of Visionaries is that they move from topic to topic, and from one vitally important concept to the next, not just seamlessly but endlessly. It's like watching Internet hyperlinking take human form. A discussion with a Visionary will begin with one topic, then jump to another (often completely unassociated) topic prompted by something as simple as a person walking past the office, an incoming email, or simply a random thought—and all delivered with the same degree of intensity.

The same process will happen with the next new thing brought back from idle time—whether it's a new business methodology, a new book the Visionary has read, a new direction to take the business in, or a new way to structure something. Whatever it is, the Visionary will introduce it with a definitive endorsement ("This is the most important change we'll ever make to how we do things around here," or "I've never read anything as vital to our business as this book"), implore everyone to get on board with this "fundamentally important" new concept, and then move on to something else.

THE SHINY-BLUE-BALL SYNDROME

The shiny-blue-ball syndrome—this pattern of bringing fundamentally important new ideas back from idle time, proselytizing it strongly, realigning everyone else around it, then moving on to something else equally fundamentally important—comes from the two basic attributes that drive every true Visionary:

1. They abhor the thought of dealing with trivia. For a Visionary, it's important to work at a highly strategic level—with big things that make big differences. So of course, whatever they become interested in must by definition be important, vital, or game-changing.

2. Visionaries have an almost inextinguishable appetite for anything new, innovative, and/or challenging.

Once those two attributes are combined, the net result is a seemingly endless stream of innovative and challenging new ideas and concepts, all of which are— guess what—fundamental and vital to the business, but few of which take root and produce genuine medium- or long-term change.

INCOMPATIBLE NOTIONS

The other trick that Visionaries can pull off with aplomb is keeping two or more entirely incompatible notions in their heads at once, and for a long time—in fact, right up until the point at which they finally have to make a decision that will require jettisoning all but one of those notions.

Because Visionaries have a high tolerance for ambiguity and uncertainty, they don't feel pressure to reconcile two opposing thoughts unless (and until) they have to. As a result, Jane may take her plan for a new product launch to her Visionary boss at 10 A.M. and receive a warm and supportive hearing, then Marcel may deliver his wholly contrary plan at 2 P.M. and receive a similarly effusive response. If Jane and Marcel trade notes, they may well wonder how their boss could apparently endorse two mutually exclusive plans. Truth is, the boss, being a Visionary, has no problem doing so, and will only make her mind up when she absolutely needs to.

THE VISIONARY'S STRENGTHS

No group or team can innovate or deliver truly creative solutions without a Visionary on board, and even a mature, well-structured business with strong reserves needs Visionary output throughout the organization if it is to avoid becoming bureaucratic and arthritic and slide into decline. Here are the main contributions Visionaries make to the groups and teams of which they are a part:

VISION

The core contribution that any Visionary brings to the organization, group, or team is, of course, at the root of the word itself—vision. The ability to see what isn't there (yet), and to motivate others to help translate that vision into reality is the foundation of any enterprise—and the Visionary is precisely the person needed to do it.

And this is vision with energy and passion. Anyone working with a true Visionary becomes aware at an early stage that their concept of vision isn't a passive one. These are not mere dreamers: Visionaries don't have an idea in the abstract—they passionately pursue it to the point where it gains traction, becomes real, and develops a life of its own.

FLEXIBILITY

One would think that the Visionary's deep commitment to a vision would make them inflexible. After all, we've heard so many stories of great innovators, laughed at by their peers, rejected by potential funders, who remained stubbornly immoveable in their commitment to the widget they've designed, and who eventually triumphed, David-like, in the face of insurmountable odds.

The reality is considerably more prosaic. Just as most Visionaries aren't dreamers, most of them aren't crazy inventors either—so wedded to their idea or concept that they won't yield an inch on how it is produced or how it finds a market. Instead, true Visionaries are eminently practical, holding to the core of their vision while remaining flexible in the detail of how it should be realized.

This is not to say that Visionaries don't sometimes get a "bee in their bonnet" about specific details—they do, and we'll see the impact of that later. But in general, the essence of a true Visionary is having great ideas, thinking at a high strategic level, and finding creative solutions to problems—all within a practical, flexible mindset that wants to see the idea, concept, or solution realized in concrete terms.

COURAGE

Visionaries like to take risks. After all, isn't the entire concept of pursuing a vision just that—one big risk? But as with the earlier strengths we've looked at, it's important not to confuse the Visionary's willingness to take risks with the cartoonish extreme of wanton carelessness.

Although it may look to some (particularly to Processors, who are highly risk-averse) that the risk-taking Visionary is simply being cavalier, the reality is that most Visionaries have a highly attuned risk detector that (mostly) prevents them from egregious overreach. They have a way of drawing from their own past experiences and comparing it to the available data that allows them to walk to the edge of risk without taking too many spills.

Put another way, the Visionary doesn't so much take wild risks as push the envelope of existing risk. For the group or team of which they are a part, this manifests itself as courage—the ability and fortitude to take decisions, pursue options, and try alternatives that other groups would rather avoid.

SIMPLICITY

Occam's razor is often popularly translated as stating that the perfect solution to any problem is the simplest one. In other words, the solution should be no more complex than it need be. Visionaries are highly wed to this idea.

Apart from their own pet notions (about which they can be stubbornly obtuse), Visionaries see through overly complex ideas, solutions, or suggestions with a laser-like intensity. This arises out of their short attention span. When it comes to detail, if presented with anything overly complex (be it a PowerPoint presentation, a report, or just a lengthy monologue), the Visionary, in an act of self-protection, will strip it down to its core, removing everything that doesn't need to be there and leaving only the vital elements.

DISPATCH

As marketing guru Seth Godin would put it, Visionaries ship. In another contrast to their less-effective brethren, the dreamers, Visionaries don't achieve fulfillment just by coming up with bright ideas. For the Visionary there needs also
to be something tangible—a real result or consequence.

Whether it's a new product rollout, enhanced profitability, or better quality control, a true Visionary won't be truly content until and unless they see a
manifest realization of that goal.

THE VISIONARY'S WEAKNESSES

Many of the weaknesses of Visionaries are an integral part of what makes them
who they are—if they didn't exhibit these characteristics, they just as surely
wouldn't exhibit the strengths we've just explored. Nonetheless, there are some
aspects of working with a Visionary that are less than optimal for those who
have to work alongside one.

BOREDOM WITH DETAIL

Perhaps the single most disruptive weakness of Visionaries is an almost path-
ological fear of getting caught up in what they would view as mind-crushing
detail.

This typically exhibits itself in ways that others find profoundly irritating:
arriving late to meetings (because the first few minutes of any meeting are always
trivial—in their view, anyway), leaving those same meetings at unpredictable
times (i.e., when detail comes to the fore), not reading background material in
sufficient depth, and failure to follow up with people and hold them accountable
(even just talking to others about *their* detail is too much for the Visionary, it
seems).

This shouldn't be interpreted as meaning that Visionaries don't understand
the importance of attention to detail—they do; they'd just prefer somebody else
took responsibility for providing it.

NEED FOR OWNERSHIP

Visionaries suffer from NIHS—Not Invented Here Syndrome. Put simply, no
matter how good an idea someone else comes up with, true Visionaries will not
be content until they have put their mark on it in some way. This may involve
tweaking some of the details or a wholesale rewrite of the entire idea, but one

way or another they must change anything novel, innovative, or new that comes their way in some manner that makes it their own.

The reason for this is simple. Visionaries, much more than Processors and Operators, derive a large part of their identity from their natural style—from being Visionaries. It's as if the very act of being visionary gives them purpose. As a result, it's hard for them to sit by and see other people's ideas adopted wholesale without their input—it makes them feel irrelevant—and irrelevance is anathema to a Visionary.

EXTREMES OF COMMITMENT

Watch a Visionary at work over time and the one thing that will amaze more than any other is their ability to swing from one extreme commitment to the next without missing a beat. Even in their leisure time, Visionaries will evangelize fervently for this newest golf driver or that fastest jet ski (Visionaries' hobbies are often expensive), having only yesterday consigned last week's fancy putter or NASA-designed scuba outfit to the garage.

The same thing happens at work—the Visionary will enthusiastically proselytize a new book, a theory, a methodology, or a guru using glowing terms that venture close to late-night infomercial territory. For the Visionary, everything is "imperative," "vital," "fundamental," and very little is "*meh*." And it's only a matter of time—often very little time—before the next, possibly even contradictory must-have or must-do book, theory, methodology, or guru comes along.

TALKING TO THINK

There is little a Visionary enjoys more than a healthy debate. Discussion is an integral part of how Visionaries work—in fact, it's how they think.

Although Visionaries can cause substantial disruption alone with just their thoughts and a legal pad, given their preference, they'd rather engage in conversation with someone, usually by setting up an Aunt Sally (a statement of firm opinion that's actually 180 degrees away from what they suspect is true), and seeing what emerges.

For a Visionary this makes perfect sense: combative discussion helps work things out. They get to discover what stands up to a grilling, and what wilts under fire—and thus, eventually, what they themselves think. Unfortunately for the person at the other end of the discussion, the degree of passion and strength of opinion that most Visionaries bring to every debate leaves the listener drained and confused, uncertain whether the Visionary was being directive (and meant precisely what was just said) or was just test-driving a notion.

LACK OF STRUCTURE

Anything with the stench of routine is an abomination to the Visionary. The idea of having their creative juices constrained by process or predictability has them climbing the walls.

Regular meetings, complicated systems, overly intrusive processes are all fine for everyone else—Visionaries can be supportively gung-ho about the need for systems and procedures in the organization as a whole—but less so for themselves.

Visionaries much prefer variety and change (in scenery, in topic, in time of day and week) than predictability and routine, so scheduling a meeting with one is an exercise in hopeful anticipation. They may or may not turn up, and when they do, they may or may not stick to the agenda you had diligently prepared, and they may or may not stay to the end—who knows?

WORKING WITH A VISIONARY

If you're the peer of a Visionary (i.e., you work *with* them, as opposed to working for them or managing them directly), you face a particular challenge—getting the best out of your interactions with your Visionary colleague while lacking the authority to impose anything on them, or to rein in their wilder tendencies.

Given what we've already seen of the Visionary's strengths and weaknesses, this can be quite a challenge. But all is not lost—here are five things that taken together will help optimize your interactions.

BE SELECTIVE IN HOW/WHEN/WHERE YOU INVOLVE THEM

Because they typically have big personalities, Visionaries tend to appear on everyone's radar a lot. They're easily noticed and don't shy from the limelight. This leads to them being frequently coopted onto teams and groups—after all, they're there, they're not shy with their opinions and ideas, so why not grab 'em and use 'em?

Truth is, Visionaries are not great utility players—they don't perform well in every environment (particularly not in those environments that require a lot of discipline and focus on detail), and because of the shiny-blue-ball syndrome they tend to overcommit.

Rather than grabbing your nearest Visionary each time you're putting a team together, consider carefully when and where to use them—rationing their involvement concentrates their impact, and you'll get better results.

DON'T JUDGE, JUST LISTEN

Because Visionaries love to talk to think, their verbal communications can, to non-Visionary listeners, often seem contradictory, or worse, glib. It may sometimes sound like your Visionary colleague is running off at the mouth, or pontificating, when what you want to hear are clear instructions, crisp directions, or a straightforward, unembellished opinion. This can cause some listeners to switch off in frustration, before the Visionary has fully thought through an idea.

Get into the habit of allowing more time when communicating with a Visionary. This allows Visionaries to get to the end of their thoughts and arrive at the conclusions you need. Be an active listener, but try not to interrupt the flow or attempt to hurry them along. Prod nonjudgmentally with questions like "So—what's the implication of that?" or "Where does that take us?" to act as bridges from one thought to the next.

When you think they've reached the conclusion of their thoughts, reflect it back to them, paraphrasing what you think you've heard in your own words to ensure you're on the same page.

ALLOW THEM THEIR VANITIES

Of the three natural styles, Visionaries typically have the largest egos. In many cases their identity is strongly linked to being a Visionary and in acting in a visionary way. They like not just to be associated with big ideas, strategic thinking, problem-solving, and cutting-edge thinking, but also to be *seen* to be associated with them.

As a result, Visionaries will often surround themselves with outward signs of their self-avowed status as an iconoclast: the latest technology (which, due to shiny-blue-ball syndrome, they'll rarely master before moving on to something new—Visionaries are classic early adopters), an office filled with tchotchkes and memorabilia (photographs featuring the Visionary front and center with people they've met or at events they've attended), the latest car, or bike, or jet ski.

This preoccupation with image can also come across as vain to the non-Visionary, but again, it's important to see this not as some form of passive-aggressive boasting or as a peacock look-at-me display, but rather as simply the outward manifestation of the inner ego-strength that makes the Visionary such a highly useful member of the team.

ASK, DON'T TELL

When working with a Visionary, one of the greatest skills you can develop is learning how to get them to adopt, implement, and support other people's ideas—including your own.

Visionaries are notoriously bad at readily accepting other people's ideas, however good they are, without fiddling with them in some way. It's almost as if they can't bring themselves to fully adopt an idea or suggestion unless they can get a smear of their own DNA on it. When you bring an idea or a proposal to a Visionary, they'll often say something equivalent to "leave it with me," and when it eventually comes back, it does so not with a yes or a no, but is instead shot through with minor or major suggestions or improvements—all designed so the Visionary can leave their own mark on it.

The trick is in approaching the Visionary not with the fully formed idea but rather with a series of leading questions designed to let the Visionary propose the idea (or some substantially similar version of it). So, rather than, say, asking your Visionary colleague to review your 15-page presentation on how to start a social media campaign, you may get better results by having an earlier discussion around the key components such a campaign might involve and soliciting your Visionary's views. Incorporating those views into your final report— maybe even giving formal credit for them to the Visionary—will supply the necessary "DNA smear" to ease acceptance and support when you finally present it.

ALLOW THEM TO CHOOSE THE TURF

Despite their aversion to routine, there will be occasions when you want a Visionary to help in a situation that is highly systematized or pro forma. Maybe you want them to attend your monthly planning meeting, or to join a project team that will be getting together weekly for six months. Under normal circumstances, you can expect that the Visionary will lack the discipline to see this through consistently, and that their attendance and contributions will be spotty at best, and at worst, they may bail on the process.

One way to minimize the possibility of this happening is to allow the Visionary to choose the venue where the meeting is being held. By allowing them to do so, they can introduce enough variety to stay interested and involved. They also get a more proprietary sense of involvement: they can view themselves as hosting the event, if not managing it, which is important to Visionaries. Just be prepared to find yourself and the rest of your team schlepping out to coffee shops, country clubs, and even the Visionary's own office, or wherever else pops to mind.

If your meetings are held virtually, this trick won't work, of course, but you have a higher chance of your Visionary showing up for virtual meetings in any case, as this enables them to multitask while the meeting is being held, thus giving their Visionary tendencies an outlet.

MANAGING A VISIONARY

Although we've mostly seen examples so far of Visionary founder/owners and senior executives, Visionaries can of course exist at any level within an organization.

And while the more senior the Visionary's position, the more likely they are to exhibit extreme characteristics (because there is less restraint and accountability), managing Visionaries at any level in the organization is a mentally exhausting process. As we've seen, they love to push the envelope and jump rapidly from one big thing to the next—so for a Visionary's manager, it often feels like trying to rein in a runaway horse.

Here are five tips to making the process less frazzled and more productive:

PLAN FOR VARIETY

Remember, Visionaries thrive on change and can't abide slavish adherence to routine or maintenance-type activities. If you don't consciously plan variety into the Visionary's schedule, they'll introduce it themselves—often with negative, unplanned consequences.

If you sit down with your Visionary on, say, a quarterly basis and agree on a work plan that allows for multiple projects and reasonably wide latitude in how to complete those projects, you will have much more predictable results than leaving it to the Visionary to find his or her own variety. It isn't fun to discover after the event that your Visionary got bored halfway through the quarter and went off the reservation with some half-baked initiative.

Plan variety and reduce the risk of those shiny blue balls appearing regularly.

RAISE ACCOUNTABILITY

Visionaries need to be held accountable more often and more rigorously than their Operator or Processor colleagues.

The reason for this is twofold. First, the act of accountability is in itself a routine, maintenance-type process, and so Visionaries naturally shy away from it. Second, because they hyperlink from one thing to the next with alacrity, the degree to which Visionaries can diverge over time from their planned goal is much higher than with an Operator or a Processor.

When you set a goal or outcome with a Visionary, put it in writing to make sure you both agree on what has been agreed, and lay out clearly what milestones will be delivered by when. Meet at those agreed times and assess progress against plan. This keeps the Visionary on track and minimizes the opportunity to hyperlink away from their assigned tasks.

ENFORCE (LIMITED) LIMITS

Trying to manage a Visionary by enforcing multiple limitations on their activities is like the Lilliputians trying to pin down Gulliver with hundreds of tiny threads—it doesn't work. Either they'll ignore what they're told, or if the restrictions are rigidly enforced, they'll get frustrated and leave.

The key to setting boundaries with a Visionary is to draw a small number of important limitations and enforce them strictly.

For example, "I can't afford to have you distracting the folks in R&D for the next six months, and I don't want to see you in there" works just fine with a Visionary. Sitting down with the entire org chart and working out a complicated matrix of allowed and restricted interactions does not.

SHORTEN THE REPORTING TIME SPAN

As we've seen, when Visionaries begin to veer off the track, the distance they can get away from their intended goal is much greater than that of an Operator or a Processor. Leave the Processor or Operator unsupervised for a while and they'll surely deviate from their initial goal, but chances are not by too much. Leave Visionaries unattended for a while and who knows where they might end up.

Set up shorter, more frequent meetings with your Visionary, but have them at different times, and in different places to provide variety.

Tip: Visionaries respond much better than Operators and Processors to informal, spur-of-the-moment check-ins—in fact, they love them. You don't need to plan all your frequent check-ins in advance—many of them can "just happen" as you bump into each other in hallways or in the car park.

JUDICIOUSLY ROTATE TEAM MEMBERS

Visionaries build very tight, loyal teams—which is mostly a good thing. Visionaries also tend to hire other Visionaries. Adding these together can result in a team of people—loyal Visionaries led by an uber-Visionary—that is too insular and too imbalanced for the good of the business as a whole.

At its extreme, this type of Visionary-dominated team can develop the overly freewheeling, high risk-taking mindset that occurred in some financial institutions in the late 2000s and which led to the near meltdown of the global economy.

Keep a judicious eye on your Visionary's team and make occasional tweaks to ensure that while the team retains an overall visionary approach, it is also balanced in composition by more pragmatic Operators and some risk-averse Processors.

WORKING FOR A VISIONARY

If you're fortunate enough to find yourself working for a Visionary, hold on—it's going to be quite a roller-coaster ride. Here are a few key reminders to keep in mind: if you can do these things, you'll emerge from the experience challenged, stretched—and happy. Get them wrong, and life could become intolerable very quickly.

KNOW EVERYTHING

Because Visionaries live in a constant state of hyperlinking from subject to subject and have so many initiatives on the go at any one time, working for them requires that you know vast amounts of information about multiple projects— or at least have rapid access to that information at a moment's notice.

And unlike those who work for Operators or Processors, you'll never know what piece of information you'll need to grab hold of next. For example, there is little guarantee that a meeting you have been hauled into with your Visionary boss will stay on the topic it was planned for—in fact, it's almost certain that the original purpose for the meeting is the one thing you'll talk about *least*.

So don't overprepare for meetings—at least not to the extent that you lose focus on everything else you and your boss are up to. Better to keep good files and a detailed journal covering the key issues on everything you're involved with and have it ready at any time. Make it easy (and quick) to retrieve information at a moment's notice and learn to roll with the punches when the subject under review once more lurches into unfamiliar territory.

BE THERE ALL THE TIME

Obviously you can't be at work 24/7—nor should you be, even if you could—but if you insist on clocking in and out at the posted office hours, you'll soon find yourself marginalized by your Visionary boss. Visionaries come and go at unpredictable times—they don't like routine, remember—and when they do arrive, they expect you to be there and to be able to bring them up to speed quickly (remember that detailed journal?).

So learn to anticipate your boss's comings and goings. Nonintrusive questioning is fine: "What time would you like me here tomorrow?" is much better than "What are you doing tomorrow, and when will you be coming in?" Most Visionaries work on a strict need-to-know basis about their comings and goings.

The good news is that many Visionaries well understand the demands they place on their employees' time, and while they expect you to work hard and play hard, they'll typically also be comfortable with you *not* being there when they are elsewhere and you need a well-deserved break.

STAY HAPPY

A positive attitude goes a very long way with a Visionary. This doesn't mean you need to be consistently cheery or oblivious to any bad news (in fact, as we'll see in a moment, quite the opposite). But an upbeat, glass-half-full approach fits well with the environment a Visionary wants to cultivate. Negativism, obstructionism, or a couldn't-care-less attitude will find you quickly reassigned.

PROVIDE A CHALLENGE FUNCTION

Once you have displayed the three characteristics above (know everything, be there all the time, and stay happy) consistently and for a reasonable amount of time, you'll begin to develop sweat equity in the form of mutual respect and trust with your Visionary boss.

A sign that this is happening is when they begin to take you into their counsel, asking for your advice. (Visionaries are notorious for lobbing questions about highly complex issues to people for whom the issue is well above their pay grade. It's one of the ways they test people.) When this occurs, it's your opportunity to provide the one thing a good Visionary boss will most value: a challenge function.

This doesn't mean arguing with your boss (never a good career move, even if most Visionaries relish a good argument). It *does* mean helping them think through the implications of what they're saying. For example, "You're wrong. That won't work, and here's why" fits firmly in the poor-career-move category, but "What are the other alternatives to doing it that way?" provides a challenge function that is both more helpful and more appropriate.

CULTIVATE BENIGN NEGLECT

I don't suggest leading with this approach right at the beginning of your relationship, but after developing sweat equity with your Visionary boss you may become adept at recognizing which of the many ideas, proposals, initiatives, and suggestions they come up with are genuinely actionable and which are merely shiny-blue-ball passing interests.

In order to stay sane—and to have the energy and other resources to act expeditiously on those things that *do* matter—most people who work for Visionary bosses learn to apply benign neglect to the more transient initiatives, on the basis that if the boss *really* wants it done, they'll return to it later.

EVERYBODY GETS TO TAKE NOTES

Later that morning—after Andy had disrupted Joanne's meeting to tell her all about "the book"—we finally made it to the comparative haven of his office.

"Andy, the purpose of today's meeting was actually to discuss your Visionary management style," I said. "Yes!" exclaimed Andy, tilting forward in his Aeron chair. "I totally forgot about that—there were some ideas I had. Joanne. . . ." Andy made to rise, and I knew where he was headed. "Hold on," I said, smiling. "Sit down, we're fine. Today was actually more helpful than you know. I learned as much from wandering around with you as I would have if we'd spent all morning sitting and talking."

Andy sat back again and blew his cheeks out. "Okay, Les. Let's get to the point. You say I'm a Visionary, and both you and Joanne tell me it's become problematical with everyone else on the team here. Can't say I like the premise, but I'll do whatever it takes to protect my business. What do we do?"

"Let's start easy," I said, "and begin by making sure we're all on the same page." Andy's face relaxed a little. I guess he thought we were going to get into something more confrontational. "I want your permission to ask everyone who interacts with you to takes some notes. Your three direct reports," I gestured outside his office at Lori and her colleagues, "Joanne, Brendan, and maybe two or three of the other senior v-p's you're most in contact with." "Notes?" said Andy. "You mean about when I'm irritating them by being too Visionary?" he smiled. "Sure. That would be interesting. Fun to read."

I paused, wanting Andy to work it out. After a moment he smiled. "Oh, I see. I don't get to read them." I smiled again. "Not the individual responses, no—I don't think we'd get accurate feedback if folks knew you'd get to see it. But I'll batch stuff together to give folks anonymity and produce a summary. Believe me, it'll still make for interesting reading."

CHAPTER SUMMARY

Visionaries cycle between active and idle mode, alternating between bursts of creative energy and recharging. They can be dangerous to be around when they come back from an idle period because of the multiplicity of ideas they generate.

Their ability to hyperlink to multiple subjects, coupled with their ability to hold seemingly contradictory viewpoints on the same subject, can confuse those who work with them.

Visionaries bring vision, flexibility, courage, and the ability to simplify seemingly complex ideas. They also bring a pragmatic approach to getting things accomplished and not overhypothesizing.

On the minus side, team members can find it frustrating to have to deal with the Visionaries' boredom with detail, their need to own all the team's ideas, and their extremes of commitment.

If you're working as a peer with a Visionary, be selective in how you involve them. Listen nonjudgmentally, and rather than forcing new ideas on them, involve them at the outset in the idea creation process.

If you manage a Visionary, schedule variety, accountability, and frequent check-ins. Enforce a few important restrictions strongly, rather than trying to enforce many limitations weakly, and make sure that individual's team isn't overdominated by other Visionaries.

If you work for a Visionary, you can build valuable sweat equity by working long hours, mastering a broad grasp of detail, and maintaining a positive demeanor. Once you've gained your boss's trust, you can begin to be more selective about what initiatives you focus on and can provide a vital challenge function.

 Scan this QR code to be taken to a web page containing case studies and examples specific to this chapter, or point your web browser to http://PredictableSuccess.com/syn-ch02.

3

THE OPERATOR
Yay...Let's Build a Rocket Ship

EVEN THOUGH I WAS LOOKING AT HIM from seventy-five feet away, the stoic set of Brad's jaw was clearly visible—and I knew the reason why.

I'd asked him to set up meetings with Carla and Tony, and despite his best efforts he hadn't been able to schedule them both on the same day. "Two. Full. Days," he'd said, only half-jokingly. Even though we were on the phone, I could tell he was glaring at me. "Two full days back at the ranch"—he meant head office—"do you know how painful that is for me? How much I need to get done? How far behind I'll be by the end of this...this..." He struggled to find a word to describe what we were going to do. "Coaching, Brad," I said, laughing. "It's coaching. Nobody will die." I knew Brad was hamming it up a little for my benefit, but I also knew that he genuinely didn't enjoy being "stuck in the office," as he would put it.

Now the fateful two days had arrived, and I was watching Brad from inside his office—he was out in the car park, where he'd been for the last 15 minutes. As soon as he'd arrived and gotten out of his car, a colleague had walked up to him, briefcase in hand, intending to leave for somewhere, but equally intent, it seemed, on confronting Brad. From the body language it was obvious Brad was being berated for something or other—in place of his usual sunnily optimistic smile he had a penitent, apologetic look, and occasionally spread his arms in surrender. When the one-sided discussion finally came to an end, I moved back to the conference table in the middle of Brad's cluttered mess of an office, where I had cleared a space for us to talk. After ten minutes, Brad still hadn't arrived. As the walk from the car park was only two minutes at best, I guessed what had happened—and stepped outside his office to confirm my suspicions. Brad was in the supplicant pose yet again. Another colleague was talking to him—well, talking *at* him—and it didn't look like he was asking after Brad's well-being.

Looking up, Brad took my appearance as his opportunity to break away and came scurrying over toward me. It looked for all the world like he was trying to make himself invisible to the rest of the office—all 220 pounds of him.

"What was all that about?" I asked. Brad smiled. "I told you," he said, whispering conspiratorially. "I don't like coming in here too often. The folks in here live in a vacuum. They get hung up on small issues. I'm a bit late on some reports that my colleagues were reminding me of on my way in." Smiling toothily, Brad lugged his briefcase—a huge, rectangular pilot's bag, bulging at the seams—onto the conference table, scattering papers from its surface. "Max!" he shouted. Nothing. "Yo, MAX!!"

A young man I assumed was Max wandered into the office and ambled over to the desk. "Yo boss," he said with a smile. "Didn't realize you were coming in today." "I'll be in for a couple of days in a row," said Brad. Max's eyebrows went up. "Blame him," said Brad, pointing his finger at me half-jokingly. Brad looked at Max, his eyes in full twinkle mode. "So?" he asked. Max's eyes narrowed for a moment, then twinkled back in return. "You got it?" he half-shouted. "You got it!"

Smiling broadly, Brad handed Max a sheaf of papers. "The entire hotel chain, domestic and international. New carpet for all six hundred properties over the next three years." Max mimicked slack-jawed amazement, and grinning crazily, the two of them fist-bumped. "You know that's put you over this year's sales target with two months still to go?" Brad adopted a mock-imperious demeanor. "I do," he said, "plus it's 15 percent of the target for each of the next two years." Max smacked the contract with the back of his hand and grinned. "Carla will be ecstatic," he said.

Brad's celebratory reverie was cut short by the trill of his office phone (his cell had been vibrating continuously from the moment he'd walked in to the office). Leaning over, Brad looked at the caller ID. "Ugh." He pulled a face and stabbed the button that would push all calls through to voicemail. "I may have, um, given that person the impression I'd be able to join a webcast this morning."

Lifting his cell phone, he turned it around so I could see the screen, filled with unread emails. "See how behind I am today, thanks to you?" I looked dubiously at Brad. "You're trying to tell me any other day is different?" I said.

He laughed. "You're right. I do always seem to make more commitments than there are hours in the day." He turned back to Max, just in time to catch him nodding furiously in agreement. "Okay—enough of that." Brad started to pull stuff out of his briefcase—two legal pads, loose papers, bulging files, Post-it notes. "Here—I think these all make sense—why don't you take it all out there and work through it. There's a bunch of customer visit reports, a few invoices to be raised, some inventory requests, and last month's stuff for expenses. Let me know if anything is missing." In contrast to the hotel contract, which Brad had handled almost reverentially, this pile of papers looked like they had been lying in the bottom of Brad's briefcase for weeks—dog-eared and intimidatingly disorganized. Nonetheless, Max happily took the stack from Brad, and was already beginning to sort and straighten them as he moved toward the door.

When Max left, I asked the obvious question. "How come I've never met Max before? Don't you ever take him on the road with you?" Brad looked at me for a beat, then through his glass door to where Max was sitting, then back to me. "Of course not," he said. "I'd never get anything done."

Before I had time to find out why someone as perennially swamped as Brad thought it was a bad idea to take his own assistant along as support, the door of his office opened again. An unsmiling woman in her late forties stood in the doorway, looking at Brad. She raised her eyebrows questioningly, but said nothing. Brad had the expression of an impish child caught with his hand in the cookie jar. "Tomorrow," he said to the woman. "I promise." She stared for another moment, then wordlessly closed the door and left.

Brad looked over at me. "I...um...sprung a few things from inventory last month. I needed them for a customer and didn't have time to fill in the paperwork. She's left me like a hundred text messages. It's all in the stuff I gave Max—he'll sort it out. She likes Max".

I smiled, but I was beginning to feel Brad's tension in my own jaw, and I was only watching from the sidelines. "Is it always like this?" I asked. "You mean when I come back to the ra...—come into the office?" said Brad. He stopped and rubbed his temples. "Pretty much. You can see why I avoid it if I can. Out there," he lifted his chin and nodded to the car park and beyond,

"I can get stuff done without distraction. They pretty much leave me alone when I'm out with customers. But as soon as I get back, it's like being caught in a spider's web: fill this in, where's that report, why did you agree to that deal, who gave you permission to take those things from inventory, this discount you gave is noncompliant, you're using last month's rate card instead of this month's. It's exhausting, but I can cope with it if it's only now and again."

"So how often *do* you come here?" Brad was over at his desk, paging through his in-tray, a stack of papers, reports, and folders that must have been 18 inches high. He'd thrown a third of them in a nearby trash can, but the remaining pile of new stuff was still considerably larger than the pile he'd given to Max. "Until recently, maybe five or six days in a month, plus a couple of weeks in the year when we have planning meetings that I can't avoid," he said. "As you saw in the restaurant, Carla and Tony would like me to be here more, but it's usually for meetings that are a complete waste of my time. Thankfully we still love our customers."

"What do you mean?" I asked. "I don't get the connection." Brad smiled. "Our customers. We love them." He extended the "o" in "love" half mockingly. "Any time there's a meeting I don't want to come in for, it's not hard to find a customer with an emergency. That always comes first." Brad glanced at his watch, and the wolfish grin disappeared. "I think it's time for us to go see Carla."

INSIDE THE HEAD OF AN OPERATOR

Compared to the towering heights of the Visionary, Operators live much more at the runway level—they work day-to-day at the coal face, selling, making, doing—transforming the Visionary's grand plans into reality.

PROPENSITY TO ACTION

The Operator's natural disposition is to action. In contrast to the Visionary's oscillation between bursts of creative energy and idling, the Operator is in a constant state of steady, forward motion—or at least, that's how they want to be. (As we'll see, barriers, many times self-imposed, often fall in their way.)

The key source of endorphin release for Operators is to get something checked off their to-do list, and they find it frustrating to sit through lengthy meetings when they could be out "doing stuff" that they deem important or a priority.

TENDENCY TO OVERCOMMIT

A direct result of this disposition to action is a tendency to overcommit (albeit only to those things that they want to do). Operators love not only to do the specific tasks directly associated with their job, but also to fix things that are broken or in need of repair. Whether it's a fridge on the fritz in the cafeteria or a strained customer relationship, Operators are always the first to put their hand up to go mend it.

Unfortunately, alongside this generosity of spirit runs an optimistic interpretation of the elasticity of time. Operators always believe they can achieve more than a realistic survey of the time available would indicate is actually possible. As a result, most Operators start and end each day with a seemingly bottomless pool of commitments, many of which will be rescheduled or renegotiated many times.

Two additional factors play into the Operator's state of constant task-juggling: a weakness for saying yes (the Operator *likes* tasks, and so finds it hard to turn them away when they are offered, however many they may already be carrying) and an in-the-moment gregariousness that takes up even more of their already overdrawn time (no matter how urgent the task, an Operator will always find time for some chat).

INNOVATION IN CLOSURE

Once focused on the task at hand, however, Operators are good finishers. Knowing that they're already overscheduled, the last thing they want to do is leave a task unfinished and have to come back to it. Also, leaving something unfinished denies them the all-important endorphin release from crossing that item off their list.

As a result, most Operators are excellent innovators when it comes to getting a task to closure. Whether it's finding a way to hot-wire an engine or devising a creative discount plan to close a deal, the Operator will find a way to get to the end of the job at hand if it is at all possible.

PREFERENCE FOR CLOSED PROCESSES

In an attempt to bridge the gap between being task-focused on the one hand and overcommitted on the other, Operators will devise their own processes—usually relatively straightforward and always highly practicable. It might be a handwritten sign on the fridge door saying "In case of outage bang here," or a five- or six-step procedure for closing high-value sales prospects, but either way it will be a simple, closed process: direct and to the point.

It will also, in all likelihood, *not* be connected to anything else within the organization. Operators know that the less they are directly connected to the slow, complex systems and processes back at the ranch, the less they will be constrained (and therefore slowed down). Consequently their own processes often have a semi-unofficial, clandestine status—detached from the rest of the organization, certainly not approved, but overlooked so long as they get the job done and don't get in anybody else's way.

DESIRE FOR AUTONOMY

Next to their desire to get things done, the Operator's most basic need is a wide degree of latitude in activities. While Operators don't have the almost obsessive need for freedom from constraints that the Visionary suffers from, they do value autonomy.

In its simplest form, an Operator doesn't mind being told *what* to do (in fact, they prefer a clear-cut set of directives to a blank sheet of paper any time), but they don't like to be told *how* to do it. They value their own skills and judgment in execution and like to be left alone to work out the "how" of a task.

THE OPERATOR'S STRENGTHS

A team or group without an Operator is basically just a talking shop. Left to their own devices, Visionaries and Processors can come up with a lot of really good ideas, and the systems and processes to manage them, but neither will do well with the follow-through required for implementation.

This ability to implement is such an obvious (and powerful) strength that it's often all an Operator receives credit for. But there are quite a number of pre-implementation areas where the strengths of the Operator are equally useful.

PRIORITIZING AND CAPACITY

Because they arrive at most team interactions already overcommitted, and because they loathe sitting in meetings talking about stuff, Operators will often be the first in the group to focus on prioritizing.

Not wanting to add unneeded commitments to their already overstuffed to-do list, Operators are much more likely than the Visionary or the Processor to ask, "Just how important is this thing, really? How does it stack up against the other things we're committed to?" An Operator will often save the team from plunging down an unnecessary rabbit hole by exposing low-priority issues that can be deferred or taken off the table.

And again because they are already so busy, an Operator is also more likely than the others to raise the question of capacity: "We can't do everything. If this *is* important enough to do, what are we going to drop to make room for it?"

REALITY CHECK

As a result of working at runway level and interacting at the front line of the organization, the Operator has a more accurate view of what's possible in the real world than the Visionary (aloft at the strategic level) or the Processor (installing the wiring and plumbing at subterranean depths). And, as Operators are the people who will likely be tasked with doing whatever is being discussed, and are likely to be the only people in the room with practical knowledge about the topic at hand, they above all are often the ones who can point out where a proposal is veering into impracticality, or at worst, fantasy.

Without the Operator's input, a Processor-dominated group or team will produce something regimented but impractical (like a telephone tree that covers every conceivable option but alienates every customer who calls), while a Visionary-dominated team without Operator input will produce a creative, soaring proposal that is entirely unimplementable.

SIMPLIFICATION

The Operator's natural tendency is to simplify. Faced with the daily pressure to complete tasks from an overcrowded list, the Operator can spot a redundant step or process from 50 feet: "Let's take out steps 3 and 5 here—they don't add anything to the whole."

This provides a vital balance to the Processor's natural tendency *toward* redundancy (because double-checking reduces risk), and to the Visionary's mental disengagement at this point (due to the discussion of boring implementation steps).

TRANSITION TO ACTION

We've all experienced what it's like to get into a state of paralysis by analysis—overthinking an issue to the point of frozen inaction—and as we'll see, this is a common mistake made by Processors. On the other hand, it's equally unproductive to spend so much time in a freewheeling brainstorming mode that the group never moves toward the practical details of implementation (a tendency of Visionaries).

The Operator is best placed on the team to recognize when it has gotten stuck in either of these modes and to help move it forward toward implementable action steps—they're often the first to call time on a brainstorming session that's gotten out of hand, or a discussion of detailed implementation steps that has become too granular.

EXECUTION

And, of course, finally—the step the Operator is built for—the actual implementation of the group's plans or ideas. Here Operators are in their element, and not surprisingly, this is the stage that they will try to get the team to as soon as possible.

This relentless push toward execution—"Let's stop talking and go get it done"—can lead to problems when the Operator is working solo, but in a team environment it provides an important counter-dynamic to the overthinking Processor and the mountaintop Visionary.

THE OPERATOR'S WEAKNESSES

An Operator's weaknesses mostly arise from two character traits: a maverick streak that impels them to work consistently outside whatever parameters are set for them, and a compulsion to speedy completion. They work to a drumming mantra of "Get it done, get it done, get it done." These two traits reveal themselves in a number of recognizable ways:

IMPATIENCE

What most often irritates those working with Operators is their impatience with delay.

An Operator will tear down any barriers that get between them and the completion of the task they are currently engaged in—and to others, that can often come across not just as impatience, but as rudeness and thoughtlessness. Reactions to an Operator's impatience usually manifest in a mild form: "Joe just lacks some social skills," or "Jen is a little challenged on the social intelligence front." But an extreme Operator can be seen as uncaring of others to the point of ruthlessness.

Relentless multitaskers, Operators often show their impatience in meetings as they thumb away at their cell phones under the table, head for the exits at the merest sign of a break, and roll their eyes when somebody dims the lights to begin a PowerPoint presentation. To the others around the table—especially the highly regimented Processor—this can seem insulting and disrespectful.

SHORTCUTS AND WORKAROUNDS

Once out in their favorite stomping ground—the front line, where the action is—Operators will do whatever it takes to complete their allotted tasks. This means taking a lot of shortcuts, and coming up with a lot of workarounds. Following along behind an Operator is an eye-opening case study in ingenuity: solutions held together with Scotch tape, conflicts resolved with on-the-spot improvisation, deals struck with little or no reference to company policy, wildly different answers to similar problems customized to suit each individual situation. Of course, due to their aversion to oversystemization, very little of this labyrinth of agreements and workarounds is ever documented.

As a result, an Operator's activities are hard to transfer to someone else. If an Operator is unavailable for a time or moves on to another job, it is almost impossible for their unlucky successors to understand all of the moving parts they inherit. In fact, it's hard to discover them all, let alone understand them, as each meeting with a customer or an employee reveals yet another bizarrely unique agreement or commitment, none of which is congruent with the organization's standard operating practices.

FORGIVENESS, NOT PERMISSION

As Operators constantly invent on-the-spot improvisations, they quickly become adept at seeking forgiveness for their sins after the event, rather than trying to obtain permission for their gum-and-duct-tape solutions in advance (which they are fairly sure would be declined in any case).

In the interest of efficiency, seasoned Operators will often store up a batch of their improvised policy infractions over a period of time before submitting to a woodshed session with their manager, at which point they will confess and seek absolution for all of their sins since the last session. This is eventually and reluctantly given by the manager on the clear understanding that the Operator will strictly adhere to standards and policies in the future.

VERBAL COMPLIANCE, ACTIVE NONCOMPLIANCE

But their compliance rarely stays the course for any length of time. Seemingly penitent, the Operator agrees to reform and adheres to standards briefly before reverting back to their previously inventive and unapproved ways.

Operators often delude themselves and others about their intent to reform. Annoyed with themselves and frustrated with what they have just done, an Operator will say all the right things and make wholehearted commitments to change, only to drift back to their old ways, disappointing those around them and straining the credulity of others.

Over time, this can make the exercise of seeking forgiveness rather than permission progressively harder to pull off, as managers and peers develop a healthy skepticism regarding the Operator's sincerity.

BECOMING A BOTTLENECK

Because of their tendency to overcommit, and their inability to effectively delegate (more on that in a moment), an Operator can quickly become the bottleneck in any team or group. As all the tasks involved in implementation get sucked into their orbit, and their frantic improvising fails to complete tasks faster than new ones arrive, the flow of activity can quickly back up right at the point where it should be moving fastest: with the Operator.

This can prove intensely frustrating for other members of the team, who, seeing how hard the Operator is working, don't understand how and why things are slowing down.

WORKING WITH AN OPERATOR

Working alongside an Operator (i.e., working with them as a peer, as opposed to working for them or managing them directly) poses three major challenges: their need to "finish stuff" can cause disruption in your area of responsibility as they coopt your people and resources to finish off their tasks and projects; they may sandbag processes and systems you need them to adhere to; and they're rarely around physically, so it's hard to get hold of them to resolve the problems they've caused.

On the other hand, their practical, action-oriented mindset is a great resource to tap into under the right circumstances: specifically, they're great team members to call on when you absolutely, positively need to get something done, come what may.

Here are some ways you can minimize the overflow effect of a peer Operator's maverick tendencies *and* get great value from having them on your team:

ENGAGE PROACTIVELY, NOT JUST REACTIVELY

We've already seen that Operators spend a lot of time asking for forgiveness rather than permission—put another way, they spend a lot of their time explaining themselves. As a result, relationships with their peers are often defensive, and interactions are often contentious and based on fighting about issues, problems, or infractions.

To really get the best out of your relationship with Operators, make time to see them (not meet with them—an Operator will recoil at the thought of adding more meetings to their schedule) when you *don't* have an issue to resolve.

Ten minutes spent with an Operator in the corridor, or at a local coffee shop, or over the hood of your car, discussing proactively what's coming up in the next week ("I see you're meeting Bloggs and Co. on Thursday—is there anything you'll need to take from inventory, so I can have it ready for you?") is worth a morning spent on an autopsy. It also helps build a stronger, less confrontational relationship.

SOLICIT THEIR ADVICE

Another great way to build a strong relationship with a peer Operator is to ask for their advice. With their strong task focus and propensity for action, good Operators can act as excellent internal consultants, particularly when you're taking an idea from the planning stage to implementation.

Twenty minutes one-on-one with a strong Operator reviewing the implementation plan for your next project will always yield good feedback. They are particularly skilled at pinpointing where you might have overcomplicated the plan or introduced unnecessary systems and processes.

If an Operator is one of your primary internal customers, ask them to sit in on your staff meetings from time to time, and as you talk through upcoming priorities with your own people, seek the Operator's input as to how you can best service their needs, and vice versa. ("Hey, I see we're going to close the warehouse for three days next month for stock-taking—can you let us know what you'll need that week, so we can get it set aside for you?")

This kind of discussion expands mutual understanding of each other's roles and will dilute the more destructive tendencies the Operator may have in riding roughshod over your department or division's needs.

BRING THEM IN FROM THE COLD

An Operator's natural tendency is to work alone and, as much as possible, outside the system. They avoid meetings if they can (usually by finding an emergency elsewhere that only they can fix), and prefer to communicate with others briefly—and virtually rather than face-to-face, if at all possible.

While this is undoubtedly irritating for everyone else who needs to work *inside* the system, it also blunts the Operator's true potential. Out of the loop (albeit by their own hand), they fail to receive vital information. Disengaged from others, they become blind to cultural changes happening throughout the organization. Never around much, they develop a reputation of being difficult. By ignoring updates and memos, their knowledge base and expertise becomes increasingly dated. Consequently, they risk becoming perceived as an out-of-touch dinosaur of rapidly declining value to the team.

A good peer will help their Operator colleagues identify the information, meetings, and interactions they really *should* be part of, and will help them understand the need to integrate more, in order to remain a vital and relevant part of the team.

HAVE LISTENING POSTS

Rather like when a lion wanders into a safari camp at night, it's important to know when an Operator peer has wandered into your domain. Particularly if you're dealing with an extreme Operator, it isn't being paranoid to make sure you have an efficient alert system for letting you know they've arrived.

Your goal, of course, is to nip things in the bud: to prevent the Operator from causing undue disruption in your division, department, project, group, or team by narrowing their options. Knowing that the last time Jorge arrived in your warehouse he coopted five stackers to find a missing item one of his customers allegedly needed that day, you'll want to know immediately the next time Jorge arrives, so you can be around to prevent any repetition.

BE FIRM AND CONSISTENT

Operators do respond to direction—so long as it is applied firmly and, most importantly, consistently. Jorge may ignore the first two or three times you tell him that he can't just take stuff from inventory without going through the required process, but once he understands that no matter how often he tries to go around the system, you'll block him, then he'll begin to comply.

This isn't Pavlovian behavioral training, by the way—Operators are largely immune to that. It's a simple calculation on their part: if the amount of effort involved in trying to go around the system has become greater than that expended in complying with the system, it makes more sense to comply. For the Operator, it's all about the shortest route to task completion.

MANAGING AN OPERATOR

Well-managed Operators are a delight. Focused on getting work done and highly effective in doing so, they lead the charge in implementation and accelerate the achievement of the group's overall goals. A poorly managed Operator is the opposite: a frustrated maverick who irritates peers and alienates those reporting directly to him, hindering real progress while getting in the way of everyone else.

Here's how to ensure the Operators reporting to you are well managed.

CLEAR DIRECTION AND INSTRUCTION

Because good Operators work hard and effectively, they're often thought of as self-starters, people who are self-directed and who can be left to their own devices. This is not true. Operators are self-directed, yes—but only *after* they've been given clear instructions to begin with. Unlike the Visionary, the Operator isn't comfortable with a blank sheet of paper and prefers to start with the goal in mind.

Since Operators achieve fulfillment by completing tasks, absent a clear direction from you, they will become frustrated and will go looking for tasks to complete—even if they have to steal them from others or invent them.

If you manage an Operator, start by clearly defining their overall goal or project, and the expected outcomes: from that foundation they can self-direct by identifying the tasks necessary to get to that goal.

WHITE SPACE

Once given clear direction, an Operator needs space within which they can work without close supervision. Autonomy is important to the Operator—while they relish being given a goal or task, they don't like being micromanaged in how they accomplish it.

So take time to establish clear boundaries for the Operator's autonomy. Whether it's in sales or medical research, service installation or pastry creation,

Operators will work best with a clear understanding of when and where you expect them to take instruction and adhere to systems and processes, and where they have freedom to work without micromanagement.

Hint: If the underlying activity has little room for autonomy and instead requires strict supervision or the precise execution of standard procedures—like performing a year-end audit or filing a patent claim—you probably need a Processor in that role, not an Operator.

ELECTRIFIED FENCE

Just as the Operator needs white space to get on with the job without micromanagement, conversely, you also must build high fences to prevent them from infringing on other people's time, resources, and staff. If you don't, you will spend much of your time placating irate peers complaining about the Operator's maverick ways.

It's pointless trying to force an Operator to comply with *every* system or process in the organization, but you can make clear from the outset the three or four absolute no's—those systems and procedures that the Operator cannot abrogate without consequence.

Make those consequences simple, overt, and clear (docking of commission, suspension, removal of privileges, loss of status—whatever it is, spell it out) and enforce it consistently and fairly. After a time, when the Operator has eventually accepted the need for compliance in these areas (and demonstrated it), you will be able to slowly extend the electrified fence to other areas.

PULLING WEEDS

We've already seen that the Operator's main weakness is overcommitment. As a result, their task list becomes unmanageable. And that's just the tasks they've actually written down—many of the commitments they've made never make it to any list.

Part of your job as a manager should be to conduct a regular review of *all* the commitments made by an Operator. Writing them all down and reviewing them individually will help reduce the actual (and psychic) burden they are carrying around by extinguishing commitments that are unrealistic, undeliverable, or inappropriate.

There are two ways in which you can help make this happen:

1. ***Provide training on task management.*** A process such as David Allen's excellent "Getting Things Done" methodology is attractive

to Operators because of its focus on next actions—something dear to an Operator's heart. And because it also focuses on "ubiquitous capture"—getting every commitment made down on paper—it is a useful tool for you as the manager in reviewing the Operator's slate of commitments.

2. **Help streamline the Operator's heavy commitment load.** Because Operators find it hard to say "No," they shy away from those conversations. Offering to do it for them ("I'm afraid I've overwhelmed Deanna recently, and I've asked her not to come fix your broken fridge next week. Sorry.") will bring a visible relief.

DELEGATION

While Operators are good "dumpers," they are poor delegators. Like Brad, an Operator can (and will) dump a lot of the stuff they don't like onto someone else—form-filling and record-keeping being prime examples.

But when it comes to truly delegating—identifying a strategically worthwhile task, handing it off to someone else (both to free up their own time and to help train and develop the delegatee), then coaching them through the best way to do it—Operators fare badly. There are three reasons for this:

1. The speed at which they work means that stopping to delegate seems like a pointless thing to do—easier just to rush on and get it done.

2. Because the Operator infrequently follows standard practice, it would (in their mind) take too long to explain the highly irregular way in which they want the task done.

3. The Operator is rarely in the same room with someone to whom they can actually delegate (the Operator is usually working outside of the office while their assistants are back at the ranch keeping themselves busy while waiting for their boss's next whirlwind visit).

As their manager, you can help the Operator by actively encouraging, modeling, and enforcing delegation. You may need to put training wheels on for a while, which includes helping them early in their job to identify important and relevant tasks and those that they can with confidence delegate to others, and checking in regularly to ensure that they have actually done so.

Persevere with this and you may end up with one of the most valuable team members any group can possess—an Operator who can delegate, and who as a result is no longer a bottleneck.

WORKING FOR AN OPERATOR

Life with an Operator as your boss can be a bipolar existence—left on your own for long periods while the boss is out on the front line, then caught up in a flurry of activity upon their return. (Notice how this is almost the exact opposite of working with a Visionary, in which case most of your work gets done when the boss is out of the office, and it's hard to get anything done when they return.)

Building a strong relationship with a gifted Operator can be a great asset to your career and personal development. Here are some ways to help get the most out of your relationship with an Operator as boss:

DON'T TAKE IT PERSONALLY

The single most important thing to remember about having an Operator boss is that while their intentions are almost always positive, their tendency to over-commit coupled with their inability to say "No" means that they frequently leave a trail of broken commitments in their wake.

For a new employee with an Operator boss, this can often appear as thoughtlessness or worse, as the employee receives frequent reassurances, such as "I'll spend next month showing you the ropes," or "Next week I'll introduce you to our best customer," only to find that those promises are either not kept, or are rolled forward week after week until they are drained of all credibility.

Understanding from the start that your Operator boss means well but that they are actually only able to follow through in a very limited number of the many promises made will save you from disappointment and disengagement.

USE FORESIGHT

Once you've recognized the "overcommitment gene," the next step is to carefully select which of your boss's commitments are truly important to your development and do what *you* can to make them happen. By being proactive about a small number of those commitments, you can dramatically increase the chances of them actually occurring.

So if, for example, your boss's commitment to introduce you to a key customer is important for your development, you might, at the point the commitment is made, undertake to contact someone to set up the meeting, or book the plane tickets or a rental car—anything to proactively move the commitment into the realm of reality.

BE WITH THEM

In selecting those commitments that you will help your Operator boss follow through with, if possible choose those that result in your spending time with the boss (physically present that is, not on the phone or in virtual conferences). Operators have an out-of-sight, out-of-mind mentality: they become engrossed in the moment, and engage with whoever is there at that point in time. As a result, they don't typically do well in managing virtual relationships.

Conversely, an Operator's natural gregariousness means that they *do* tend to build strong bonds with those they spend time with (this is one of the reasons there are so many Operators in industries that value relationships, such as sales, and in the entertainment and restaurant industries, for example). By carving out time with your Operator boss, you're creating the environment to build a strong, enduring relationship.

RUN (POSITIVE) INTERFERENCE WITH PROCEDURES

Once you have actively helped your boss follow through on a selected number of commitments, during which you've spent time together, and having used that time to build a relationship, you can begin to do the one thing an Operator values above all in an employee—run interference.

As we've seen, the Operator's mindset is akin to a 300-pound defensive lineman who finds himself holding the football seventy yards from an open goal line. He's going to put his head down and charge, and best of luck to anyone who gets in his way. In just the same way, your Operator boss wants to reach the goal line multiple times a day, and the more you can run interference with those who are getting in their way, the better for both parties.

This doesn't mean that you will follow the same playbook as your boss— crushing the opposition—quite the opposite. As the Operator's trusted wingman, you can bring added value to the organization as a whole by anticipating those systems and processes your boss is likely to need to interact with and smoothing the way for those interactions: fill out the forms to grab some parts from inventory (so he doesn't just walk in and grab them); take your boss's broken laptop to IT while she's in a meeting elsewhere (so she doesn't just hijack somebody else's computer as soon as she comes out of the meeting); or call ahead to Accounting to give them a heads-up that your boss will need an A/P report on Friday morning (otherwise, he'll demand it immediately on Friday morning).

Everyone wins when you can play this role—your boss gets what he or she wants, other people in the organization don't feel trampled over, and you get to see the inside of all parts of the organization—and to hone your negotiation skills.

FIND SPACE TO BE COACHED AND MENTORED

Operators are great mentors and coaches—in theory. They have good hearts, know their business well, love to talk, like to see other people develop, and enjoy teaching. In fact, you'll find many Operators coaching their son's little league or their daughter's soccer team.

At work it's different. There, the time needed to mentor or coach disappears under the weight of their task list and their existing overcommitments.

The key is to carve out slices of time in their down periods between task completion, then ask the right questions. Grab a cup of coffee with your Operator boss on the way from one meeting to another, ask "How did you get her to agree to a 7 percent discount when 10 percent is standard?" then listen carefully. Same at lunch. Same in the airport. Same in the car.

If you want to be coached and mentored by an Operator (and you do), there's no point waiting for them to turn up for a prescheduled mentoring meeting. You need to be there, with them, as they go about their daily business.

BRAD LOOKS IN THE MIRROR

"We're not going to see Carla today, Brad." Brad looked up at me, clearly conflicted. I could tell he liked what he'd just heard, but was confused. "But I've already set it up," he said, "and Tony, tomorrow. You told me to." A hint of exasperation came into his voice. "That's why I came in!"

"I know, and I'm sorry. I'll speak to them both and sort it out. It's my fault, not yours. I'll make that clear." I motioned Brad over to the conference table. "We will see them, later. Maybe in a couple of weeks. But it's too early to see them now."

Brad sat down and looked at me quizzically, and a little angrily. "What's going on here, Les? I've got a lot going on, and I pulled a lot of client meetings to be here today and tomorrow—at your request. I'm not going to take it kindly if you tell me I've wasted my time."

"It isn't a waste of time, Brad—very much the opposite. When you explained the problems you were having with Carla and Tony, I assumed from what you told me that most of the problem was with them."

I paused to let Brad reflect on what I'd just said. After a moment he hooded his eyebrows and stared at me. "You're telling me this is all my fault?" he said. "Based on what—forty-five minutes in my office—you're telling me that the way those two have yanked me around in the last few months is *my* fault?" Brad's voice had risen. I could see Max swiveling in his seat to catch a glimpse at what was happening.

"Brad, relax. I'm here to help you. But I'm not going to blow smoke in your eyes, and you wouldn't want me to." Brad's eyes unclouded a little. "Let's just say there's a degree of contributory negligence on your part. And that if I can spot it in forty-five minutes, then it needs work. Let me talk to the folks that work with you here"—I gestured out to the office—"over the next two days, then maybe we can talk about going to see Carla and Tony."

Brad grunted and looked at me with the faintest of smiles, then out the window of his office, then at his pilot's bag. "So, I get to go back outside?"

CHAPTER SUMMARY

Operators are intensely task-focused and will do whatever it takes to complete the job they have in hand—even if it means working outside the system and ignoring standardized procedures in order to do so.

Because of their propensity to action, Operators can provide an effective reality check for groups and teams, help eliminate unnecessary implementation steps, and identify redundant or overly complicated systems and processes.

It's important to give an Operator latitude in how they do what they do. Micromanaging Operators is ineffective and can cause intense frustration on both sides.

Working alongside an Operator can be frustrating because of the Operator's impatience with delay, and their maverick approach to systems and processes. This makes relationships with Operators defensive and issue-oriented. If the relationship can be moved to a more proactive footing, potential areas of conflict can be identified early and problems avoided.

Effectively managing an Operator requires clear direction, providing autonomy, being consistent in enforcing boundaries, and helping them prioritize and delegate.

Working for an Operator can be frustrating, as they're rarely around and aren't good delegators. It is important to physically accompany your Operator boss in order to develop a trusted relationship. Once you've done so, you can find ways to run interference (facilitate their interaction with the organization's systems and procedures), and you may be able to tap into high-quality coaching and mentoring.

 Scan this QR code to be taken to a web page containing case studies and examples specific to this chapter, or point your web browser to http://PredictableSuccess.com/syn-ch03.

4

THE PROCESSOR
Not So Fast. Where's Your Requisition Slip?

BRIANNA'S DISCOMFORT WAS PALPABLE.

It was my idea to meet at the local Starbucks. I had shadowed Brianna for the entire day before, from her on-the-dot arrival to her equally timely departure, and I felt the need for a change of scenery. Almost all of Brianna's work life seemed to revolve around her office, the meeting room next door, and her subordinates' cubicles.

Brianna was obviously at home in her work environment, and when at the end of the previous day I had suggested that we start this morning by meeting at a coffee shop, she had looked at me with a mixture of distaste and reluctance. "I have a lot to get through tomorrow, Les," she'd said, gesturing around her office. "Can't we do it here? I have access to anything we might need, and we won't waste time driving there and back."

My plea that I needed a change of pace and that I wanted to discuss some things with her in a more relaxed environment had prevailed. Now here we were, each of us with a hot latte, staring at each other a little uncomfortably, though for different reasons.

"You seem a little tense, Brianna," I said. "Is it really that nerve-racking to be separated from your files and the computer monitor?" I'd meant it to be a lighthearted comment, to try to put Brianna at ease, but she answered in a far-from-lighthearted tone. "As I said yesterday, Les, I have a lot to do today. My schedule's pretty tight, and I don't have a lot of time for shooting the breeze.

I don't mean to be rude, but can we get started?" She already had her lab book out on the table, and she started to head it up with the date and a topic, something I'd watch her do repeatedly the day before.

"You won't need the notebook, Brianna," I said. "I just want us to talk—informally. Not for the record." Brianna paused in her writing and looked at me for a beat. She sighed, putting her pen down in a manner that made clear she didn't think this was a good idea—at all. "Okay", she said, sitting back. "Shoot."

The previous day had passed uneventfully enough—Brianna spent much of it on the phone and in meetings with her staff and the occasional visitor, each meeting preplanned and tightly choreographed, just like the meeting I'd had with her a few weeks previously. Between meetings, Brianna worked sequentially through a stack of files she had laid out that morning, updating notes, entering information into her computer, threading papers and documents into their proper place.

As she'd completed the work on each file, she placed it in her out tray, which her assistant emptied at lunch time and at the end of the day, presumably to return them to their correct spot in the two vast filing cabinets. Coffee breaks at 10:30 A.M. and 2:15 P.M. were used as an opportunity to browse websites Brianna needed to stay current with for her job (all neatly categorized and stored in her browser's favorites bar for easy access), and at noon Brianna had headed off to the nearby gym, her only break away from her office that she took that day.

Only twice in the entire day had I seen Brianna knocked out of her relentlessly productive stride, and on both occasions her boss, Riya, had been the cause. First, at 9:30 Riya strolled into Brianna's office, a broad smile on her face, carrying a coffee and a small box containing doughnuts. "I didn't bring you any coffee, Brianna," she said, nodding to a coffee pot on a table in the corner of Brianna's office. "I know you like your own brew. But I did bring doughnuts. Here." She handed the box to me and sat down in the remaining visitor's chair.

I saw Brianna glance quickly down at her printed daily agenda while Riya got settled. It was clear that this was an unexpected visit, and Brianna was recalculating the effect on her schedule. "Good morning, Riya," she said, waving away the doughnut box I was proffering. "What's up?"

Riya plunged into an enthusiastic description of a new rebranding initiative her team was working on. She had been speaking for only a minute or two when one of Brianna's colleagues—I assume the person Brianna actually *did* have a scheduled meeting with—appeared in the doorway.

Riya's and Brianna's response to the situation couldn't have been more different. Riya continued talking and with a generous smile and an apologetic this-won't-take-a-minute expression waved the employee off. Brianna had simply stood and beckoned her visitor in, indicating incontrovertibly that the unscheduled chat with Riya needed to end so she could return to her scheduled routine.

After another 45 seconds or so of her monologue, Riya seemed to realize the situation and came to a halt. After a slightly awkward how-are-you exchange with Brianna's subordinate, she left, coffee still in hand.

The second time when Brianna seemed thrown was when Riya had phoned later in the day. Piecing together the discussion from the one side of it I could hear, it was clear that Riya was trying to extract from Brianna her view on how the new rebranding initiative would go down with the more active investor groups. It was equally clear that Brianna felt she was in no position to offer any sort of an opinion based on the short discussion she'd had with Riya that morning. The call had ended with Brianna sounding flat and disengaged from the topic, and Riya, from what I could hear, sounding exasperated.

And now here we were, and it was Brianna looking exasperated—with me.

INSIDE THE HEAD OF A PROCESSOR

As we've seen, Visionaries are at their most productive (and most engaged) when working at the leading edge of strategy and innovation, while Operators prefer to be at runway level, transforming the Visionary's grand plans into reality.

Except in the simplest of enterprises, without an effective Processor on the team to build and maintain the systems and processes needed to support their efforts, both the Visionary and the Operator will quickly become overwhelmed by the complexities of execution: put simply, without the Processor's efficiencies, the Operator cannot effectively implement the Visionary's strategies in anything other than the most basic of environments.

In many teams the Processor is the unsung hero: co-equal with the Visionary and Operator to the team's success, they nonetheless do much of their work deep in the bowels of the organization, installing the plumbing and wiring that not only enable the enterprise to work, but which also free the Visionary and Operator to do what they do best—envision and execute.

NEED FOR ORDER

Processors feel compelled to bring order to all they see. They're easy to recognize not just in business, but in every walk of life—Processors color-code their wardrobes, arrange their books by subject, and know the replacement date for their water filters.

Furthermore, this act of bringing order to chaos is rarely a one-time-only, standalone event—Processors are true systems thinkers, and in the act of bringing order (whether to their wardrobes, their books, or their filters), they will usually set in place a system or process to ensure that the order is maintained over time.

Processors love a well-designed system in and for itself—they see beauty in its patterns and take satisfaction, even comfort, from the sense of control that order brings.

So, unlike the Operator—who's first thought when faced with a task is "Let's get started"—a Processor's first thought is "What system or process can I put in place to ensure that this task is performed consistently in the future?"

RISK-AVERSE

Allied to the Processors' need for order is their aversion to risk. The key reason for introducing systems and processes is, after all, to minimize the risk of something going wrong in the future. To the Processor, the best system is therefore the one that most reduces risk.

The Processor's risk-aversion often manifests itself as resistance to change. After all, thinks the Processor, if I have developed a system that manages risk effectively, why would I want to change it? Doing so will only open up the possibility of letting more unwanted risk into the system.

For those working alongside the Processor, this often comes across as intransigence. They hear the Processor saying, in effect: "We did it this way yesterday and nothing went wrong. We did it this way last week and nothing went wrong. We did it this way all of last year and nothing went wrong. So why do you want to change things now?"

WHERE'S THE DATA?

For a Processor, data is all important. More precise than experience, more accurate than judgment, data is the fundamental currency in which the Processor trades.

Often, Processors will extract the data from whatever they see, hear, or read and discard the rest. Your 47-slide presentation may contain prose as captivating as the Gettysburg Address, but if you want support from the Processor for your proposal, it better also contain the relevant hard data.

Due to their preference for objective fact over subjective things like anecdote, opinion, and personal judgment, Processors most often turn up in those parts of the business that value data, such as accounting, engineering, human resources, information technology, and legal services. When Processors appear in the right-brain parts of the business, such as marketing and research and development, it's usually in support roles in which they unearth and analyze underlying data, rather than in lead roles that require creative or subjective interpretation.

FRUSTRATION WITH AMBIGUITY

The Processor's need for data isn't entirely unemotional. Most Processors have a deep respect for the integrity of the information they work with and can become irritated or confused when others treat data ambiguously or show a lack of precision.

Tasked with jobs that require precision, Processors find it perplexing when others don't respect that need for precision—especially when they depend upon that input to do their job right. Whether it's a Visionary bragging to a contracts manager about their "million-dollar deal" only for the contracts manager to later discover that the deal is in fact for substantially less than a million dollars, or an Operator responding "somewhere between 5 and 10 percent" to a quality control manager's request for the current quality defect rate, for a Processor, the imprecision of such statements is frustrating.

As we'll see later, frequent use of broad, sweeping statements will eventually, in the eyes of the Processor, undermine the credibility of the people making those statements, which in turn produces underlying tensions in the team as a whole.

DOING IT RIGHT

It is important for Processors that whatever they do, they do it right. Inexactitude and imprecision is loathsome to them—they dislike it in others, and they won't tolerate it in themselves.

While this is usually a good thing—bringing precision is why the Processor is there, after all—on occasion Processors can become so preoccupied with "doing the thing *right*" at the expense of "doing the right *thing*" that they lose sight of the organization's overall business needs. When this happens, they can end up spending too much time and energy on the accuracy and precision of a process that is of little or no value to the enterprise.

THE PROCESSOR'S STRENGTHS

A Visionary and an Operator can achieve quite a lot together—the Visionary comes up with great ideas, and the Operator makes them happen. In a simple environment (a very small business, or a team dealing with a relatively minor matter) this Visionary-Operator combination is often enough. But, as soon as complexity enters the picture, a Processor is needed to bring consistency and systematize the implementation process.

Here's what a great Processor brings to any group or team:

CONSISTENCY AND REPEATABILITY

It's one thing to come up with a whizbang idea. It's another to go out and make it happen. It's a third—and equally important—thing to make that idea happen *over and over again*, day in, day out, with the same quality and consistency each time.

So while a Visionary may, for example, come up with a plan to upsell channel A customers to your higher-margin product B, and the Operator can implement it with their best customers, it's the Processor who provides repeatable consistency. Processors are the ones who will design the training program for the sales force, produce the supporting materials, craft a bonus scheme, identify all possible upsell target customers, and order the required number of product A.

Visionaries are renowned for moving from one thing to another with little consistency or continuity, and Operators, as we've seen, are relentlessly focused on the task at hand. Processors deliver the systems and procedures that ensure consistency of execution time after time.

SCALABILITY

Systems and processes that enable repeatability are good. Those that enable scalability are even better.

Take the previous example. Let's say you've had a resounding success up-selling channel A customers to the higher-margin product B. What if you now want to upsell them to product C? Or introduce channel F customers to product G? Does the new process (upselling A customers to product B) scale easily? Can it cope with the added capacity involved? Was it designed with modularity so we can easily add a new product or channel? Or will doing so cause the system to collapse under its own weight or become unduly complex?

Building scalable systems is the highest added-value activity a Processor can engage in. The best Processors know that good systems design enables revenue growth by ensuring efficient repeatability. They also know that *great* systems design enables revenue *and* profit growth by ensuring scalability.

ACCURACY

On a more mundane, but equally important, level, Processors bring accuracy to any enterprise's planning and implementation. Left to their own devices, both Visionaries and Operators will make do with round-sum guesstimates and imprecise data. While this is generally sufficient in the early days of a business when the enterprise is relatively simple and profitability is high, once it becomes even medium-sized, its growing complexity makes such imprecision highly dangerous and expensive.

As we'll see in later chapters, the early successes achieved by the Visionary and the Operator while working with less than precise information often inure them to the value of a good Processor. They are likely to say, "We knocked it out of the park often enough without all this number-crunching." But once they've been humbled by a costly error as a result of depending on finger-in-the-air estimates, the true value of the Processor becomes apparent.

CONTROL

A good Processor will give their Visionary and Operator colleagues an enhanced sense of control.

As we've already seen, the Processor possesses two skills, neither of which come easily to the Visionary or Operator: fluency in slicing and dicing data, and proficiency in the design of systems and processes. Combining these together brings something previously unavailable to the enterprise—a management dashboard to anticipate and monitor results.

Previously, the more visceral management styles of the Visionary and Operator depended mostly on experimentation and observation to determine whether or not a particular initiative or activity was successful. Now, with the Processor on board, data can be transformed into spreadsheets, projections, and reports showing direct correlation between cause and effect. What happens if we tweak the discount on product A by 10 percent, or if we start a second shift, or "if we close the store in Poughkeepsie? A Visionary or an Operator will take an anecdotal stab, but a Processor will crunch the data.

Similarly, when reviewing actual results, neither the Visionary nor the Operator possesses the attention to detail (or, usually, the time) to produce accurate statistical analyses, so their conclusions as to what worked and what didn't—and why—tend to be similarly subjective and anecdotal. The Processor brings a data-focused perspective that adds an objective statistical analysis to the Visionary's and Operator's hunches (one of the reasons Processors have developed many superb business analysis tools, such as lean, six sigma, and kaizen).

CLINICAL PERSPECTIVE

Left on their own, the Visionary and Operator will manage the business (or the group or team) on a visceral level. They depend mostly on their gut—personal experience and judgment—to make decisions. A ride up in an elevator together can result in a decision to launch a new product or start an entirely new division. Stumbling across a one-off opportunity in a foreign city can lead to opening an office there. Meeting an impressive individual at a dinner party can lead to an offer of employment.

The arrival of the Processor changes this dynamic—and for an enterprise of any complexity, usually for the good. Resistant to such off-the-cuff decision-making, the Processor adds a sharper, fact-based perspective that is more analytical than previously. They question hunches and demur on impulsive decisions. They apply objective criteria to key business issues and discourage flamboyant gestures.

The Processor's clinical approach causes tensions in the team at first because it slows down decision-making, but, though resisted by the others initially, in fact, it is good for the enterprise in the long run.

THE PROCESSOR'S WEAKNESSES

The Processor usually arrives on the scene later than the Visionary and the Operator (essentially because the role of the Processor becomes necessary only when the organization develops complexity). Because of their later arrival, the Processor's weaknesses can often—unfairly—appear glaring at first to the

Visionary and Operator, simply because they haven't had to deal with them before. Having become accustomed to each other's weaknesses (which they by now view as quirks), the Visionary and Operator need patience and self-aware-ness to recognize and work with these aspects of the Processor's working style:

INVARIABLE PACE

Processors work well with recurring, sustaining activities, such as producing periodic accounting statements, regular updating of operating systems across the network, monitoring patents and agreements to make sure they aren't allowed to lapse—these are all ideal Processor tasks that can be completed at a steady, predictable pace.

When a change of pace is required—for example, producing a quick-and-dirty set of accounts for a possible acquisition target, fixing a broken laptop right away, or hammering out a draft legal document to cover an unexpected event—Processors often find it hard to respond swiftly. This is for two reasons:

1. Their inherent desire to work thoroughly and carefully to cover all the bases.

2. The degree to which their schedules are dictated by their other routine but important responsibilities.

This inability to easily switch gears can be seen by others as truculence, or as the Processor in some passive-aggressive way passing judgment on the impor-tance of the I-need-it-now activity. A Processor who repeatedly fails to change speed when needed risks being labeled as "just not getting it"—implying that they work in a vacuum and have little or no understanding of the commercial pressures the organization is working under.

RESISTANCE TO RISK AND CHANGE

That Processors are by nature leery of both risk and (what they view as) unneces-sary changes in the status quo can place the Processor team member in the unpleas-ant position of being seen by their Visionary and Operator colleagues as stubborn, or worse, as actively undermining the organization's growth and development.

Because the Processor holds the key to developing the systems and pro-cesses needed to institutionalize what the Visionary and Operator want to do, this resistance to change on the part of the Processor can often lead to acute tension, as the Visionary and Operator, accustomed to working fast and flexibly, find themselves negotiating with a Processor each time they want something changed in the way the organization does business.

OVERANALYSIS

Their need for precision sometimes makes it hard for a Processor to say "enough" and bring the analysis of data to a close. With the team waiting eagerly to hear what effect a new product launch has had on overall market share, or how a focus group responded to a rebranding exercise, the Processor is calling for "just one more month's test data," or asking that the focus group be repeated to include females between 25 and 35 years of age.

This reluctance on the part of the Processor to reach a conclusion until all the data is in frustrates the rest of the team who need to make a decision, and it often leads to an attempt at compromise. The Processor is promised access to the additional data, if they will provide an interim conclusion based on the information already in hand. The Processor resists doing so, because reaching a conclusion without having all the relevant data is risky, and, well, just plain wrong.

The net result is that (yet again) it appears that the Processor doesn't understand how important it is for the business to make timely decisions and, at worst, is being willfully obstructive.

DEFAULT TO NO

Ask a Processor whether such-and-such a thing can be done, and (unless it is something that happens every day—the organizational equivalent of the sun coming up) the default answer will be "No."

Processors take this negative stance for two reasons:

1. Their aversion to risk tells them that if something *can* go wrong, it *will* go wrong—and so many things can go wrong with any specific course of action that it's almost certain it won't turn out well.

2. Processors don't like to be proved wrong, as they believe it undermines their status. Saying yes to something could end up looking like a bad decision. That saying no was a bad decision is much harder to prove.

Consequently, Processors often gain the reputation of being negative, seeing the downside of anything out of the ordinary.

LAGGING INDICATOR

Bring a team together and ask the questions "Where are we headed? What does the future hold?" and Visionaries will dominate the discussion. Ask the questions "Where have we been—what happened last month / quarter / year?" and all heads turn to the Processor.

Processors are often regarded as lagging indicators—excellent at autopsies, but not so valuable in brainstorming or planning sessions.

There are of course exceptions to this rule. There are forward-looking Processors who prove themselves invaluable in bridging the gap between past performance and future plans, but they are less frequently encountered.

WORKING WITH A PROCESSOR

The Processor often fades into the background. Less naturally gregarious than their Visionary and Operator colleagues and spending most of their time closeted away, when the team gets together it can sometimes seem like the Processor is the somewhat awkward "odd man out."

Here's how you can help draw a Processor more tightly into the team and help them integrate to best effect:

RESPECT THEIR PRINCIPLES

Turning up on time for a meeting is important to a Processor. Being prepared for the meeting is, too. Showing respect for the agenda and staying focused throughout is, to them, common courtesy. Closing the meeting with a clear understanding of what will happen next and following up with a memorandum of the meeting is, to them, right and proper.

Complying with any or all of these steps is at least negotiable to an Operator and downright asphyxiating to a Visionary. But if the Processor's principles are consistently trampled on, with people arriving late and leaving early, wandering from topic to topic, and with the meeting breaking up without concrete next steps, the Processor feels adrift, and their respect for the other participants is weakened.

Every meeting the team holds need not be highly and formally structured, but to build a trusted relationship with the Processors on the team, at least conduct them in a way that is consistent and respectful.

LISTEN

Ask any Processor what most irritates them about interacting with their non-Processor colleagues and they'll universally complain that they don't get a fair hearing. Watch a Processor present to a group and you'll see the dynamic in action: their listeners begin to multitask, grow antsy, and try to hurry the Processor along.

This is often the Processor's own fault for providing information in such grinding detail that their audience is lost right out of the gate. As we'll see in later chapters, there are many ways to help them improve their presentation skills, but a great first step is to simply summon up patience and listen actively to what the Processor is saying.

Give them clear time boundaries (longer than you might allocate to a non-Processor) and hold them to that limit, but during their allotted span, pay attention.

CHALLENGE CONSTRUCTIVELY

One of the easiest ways to alienate Processors (and to lose the benefit of having them on the team) is to criticize what they say in a manner that forces them to own and defend the data they present.

Often when a Processor presents data that's hard for the team to hear (say, a negative earnings report, or a less-than-spectacular new market impact analysis), the other members of the team react by attacking the data, and by extension the person presenting it. This places the Processor in the position of defending the data, thus neutralizing the role as an impartial analyst on the team's behalf.

As their peer, learn to challenge data presented by a Processor constructively and dispassionately. An open question like "Do we have any information that explains why only 3 percent of the test group liked the new cat food?" extends the discussion and enables the Processor to help the team, while an attacking statement like "That can't be right—I fed the stuff to my 17 cats all week and every one of them loved it" personalizes the discussion and forces the Processor into a defensive stance.

GIVE CREDIT

When a quarterback throws a 70-yard touchdown pass, the defensive linebackers rarely get credit for creating the pocket of safety from where the ball could be thrown. When a team devises a strategy that steals eight points of market share from a competitor, or a group develops a vaccine that eradicates an illness, it's rarely the Processors on the team that get the public credit.

Take time to thank the Processors on your team for their contribution. Don't always send the charismatic Visionaries or the hard-charging Operators out in front of the cameras or up to the C-suite to receive the accolades. Processors may not need the limelight to the extent that Visionaries do, but that doesn't mean they don't appreciate it when they get it.

HELP THEM TRUST YOU

Above all else, put in the hard work to build the trust and respect of your Processor colleagues. For a Processor, trust comes directly from credibility—if what you say is credible, and what you do is congruent with what you say, then you will gain their trust.

A surprisingly large amount of that credibility is based on your verbal communications. If you use sweeping, unsupportable statements, base strongly held opinions on a few anecdotal pieces of evidence, or frequently use hyperbole or exaggeration, you undercut the Processor's ability to lend credence to what you say, and they will find it difficult to trust you.

When building a relationship with a Processor, the old adage holds true: stick to the facts, say what you mean, and mean what you say.

MANAGING A PROCESSOR

One of the greatest resources any manager can have is a healthy, strong relationship with a competent Processor—one who can deliver good data quickly and accurately, and can provide competent analysis of that data.

Here's how to build successful, mutually rewarding relationships with the Processors on your team.

SET PRECISE GOALS

When setting goals for a Processor, be precise about what you want to achieve—not just the output itself, but when you want it, and what the final result should look like. Be overly specific—until you've been working with them for some time, don't assume that Processors will get the drift of what you want from an unstructured, informal chat.

Saying "I want to be regularly updated on our patent filings" could result in a 13-tab spreadsheet sent to you each morning with every change in patent status (however insignificant) color-coded and cross-referenced to the original filing document. Be specific: ask instead for a one-page, monthly summary of those patents that have been declined or reached final clearance. In return you'll get what you want *and* save the Processor from spending a large amount of time on unneeded detail.

IMPROVISE SPARINGLY

Any good manager needs to improvise at times—sometimes a lot. To get the best from the Processors on your team, however, you will need to shelter them from much of that improvisation. Processors contribute best when working within clearly defined boundaries, and moving those boundaries too often will cause them to freeze with uncertainty.

Rearranging the organization chart and reassigning people frequently, changing roles and responsibilities, even moving the physical location where they work can all elevate Processors' stress levels and make them feel uncertain.

Processors don't make good "beta-testers." If there is something you wish to experiment with, if possible try it first with your Visionary team members, then ask the Operators to take a look. Only introduce it to the Processors when you're sure that your new initiative is likely to become permanent.

IMPOSE COMMERCIAL PRIORITIES

Left to their own devices, Processors will prioritize given tasks in ways that make sense to them, usually based on their work schedule: batching tasks that go together, scheduling others in a logical chronological sequence, leaving others for slow days in the week or month. Because Processors usually work away from the front line of the business, this prioritization can often bear little correlation to the organization's overall commercial priorities.

As their manager, one of your roles is to help Processors better understand the organization's goals and needs, in order for them to better prioritize their work. Making clear, for example, that fixing failed point-of-sale computers in your retail outlets is more important than rolling out Linux update patches across the network may seem like a no-brainer to you, but can be an "a-ha" for the systems-focused Processor.

HAVE PATIENCE

Of the three natural styles, Processors work most carefully—and therefore most slowly. Their focus on detail and precision dictates it. Sometimes it's easy to forget that this is why you hired them in the first place, and become frustrated with their seemingly plodding pace.

The frustration will usually be generated less by the speed of the actual work itself—they do that away from direct glare—than by the speed of their communications. When asked a question, Processors will often respond not with a direct answer to the question but with a lengthy explanation—which may or may not lead, eventually, to a direct answer. Ask them to make a presentation on any topic, however straightforward, and the Processor will arrive with a slide presentation, each slide dense with numbers and statistics.

Irritating as this might be, it is important to allow Processors to show their work—not doing so invalidates the process for them and drains your credibility in their eyes. (After all, how can you accept their recommendations if you don't know the data on which they are based?) This will change over time as you build a relationship, and as they learn that you actually trust their judgment and don't need to always see how they derived a particular answer. But at the outset it is important to have patience and allow the Processor time to lay out a case.

RESTRAIN YOURSELF

Processors respond well to calm, even-tempered, moderate communications. Flamboyant egos, florid speech, overuse of adjectives, dependence on anecdotes to make a case—these are all things that lack credibility to a Processor, and if used extensively, cause one to withdraw.

Learn to tone it down when you're interacting with a Processor. Address one subject at a time, slow down your speech patterns, stick mostly to the facts, and use hyperbole sparingly. When you're going to meet with a Processor, prepare a little more in advance than you would for a Visionary or an Operator; improvisation and winging it will unsettle a Processor. Arriving in possession of the relevant facts and knowing clearly what you want to communicate will help pace the discussion and keep it on an even keel.

WORKING FOR A PROCESSOR

There is no doubt that working for a Processor is much easier if you are yourself a Processor. Their need for control, adherence to system and routine, their risk-aversion and unrelenting focus on precise detail are very hard for a non-Processor to cope with for prolonged periods. Nonetheless, the keys to a happy and successful working relationship with a Processor manager are the same irrespective of your own personal style.

UNDERSTAND THEIR RHYTHMS

Viewed from a distance, Processors appear to work at a seemingly steady pace, rarely varying from routine and plodding predictably through each week and month. Underneath this seeming homogeneity, however, there are patterns and rhythms to their work: this report is produced every Thursday, that one on the last Wednesday of each month; we visit this factory every alternate month, this one on the others; if profit is down by 5 percent or more we look at this, if it's up by more than 5 percent we look at that.

Understanding the patterns your boss has established—for herself and for the group as a whole—will enable you to match the flow of your own work with that of your boss and the Processor-managed unit, and respecting them will accelerate your acceptance into the wider group.

PLAN AHEAD TO GET ACCESS

Working for a Processor is a two-way street: not only are you helping the person get work done, but you will also have assigned projects with which you will need the boss's help.

However, Processors tend not to operate an open-door policy (whatever they may say, and however wide their doors may actually be open). They have highly structured schedules with carefully planned priorities that they fully intend to complete within their allotted time. Wandering in for a brief chat about something you'd like their help with isn't going to produce optimal results.

Instead, plan ahead—when you first receive a project assignment, agree on checkup times as part of the project planning process. Build in short visits— 20 minutes or so—to give them a high-level overview of progress and to seek confirmation that you're on the right track. If the project is a longer one, build in monthly review meetings—30 to 45 minutes—when you can go through the project in more detail.

And if you positively, absolutely need to get some ad hoc advice on the fly, don't just walk in expecting an audience—grab your Processor boss early in the day and ask what time would work best to meet.

DECODE THEIR PRIORITIES

As we've seen, Visionaries let their priorities be set by the "shiny-blue-ball syndrome"—whatever is newest and most intellectually interesting sets the agenda, until the next thing comes along. Operators start the day focused on their task list and from then on live the day in the moment.

For a Processor, improvising from day to day as the Visionary does, or having an unfinished task list rolled over day after day like the Operator, is anathema. Alone among the three natural styles, Processors not only assign priorities to their tasks; they then plan their time carefully to ensure that those priorities are completed on time.

When working for a Processor, anticipating their priorities and ensuring all backup work and supporting information is available in a timely manner is the shortest route to trusted status. Learn by observation and by asking direct but nonintrusive questions: "I noticed you run the 90-day A/P report every Thursday morning—would it help if I moved the cash allocation up from Friday to Wednesday night, so Thursday's A/P report would be more up to date?"

BRING DATA, NOT SURPRISES

Processors react negatively to surprises (even, sometimes, when they are good surprises) because surprises are just another form of change from the status quo. Outliers—anything acutely different from the norm—similarly concern them, as their existence indicates a breakdown in risk control or the collapse of a process somewhere in the organization.

Consequently, it's not helpful to confront a Processor with a bald statement of fact if that statement is a surprise. The blunt statement "Profits are down 10 percent this quarter" will likely elicit a highly negative reaction and a demand for truckloads of supporting data to be submitted for review and analysis.

On the other hand, most Processors have a keenly logical mind and a belief in the importance of data, so by leading instead with the key underlying factors, rather than the blunt result itself ("Last month the new promotion on the West Coast came in at the lowest range of our projections, and our commodity costs rose by 7 percent"), most Processors will get to the conclusion—and accept it—fast ("Huh. That must have had about a 10 percent impact on profits, right?").

INNOVATE ITERATIVELY

The concept of "innovation" can make a Processor apprehensive. The idea of "improvement" will always delight them. The notion that something can be done better, more efficiently, is an attractive one to a Processor—much more so than the concept of wholesale change.

So, if you see the opportunity to innovate, if at all possible present it to your Processor boss as a series of steps—iterative improvements on an existing system or process, rather than an intuitive leap from A to B. You'll receive a much more sympathetic hearing and a higher likelihood of getting a "Yes".

BRIANNA

"Brianna, I know you're frustrated right now and just want to get back to the office." Her expression confirmed that there was little doubt I was right. "I'd love for you to take a moment to tell me why you're feeling that way." I paused. I could go on to explain why this was important for me, but I wanted to see if Brianna could work it out for herself.

"Well, not to sound like a broken record, but as I've already said a few times, I've got a lot to do." I nodded but stayed silent. I knew there was more to Brianna's frustration than just her workload. After a moment staring at her latte, she said: "And I'm not sure where this is going. It was strange having you sit with me all day yesterday. I mean, I understand the stakes here—Riya and I aren't exactly clicking, you saw that yesterday, and I want to do all I can to help, but it's awkward being under the spotlight like this."

"Anything else?" I hoped a gentle prod would bring out whatever else was annoying her. I sipped my coffee and waited. After a long pause, Brianna turned her eyes back to me, and I saw her shoulders slump a little as she let out some of the tension she was carrying. "I guess I'm annoyed with myself for how I handled that situation with Riya yesterday. Doubly so because you were there to witness it." She uncrossed her legs and sat forward. "I'm sure Riya has explained to you that this has been happening more and more recently. We meet, we talk, but we seem to be talking past each other. It's like we've lost the ability to connect." She paused again. "If we ever had it."

"What do you mean," I asked, "by 'If you ever had it'?" Brianna stared at the coffee table and thought for a moment. "I guess the problem was there from the start, but neither Riya nor I wanted to admit it. We've admired each other professionally for so long, met so often at industry events, it was a shock to me when I found out almost right away that we're incompatible. And I guess it's the same for her, too."

"What makes you say you're incompatible?" I asked. We were getting close to the core of the problem, and it was important for Brianna to see at least the possibility of a solution for herself. "Why use that particular word?"

"Because that's what the problem *is*, seems to me. You saw it in action yesterday. I know Riya has already talked to you about it. It's like we're on different wavelengths. Professionally, Riya operates in a way I'm not comfortable with—she jumps around from one thing to the next, everything is always important, always urgent, and she marches to her own drum—I can't tell when she's going to drop in to my office next, or call me in to some meeting I wasn't even aware was happening. And I have no idea from one day to the next what she's going to ask me—she's always asking my opinion on stuff that I know nothing about."

I waited for Brianna to compose herself after what I knew for her was a difficult speech to have given. It was as open as she'd been with me since we'd started working together a few weeks previously.

"What if it's not incompatibility, but just a lack of understanding?"

"You mean that Riya doesn't understand what motivates me? Or why I need to do things in a certain way?"

I nodded. "Or you her."

Brianna drained the last of her coffee and stared at the wall opposite for a long minute. "That would mean we have a chance of making this work," she said.

CHAPTER SUMMARY

A Processor thinks logically, is compelled by data, not anecdote, and likes to bring order to situations. They tend to be risk-averse and do not cope well with ambiguity or imprecision.

Having a Processor on your team will bring to the table consistency, scalability, accuracy, and an objective perspective. A good Processor will also assist the other team members in identifying key metrics to use in controlling the enterprise.

Some Processors can overanalyze data to the extent that others find frustrating. Their resistance to both risk and change, their relatively steady pace of work irrespective of the need for urgency, and the fact that they often respond to requests by saying no can make them a challenge to work with.

Working with Processors can be made easier by respecting their need for order, listening to them and challenging them constructively, giving credit where due, and refraining from hyperbole and exaggeration.

If you are managing a Processor, set clear, precise goals, make sure the organization's overall commercial priorities are understood, and have patience and improvise sparingly.

If you work *for* a Processor, you will benefit from gaining an understanding of the underlying patterns or rhythms to the work, and similarly understanding their priorities (which aren't always obvious). Be careful in communicating big surprises or bad news, and plan ahead to get access to their mentoring and coaching skills. Innovate incrementally, not in giant leaps.

 Scan this QR code to be taken to a web page containing case studies and examples specific to this chapter, or point your web browser to http://PredictableSuccess.com/syn-ch04.

5

GRIDLOCK

The Hidden Death-Grip That Silently Paralyzes Every Group

WHY IS IT THAT THE Visionary-Operator-Processor triangle is so unstable? What is it about the combination of these three styles that dooms them to almost certain gridlock right from the outset?

The key is in remembering that these are *natural* styles that are part of who we are. Each of us tends toward one style by default, and usually have traces of the others, too, sometimes strongly so—but almost always we have one dominant natural style. When we're placed in group situations, the attributes that characterize our natural style cannot help but come out.

Precisely because our Visionary, Operator, or Processor style is so natural—because we don't think about being one or the other, we just *are* one of them—there is an equally natural tendency to assume that what we want (as a Visionary, Operator, or Processor) is also what's best for the group or team as a whole.

So when the Visionary, Operator, and Processor find themselves together in a group situation, they each think, talk, and act in accordance with their natural style, resulting in three wholly different agendas being pursued. As we shall see, those agendas are in many areas irreconcilable, so that the group stands little chance of reaching agreement and will usually end up compromising at best and gridlocked at worst.

V-O-P NUMBERS AND COMBINATIONS

Before we explore the reasons why this gridlock occurs—and, in Part II, examine how to fix it—first, a word about numbers and combinations of the V, O, and P styles.

For ease of understanding we will continue to refer to the Visionary, Operator, and Processor in the singular. This is not, however, to simplistically assume that all groups are comprised solely of one of each. Teams naturally vary in size and composition, with different combinations of Vs, Os, and Ps.

Nor, of course, do Visionaries, Operators, and Processors form entirely homogeneous groups. While all Visionaries, for example, share to a greater or lesser extent the characteristics described in chapter 2, each Visionary is not a clone of the next, any more than are Operators or Processors. We are all distinct personalities irrespective of our natural style.

But when it comes to the reasons why teams gridlock or compromise, it is not the *differences* between the individual Visionaries (or Operators, or Processors) that are problematic—it is what they *share* that causes the team to become dysfunctional. As we'll see, the team's dysfunction springs from the interaction of those characteristics common to all Visionaries (as discussed in chapter 2), Operators (chapter 3), and Processors (chapter 4).

So in understanding how V's, O's, and P's interact, their numbers don't matter—the Visionary's contribution to gridlock (as detailed in the rest of this chapter) will manifest itself whether there is one Visionary in a group or five. Same with the Operator and Processor roles—having more than one of either on the team doesn't change (in fact, only amplifies) the underlying patterns we'll see in this chapter and in Part II.

WHY GROUPS AND TEAMS GRIDLOCK

There are three main reasons why, once they're placed in a group or team environment, the Visionary, Operator, and Processor are destined to arrive at gridlock or compromise: they each have different motivations, different goals, and different perspectives.

1. Different motivations. The single most powerful differentiator between the three natural styles is in the answer to a question fundamental to all of us: what motivates us? As we'll see, the Visionary, Operator, and Processor are each motivated—and can therefore only ultimately be satisfied by—very different compulsions.

2. Different goals. Separate and distinct from an individual's intrinsic motivation is the ultimate goal they are seeking. A team of 11 soccer players will take the field with the same ultimate goal—to beat the other side and win the game—even if they each have different motivations for doing so (one may be in it for the glory, another for monetary reward, yet another for sheer love of the game).

We've already seen that the Visionary, Operator, and Processor share different motivations, but even more destabilizing for the group, unlike the 11 soccer players, they rarely begin with even the same ultimate goal.

3. Different perspectives. Not only do the Visionary, Operator, and Processor have irreconcilable motivations and different goals, but they each see the environment within which the team operates in entirely different ways.

If you were to ask an airline pilot, a train engineer, and a submarine captain to describe their immediate work surroundings, you would expect to hear entirely different—and incompatible—descriptions. When the Visionary, Operator, and Processor get together, this is precisely what happens—except each is convinced that only their view is the right one.

Let's examine each of these three factors in more detail:

MOTIVATION

We are all driven to obtain satisfaction from what we do. Even with the most mundane task, there is something within us that craves fulfillment as a result—we wash the kitchen counter because it gives us a sense of cleanliness, or we water the flowers for the enjoyment we get from how they look and smell.

The same principle applies at work—we have a (perfectly normal) need to obtain satisfaction from our daily tasks. The difficulty for a team or group, however, is that the Visionary, Operator, and Processor approach what they do with very different internal motivations—so different, in fact, that most teams are headed for paralysis from the get-go precisely because the motivations of the individual members are mutually incompatible.

ENDORPHIN RELEASE

When we do something we enjoy, a chemical change occurs: endorphins are released by the pituitary gland into our bloodstream, eventually reaching our brain and producing what is commonly called an *endorphin rush*.

Although it's most commonly recognized as a consequence of intense physical activity (like the so-called runner's high), we are all, in fact, generating mini-endorphin rushes all day long, simply by doing those things that satisfy us.

By looking at what gives each of the three natural styles their endorphin rush, we can see clearly how each is differently—and incompatibly—motivated.

THE VISIONARY: START AND SOLVE

Visionaries are most motivated by two things: (1) Starting—getting involved with something new and exciting; and (2) Solving—finding the solution to a problem.

Starting something—whether it's a new business, a new fitness regime, or a new book—is the most fundamental source of endorphin release for the Visionary. And because endorphin release is addictive, the Visionary can end up chasing a constant stream of new things—new ideas, new technology, new ventures—anything that will satisfy the need to be in at the start of yet another new thing.

The obverse of this is that for most Visionaries, the least fruitful source of endorphin release is in finishing things. Finishing something off can be a lengthy, tedious process, and most frustratingly (for the Visionary), finishing *this* thing delays starting *that* thing—which, of course, they would much rather do.

Solving something is the other main source of the Visionary's endorphin release, specifically, finding an elegant solution to a nontrivial matter. A sledgehammer solution—forcing something into place, much in the way an Operator will approach a problem—won't work for the Visionary, as it doesn't provide the necessary finesse and intellectual challenge.

Similarly, working on a trivial matter will only interest the Visionary in short bursts. For real satisfaction, they need to be engaged in issues that are of relatively high importance. For this reason Visionaries will often become uninterested and disengaged when working on matters they judge to be tactical or mundane.

This need to solve things is at the heart of the Visionary's visceral reaction against the drudgery of day-to-day upkeep activities: every minute spent going through the motions of a predictable routine is a minute lost to creativity and invention—and a minute without their endorphin rush.

THE OPERATOR: FINISH AND FIX

The two most satisfying activities Operators can engage in are (1) Finishing, i.e., completing a task on their list; or (2) Fixing, by making something work that wasn't working before.

Finishing things is the bass beat to the Operator's sound track: thrumming along in the background, the imperative to complete one task then move on to another is the common thread that gives their day meaning. Having tasks to complete is so important to Operators that they will often overcommit, taking on more tasks than they can possibly complete, rather than risk finding themselves stranded with nothing to do.

The physical act of striking an item off a to-do list can in itself produce an endorphin rush for an Operator. (This is such a strong motivator for some that I've known extreme Operators who will retroactively enter an already completed task into their to-do list, just so they could get a buzz from striking it off as complete.)

The downside of the Operator's need to complete tasks is that they become impatient with anything that gets in the way of doing so: sitting in meetings, filling in forms, following protocol—to the Operator these are all simply barriers on the way to the endorphin rush of crossing something off their task list.

Fixing something is the Operator's creative outlet—a way in which to improvise and experiment from time to time. When they're not busy finishing things, Operators can easily be talked into looking at a problem and finding a way to fix it. Over time, many gain a reputation of being good problem-solvers, and their peers and colleagues will often gravitate to them with their own problems.

Unlike the Visionary, the Operator is not concerned about finding elegant solutions to high-level issues; instead, the Operator gets their rush from finding highly practical solutions to practical problems. Their motto is "the simplest solution is always the best one," and they have no qualms about forcefully imposing a solution if they believe it will fix the problem, however inelegantly.

As with finishing things, Operators become easily frustrated with anything they see as standing in the way of fixing something—an overly complex process or a cumbersome policy is simply something to be circumvented.

THE PROCESSOR: SYSTEMATIZE AND SUPERVISE

The Processor's two main motivating drives are (1) Systematizing—bringing order to chaos; and (2) Supervising—controlling and managing that which they have systematized.

Systematizing is the Processor's first reaction in any situation—how can I bring order to what is before me, make sense of it, and make it easily replicable?

For a Processor, the endorphin rush comes from seeing *their* systems—not just any systems—in action. A recently appointed IT manager will feel a visceral need to standardize the existing patchwork of servers; an incoming accountant may design a new standardized weekly accounts receivable report, and the new vice president of HR will set about consolidating the sea of individually negotiated salary and bonus packages into a single coherent compensation system.

And it's not just in the big things, either. For the Processor, something as simple as an up-to-date, well-annotated set of replacement bulbs and batteries in the garage at home, or a perfectly aligned, color-coded row of shoes in their closet can produce the same effect.

The downside of having systemization as such a major motivator is that the Processor can lose sight of the bigger picture—specifically, how important what they are systematizing is in the wider scale of things. We'll see in the next chapter how this loss of perspective can cripple the team by producing frustration and disengagement in the other team members.

Supervising is the second way that Processors achieve fulfillment—by managing what they have systematized to maximize efficiency and reduce risk.

Processors have an innate desire to control the environment within which their systems and processes operate lest risk and noncompliance creep in, destabilizing the systems they have worked so hard to establish.

Because of this need for control coupled with a fear of destabilization, Processors often build high walls around their domains, making it hard for others to interfere with their way of doing things. And because Processors are often in parts of the business where they are subject matter experts (IT, HR, accounting, audit, and legal are good examples), they can often use their professional expertise as a way of discouraging others from trying to interfere with what they do.

HOW THE DIFFERING MOTIVATIONS INTERACT

These differing motivations (start and solve, finish and fix, systematize and supervise) impact the teamwork of the Visionary, Operator, and Processor primarily by preventing them from cohering as a team in the first place.

While each of the natural management styles finds it relatively easy to band together with others of the same style—a group of Processors, say, will easily come together in groups to agree on enterprise-wide standards, or a group of Operators will share workarounds on how to solve common problems, or a bunch of Visionaries will gather to brainstorm creative ways out of a difficult situation—the disparate, conflicting nature of their motivations works to prevent the Visionary, Operator, and Processor from becoming a true team.

This happens for two reasons:

1. They each obtain their own satisfaction in mutually exclusive activities.

The activities that the Visionary, for example, is motivated to engage in—brainstorming, blue-sky thinking, strategic planning—don't occur where the Processor lives: behind the scenes producing manuals, research, analysis, systems, and processes. Similarly the things that a Processor likes to do don't occur at the front line where the Operator is making the sale, delivering the service, or installing the product.

Hence the Visionary, Operator, and Processor mostly live their institutional lives apart from each other, and they don't develop a natural tendency to work together. It isn't in their genes to move into teamwork mode when presented with a problem. Instead, they work in silos, each reaching out to the other only when absolutely necessary.

2. They feel pain when forced to spend time in the other's company.

Of course, in an organization of any size, it's impossible for colleagues to entirely avoid being in each other's company, both professionally and personally. And when it does happen, the Visionary, Operator, and Processor soon discover that they have a visceral dislike of the environment in which the other operates.

The freewheeling, unstructured, jump-from-topic-to-topic world of the Visionary is confusing and disorienting to the Operator and Processor; the insistent, relentless task focus of the Operator is boring to the Visionary and glaringly inefficient to the Processor; and the highly structured, systems-dominated world of the Processor is claustrophobic to both the Visionary and the Operator. As a consequence, the differing internal motivation driving each of the Visionary, Operator, and Processor turns out to be not just an inconvenience but a fundamental barrier to their coming together as an effective team in the first place.

So what happens when there is no option—when the Visionary, Operator, and Processor *must* work as a team, either because they sit together on a board or other group, or because they've been given a task or issue to jointly resolve? Well, that's when the second impetus to gridlock shows up.

ULTIMATE GOALS

It's usual to approach a task with some idea of what the end goal is. Whether fixing a broken fridge (so it will work again), running an accounts payable report (to bring in some cash), or embarking on a global rebranding exercise (to raise market share), we usually have a good idea of what we're trying to achieve at any point in time. And, if a group or team can agree on what the ultimate goal is, they increase their chances of reaching it—even if, as we've just seen, their individual motivations for getting there vary.

Put a group of Visionaries, Operators, and Processors together, however, and something interesting will quickly emerge: they will each approach the same task with a fundamentally different goal in mind. This arises partially out of the differences in their internal motivation (as we explored in the section above), but also because they see the world in fundamentally different ways.

DEFAULT GOAL

In essence, the Visionary, Operator, and Processor each have a different "default goal"—a different underlying trigger for when something is done or complete—which in turn dictates how they each respond in group situations. And those differences in how they respond ultimately bring debilitating confusion and tension to their group interactions.

Although it's a highly simplistic comparison, this innate response bias of the Visionary, Operator, and Processor is a little like that of different breeds of dog: when I approach my King Charles spaniel, his natural response is to assume we're going to play and will roll over looking for tickles; my Golden Retriever will assume I'm bringing a treat and will sniff my hands; the pit bull next door will assume I'm infringing on his territory and will bare his fangs. Similarly, when the V, O, and P are faced with a task—whether simple or complex—differing default assumptions about what the end goal is cause the Visionary, Operator, and Processor to respond in predictable but often incompatible ways.

THE VISIONARY: SOLVE=TALK AND THINK

When faced with a challenge, the Visionary's default assumption is that the ultimate goal is to *solve* it. For the Visionary, the purpose of working together as a group or team is to find an answer to the problem—an original and unique answer if at all possible. Once that answer has been found, to the Visionary the job is complete and the ultimate goal has been achieved.

This need to solve things triggers two responses by Visionaries when they find themselves in group interactions: to *talk* and to *think,* often simultaneously.

As we've already seen, Visionaries love to talk, and one of the reasons they do so is because it's how they solve things: setting up a working hypothesis and seeing if it will withstand debate. Consequently, a group or team that includes a strong Visionary will find that many of their interactions will begin with the Visionary talking—seemingly randomly but usually with the goal of discussing (or arguing) their way to a solution for the problem.

Problematically for the rest of the team, once the answer has been found, in the Visionary's perspective the group has reached its ultimate goal. This is not to say that the Visionary doesn't understand at an intellectual level that there is still much for the team to achieve—to implement the answer and to construct relevant systems and processes around it—just that they see all those things as "mopping up," rather as a team of junior doctors and nurses will mop up after a surgeon has completed a difficult procedure.

As a result, their participation in the rest of the interaction will typically decline: they'll become distracted and begin to multitask, or at worst, will disengage completely to go do something less mundane.

There's one other thing to notice about the Visionary's default goal: because they believe that the ultimate goal of the group is to solve something, they don't do well in groups or teams that don't actually have a problem to solve. Placing a Visionary on the Audit Review Committee, or the Plant Asset Maintenance Kaizen is rarely helpful. They become easily bored by the lack of challenge, and either disengage or take the group into unnecessary detours, looking for a problem they can solve.

THE OPERATOR: ACT=DECIDE AND DO

In stark contrast to the Visionary, for an Operator, solving a problem or issue is only the beginning, merely a necessary stepping-stone to the ultimate goal: *taking action.*

As we have already seen, until they have an action list in their hands Operators feel irrelevant and underutilized. Up until the point in a group or team interaction at which those action points are agreed, the Operator will often display signs of agitation and impatience—to them, all of this Visionary problem-solving is fine as far as it goes, but until it is translated into action it is of little practical use to the Operator.

Because the ultimate goal is action, the Operator brings two default responses to group or team interactions: they want to *decide* and *do*. Although they understand the need for (and will participate in) the Visionary's talk-to-think problem-solving, from an early stage they will push the group to begin making actual decisions.

Once those decisions have been made, the Operator quite simply wants then to go *do* them—to implement those decisions. This is the point when the Operator feels the ultimate goal has been reached: they have an action list, so the group's work is over. And as we'll see in a moment, that causes problems for the Processor.

Notice that as with the Visionary, putting an Operator into a group or team that doesn't have real-world actions as part of its mandate will produce less than optimal results. For example, Operators don't do well in study groups that are being asked to make recommendations, because recommendations are theoretical and don't allow the Operator to actually go *do* anything.

THE PROCESSOR: CONTROL=ANALYZE AND ALIGN

If for the Visionary the ultimate goal is to solve something, and for the Operator it is to act, then for the Processor it is to *control*.

For the Processor it is not enough merely to see the answer to a problem, or even to implement that answer—for them, the ultimate goal has not been achieved until they have wrapped the solution and the resulting actions in a controlling cocoon of systems and processes.

To get the group or team to this point of control, Processors bring two default responses of their own: they want to *analyze* and *align*.

If there is an outspoken Processor in the group, the analysis may start early in the group interaction in the form of questioning during the Visionary's talk-to-think problem-solving process: Where is the Visionary getting this idea from? Where is the data that backs this up? Why would this option be better than that one? For the Visionary, who is merely trying to get his or her creative juices going and doesn't intend for any of their spitballing to be taken as gospel, this can be highly annoying.

Most frequently, the Processor's need for analysis will peak at the point of transition from the Visionary's problem-solving process to the Operator-satisfying decision-making process. Once it becomes clear that actual decisions are about to be made, the Processor will intervene: Are we sure what we have come up with is the right answer? What other data can we look at before we start making decisions? How have other groups and teams dealt with similar situations? What are our benchmarks, our metrics and key performance indicators? (At this point it is the Operators' turn to feel frustrated, as they simply want to take the decisions and get on with implementing them.)

The second step for Processors in reaching their ultimate goal is to *align* the team's output with the rest of the organization's systems and processes. For Processors, the motto "The job's not done until the paperwork is complete" is both important and self-evident—and until that's done, the team has not reached its goal and its work is not finished.

As is self-evident, and as we will see in more detail in the next chapter, the fact that the Processor does not believe that the group has reached its ultimate goal until it has put controlling systems and processes in place is something that the Visionaries and Operators on the team can intellectually understand, but which they find frustrating and a source of great tension—primarily because by this point both *their* goals (a solution for the Visionary and an action list for the Operator) have been reached.

HOW THE DIFFERING GOALS INTERACT

For Visionaries, the team goal is a creative and elegant solution or idea; for Operators, it's actionable decisions; and for Processors, it's analyzing and aligning those decisions with existing systems and processes. These differing views of what the team is to achieve may seem superficial, even childish, but they are so fundamental that they critically impact the ability of most teams to perform effectively. This is for two reasons:

1. It prevents genuine sharing and silo-izes group interaction.

The whole point of getting a team together is to pool the knowledge and skills of the participants. After all, if a single individual has the entire answer to any issue or problem, a group or team is unnecessary. But when the Visionary, Operator, and Processor get together, their differing views of the ultimate goal of the group prevents them from pooling their knowledge and experience, and instead of coalescing as a team they end up acting more like a group of relay runners.

First, the Visionaries work through the brainstorming, creative part of the group interaction, with the Operators contributing only to the extent necessary to nudge the discussion along to the decision-making phase, and the Processors either not contributing or doing so in a way that is interpreted by the others as negative or mechanistic.

Next, the Operators take over, translating the agreed solution (or idea, or proposal) into actionable tasks. At this point, the Visionaries begin to zone out, and the Processors start their engines—auditing the transition process from idea to plan in a way that frustrates the Operator (who wants to get out the door and begin working).

Finally, the Processor takes the agreed decisions and begins the process of integrating them within the systems and processes framework of the organization—with little contribution from either the Visionary or the Operator, who both believe that the group's main purpose has already been achieved. This is frustrating for the Processor, who knows that both the Operator and the Visionary will soon enough be complaining that adherence to those self-same systems and processes is onerous.

And so, because of their fundamentally different views of what a team is there to achieve, instead of rich peer interaction from start to finish throughout the process, the team is reduced to one or more of the Visionary, Operator, or Processor nursing the process through each separate stage, without the benefit of substantive input from the others.

2. It undermines unity.

One of the pillars of the British parliamentary system is the concept of "cabinet responsibility." This states, in essence, that irrespective of how much members of the cabinet disagree in discussion about a specific issue, once a decision is made, it's upheld by the entire cabinet.

As we've just seen, the difference between each of the Visionary, Operator, and Processor's view of the ultimate goal for the team turns what should be a joint discussion and decision-making process into a series of "baton hand-offs" as each of the Visionary, Operator, and Processor do their part more or less independently. This in turn produces decisions that are brittle and devoid of the richness that should come from their pooled knowledge and expertise.

This collision of different goals also results in a breakdown in the concept of cabinet responsibility and a lack of unity in implementing and upholding the group's decisions. Because they weren't an integral part of the initial brainstorming, for example, once outside the group environment, Processors can distance themselves from the idea: "I thought it was a dumb idea from the outset. I'm only sorry we have to put all these systems in place to account for it." Similarly the Visionary can wash their hands of the pain of implementation: "I only came up with the idea—I would never have implemented it like that, if you'd asked me," and the Operator can return to the front line, grumbling about both: "This solution is way overcomplicated—and wait till you see the paperwork we have to complete!"

Of course, it's only a matter of time before this griping and blame-throwing gets back to the other team members, ratcheting up the already fast-growing tensions between the Visionary, Operator, and Processor.

PERSPECTIVES

The third fundamental difference between the Visionary, Operator, and Processor lies in how they perceive their surroundings. Just as each has a distinct view of the team's ultimate goal and is motivated differently to reach that goal, each also holds a different perspective of the environment within which the team works to achieve those goals.

This is rather like the differences in perspective seen by a player, a coach, and an owner at a football game. The player views things from the center of the action, the coach gets an eye-level view from the sidelines, and the owner sees things from the lofty heights of the VIP booth in the stands. Taken together, these differences in perspective *should* lead to a greater understanding of the game and of how the team played, with the player, coach, and manager each sharing different perspectives and enriching everyone's understanding of what worked and what didn't.

But what if the player, coach, and manager each believe that only *their* perspective is valid? What happens if they disparage, disrespect, or simply ignore the views of the others? That's typically what happens when Visionaries, Operators, and Processors get together.

THE VISIONARY—MOUNTAINTOP: PATTERNS AND PERSPECTIVE

The Visionary's perspective is from on high, circling the target at 30,000 feet, zooming in on matters of interest, and moving from mountaintop to mountaintop with consummate ease.

The great benefit for any team in having a Visionary operating at this level is, of course, that they see a much broader expanse—a greater canvas to work on, if you will—than the Operator and the Processor. It's the Visionary who gets the "big picture." The downside is, from that elevation, the Visionary often sees a canvas so broad that the Operator and Processor stand little chance of covering even a small percentage of it (we'll see the implications of this in the next chapter).

This elevated perspective means that the Visionary's "view from here"—the way in which they see their surroundings—consists primarily of two things: *patterns* and *perspective*.

Seeing patterns is the Visionary's stock-in-trade. From their lofty perspective they become adept at recognizing connections, cause-and-effect, and cycles in the mire of data and events that the Operator and Processor are embroiled in. It can seem at times like the Visionary is viewing with 3D glasses what the Operator or Processor can see in only two dimensions.

The main consequence of their ability to see patterns in seemingly unconnected data is to provide the group with "a-ha!" moments—breakthroughs in which by connecting two dots that seem previously unconnected, the path to their overall goal can be substantially shortened. Whether it's by linking a rise in product returns to a change in subcomponent supplier, or by recognizing before anyone else that a seemingly disparate series of company mergers presages consolidation of an entire industry, the Visionary's pattern recognition is a substantial asset to any enterprise.

The second recurring element in the Visionary's landscape is that of strategic perspective. Because of their elevated viewpoint, they often see before—and more clearly than—others the relative importance of issues faced by the enterprise, group, or team. Just as for a soldier on the ground, fording the next stream may seem like a major challenge calling for the employment of substantial resources while to the general watching from a nearby hilltop the stream is of less consequence than the mountain range beyond, so it is with the Visionary: from strategic heights, the Visionary sees the terrain surrounding the current focus of action and can best assess and prioritize the challenges facing the group.

This sense of perspective—the ability to accurately assess the relative importance of this problem versus the challenge—is a great strength, but it does expose the group to sudden changes of direction if the Visionary sees a fundamental shift in priorities. If the Visionary in a team is also its leader, the team can find itself darting from one direction to another like a shoal of fish—which rapidly becomes tiring and disorienting for the other team members.

THE OPERATOR—RUNWAY: OPPORTUNITY AND OBSTACLES

While the Visionary views the scene from lofty heights, the Operator's view is at runway level, on the ground where the action is. If the Visionary is the general on the hill, the Operator is the soldier on the field, executing the strategy and responding to changes in the local terrain.

Because their focus is on execution, on getting things done, the two major elements that comprise the Operator's landscape are *opportunities* and *obstacles*.

The opportunity to execute is what the Operator lives for. Because each day stands or falls on the degree to which the Operator can make a real impact by completing tasks, so their view of their surroundings is through that filter—where is the next opportunity for me to execute?

This perspective means that the Operator is constantly in motion, seeking the next opportunity to execute on the plan. To an outside observer this often looks like Brownian motion—seemingly random shifts in direction—but to the Operator, so long as each action leads closer to the overall goal it all makes sense in the end. For the others in the group (particularly for Processors with their need for order and structure), the Operator's opportunistic get-it-done-at-any-cost approach can seem inelegant and frustratingly inefficient.

The second key feature of the Operator's landscape is obstacles—hurdles that prevent them from completing their tasks. This is to be expected—it's not as if Operators are wandering around looking for obstacles, it's simply a statistical certainty: if your main goal is to complete a series of tasks, it's bound to be the case that some obstacles to the completion of those tasks will emerge. For an Operator, the appearance of an obstacle isn't a cause for gnashing of teeth or even undue concern: it's simply something natural in the scheme of things, an expected feature of the landscape.

Consequently, to an Operator, overcoming obstacles is just as much a part of the job as the actual completion of a task. The two have a yin and yang relationship: overcome this obstacle to complete that task; complete this task and encounter a new obstacle. And as we'll see in the next chapter, this almost robotic perseverance in the face of any obstacles causes problems for the group as a whole, particularly when by overcoming those obstacles the Operator causes major disruption for others.

THE PROCESSOR—SUBWAY: COMPLIANCE AND CONTINGENT LIABILITY

The Processor is by the nature of their role typically working at a subterranean level in the organization. It is they who put in place and maintain the wiring and plumbing of the enterprise: the systems and processes that underpin its activities and make everything flow efficiently. Like a quartermaster who ensures the troops have what they need to execute the battle plan, so the Processor designs and implements the organizational linkages between effective strategy and efficient action.

When the Processor surveys their landscape, they see two things loom large: *compliance* and *contingent liability*.

For the Processor, everything in the organization has only two possible states: it's either compliant with existing systems and processes or it's not. If it's the former, the Processor can ignore it—the systems and processes will take account of it. If it isn't—if it's another wild change in direction by a Visionary, say, or another improvised solution to a problem by an Operator—then the Processor must find a way to integrate it with the existing system, to make it comply.

For this reason, the Processor's view of the surrounding landscape is essentially based on compliance: is what I'm seeing in accordance with our systems and processes (in which case all is well), or is it an exception (in which case I need to get my hands on it and wrestle it into compliance)?

The second prominent feature that the Processor scans the landscape for is the possibility of contingent liability. This can arise in two ways: from unacceptable risk, and from actions that cannot be made compliant to existing systems and processes.

For a Processor, the perfect environment is one in which the status quo is not threatened, so naturally they are on constant guard against anything that could adversely affect the status quo, and these two categories—high risk and noncompliant actions—pose the greatest threat.

Of course, this is why Processors are hired in the first place, and their ability to spot and eradicate risk is a highly valued one in the enterprise as a whole, but during team interactions this constant scanning of the horizon by the Processor to spot anything noncompliant becomes wearing to the Operator and the Visionary, and to them appears to be at best passive-aggressive negativity, and at worst rampant bureaucracy.

PARALYZING PERSPECTIVES

In summary, when they get together to work as a team, the Visionary, Operator, and Processor see the exact same landscape through different lenses. The Visionary sees patterns and perspective, the Operator sees opportunity and obstacles, and the Processor sees compliance and contingent liability.

In the best of worlds, this should work to the team's advantage. Like the Indian fable of the blind men and the elephant, by pooling each of their different perspectives, the Visionary, Operator, and Processor should be able to formulate a combined view of the issue they are working on that is greater than that each of them individually possesses.

The problem is that as we've already seen, because of their different goals and motivations these three rarely pool their perspectives, and instead they become confused and frustrated with the others, who are (to them) quite simply seeing things wrongly.

There are two main reasons why Visionaries, Operators, and Processors fail to pool their perspectives, thus robbing the group of the benefit of a fully rounded view of the landscape:

1. They lack respect for the other perspectives.

Truth is, the Visionary, Operator, and Processor have limited respect for each other's perspective. This isn't to say that they necessarily exhibit active *dis*respect for each other (although at later stages in the team's interaction they certainly may), more that they are disengaged from—and uninterested in—how the other's perspective differs from theirs.

This comes from the fact that these are *natural* styles—being a Visionary, Operator, or Processor is an integral part of who we are, so naturally we at least subconsciously assume that our position is right and that the others are wrong, even if we're much too sophisticated to actually say so.

2. They find the act of sharing too painful.

The second reason that the Visionary, Operator, and Processor don't share perspectives for their common good is that to do so would entail spending even more time together in an even more meaningful, intimate way—and as we've already seen, when they get together, their differing motivations and goals lead not to a collegial pooling of knowledge, but instead to each adopting an independent stance, rarely working together in a meaningful manner.

In the next chapter we'll see in more detail how this inability to work together exhibits itself, and how to fix it.

CHAPTER SUMMARY

The combination of Visionary, Operator, and Processor is an inherently unstable one, which leads to the group or team compromising or gridlocking instead of performing effectively.

The three main reasons for this are that Visionaries, Operators, and Processors each have different inherent motivations, each view the team's ultimate goal differently, and each see the surroundings in which they work differently.

The Visionary is motivated to start new things and to solve problems. They believe the group's primary purpose is to solve problems, and to do so they talk and think. Their view of the landscape in which they work is dominated by patterns and perspective.

The Operator is motivated to finish tasks and fix things. They believe the group's primary purpose is to take action, and to achieve this they *decide* and *do*. Their view of the landscape in which they work is dominated by opportunities and obstacles.

The Processor is motivated to systematize and supervise. They believe the group's primary purpose is to control, and to do so they analyze and align. Their view of the landscape in which they work is dominated by compliance and contingent liabilities.

These varying perspectives severely impact the team's ability to work effectively by preventing the Visionary, Operator, and Processor from naturally coalescing into a group; reducing the degree of interaction when they do; and preventing them from agreeing on a common view of what they are trying to achieve.

 Scan this QR code to be taken to a web page containing case studies and examples specific to this chapter, or point your web browser to http://PredictableSuccess.com/syn-ch05.

Part II

THE SYNERGIST

Transforming the Group by Transcending
Personal Agendas

6

LIMPING TO THE END LINE
How Visionaries, Operators, and Processors Hobble Group Success

IN THE LAST CHAPTER WE SAW *why* Visionaries, Operators, and Processors end in compromise or gridlock when they work together—because of the incompatibility of their different motivations, end goals, and radically different viewpoints on their work environment.

In this chapter, we'll look at *how* compromise and gridlock happens. In particular, we'll see what it looks like when the three incompatibilities show up in the team's interactions and hobble the team's ability to succeed. Next, we'll look at the most common remedies teams try in order to overcome gridlock, and we'll see why they don't work. Finally, we'll take our first look at the only answer to the team's instability: the Synergist.

FOUR PHASES

There are four phases through which every V-O-P team passes: formal meetings, informal communications, meetings redux, and endgame.

1. Formal meetings. They're what teams are formed for, right? Well, no. Teams are formed to actually achieve things, but having a meeting, then another, and another is the time-honored way that teams are expected to achieve their goals. So when a team is formed, the first (and second, and third) thing they do is to get together in a meeting. It's here, in the initial V-O-P meetings, that the three incompatibilities first show up, not merely as abstract concepts but unavoidably personified in the Visionary, Operator, and Processor participants. And as we'll see, it's not long before the team has its first encounter with gridlock.

2. Informal communications. When it soon becomes clear that the V-O-P team is producing little in the way of meaningful results when it meets formally, the second phase begins: supplementing the formal meetings with informal communications, mostly one-on-one among the Visionary, Operator, and Processor paired in various combinations. The rationale for this is simple: "Since we don't seem to be able to get our act together in the formality of a group environment, let's see if we can work this out on the sidelines." Unfortunately, the same incompatible differences still exist among the Visionary, Operator, and Processor, and it doesn't take long for the informal communications to gridlock just as much as the formal meetings.

3. Meetings redux. As it turns out, the informal one-on-one communications cause the Visionary, Operator, and Processor even greater discomfort than the formal V-O-P team meetings ever did. As a result, it's not long before they move into phase 3: a return to the group environment. This time, in an attempt to avoid the sterility of their first round of meetings, the V-O-P team changes the way in which they meet. By focusing on decision-making alone—"getting down to business right away"—they seek to speed the process and minimize their time together, thus avoiding the gridlock-inducing quicksand of lengthy V-O-P interaction.

4. Endgame: Compromise or gridlock. Unfortunately, the Visionary, Operator, and Processor are who they are, and trying to suppress their V-, O-, or P-ness never lasts long—however short the meetings are. After one or two micromeetings, the V-O-P interactions reappear, taking the team back all the way back to phase 1: sterile formal meetings.

At this point, the team will usually reach for one or more of four commonly used tools to try to fix their dysfunctionality, but because each of these tools (as we shall see) deals only with the *effects* of the dysfunctionality, not the root cause, none of them work in the medium- or long-term, leaving the team mired in gridlock.

Let's look at each of these four phases in more detail.

PHASE 1: FORMAL MEETINGS

When a team is formed, the first meaningful task they have is to meet. The purpose of a team, after all, is to pool the combined knowledge, experience, and skills of a group of people, and that happens through meetings—formal and informal, synchronous and asynchronous, virtual and actual. Accordingly, most teams begin by scheduling one or more formal meetings, and with them the breakdown of the V-O-P team begins.

How each of the Visionary, Operator, and Processor functions in meetings is the most obvious, outward demonstration of the problems the V-O-P team faces. Simply by observing the physical interaction of the Visionary, Operator, and Processor, it's easy to see how the possibility of the group's success is hobbled. Let's zoom in for a moment on the specific characteristics that each brings to the formal meeting environment by briefly recapping what we saw in the earlier chapters:

HOW THE VISIONARY SHOWS UP

In terms of physical presence—actually turning up at meetings—the Visionary is the least predictable member of the group. Their mercurial nature, short attention span, and need for novelty combine to make it a coin toss as to whether or not they'll be there when you need them.

And when they do turn up, the Visionary is highly likely to undermine the group's ability to deliver substantive results by introducing new, unconnected topics to the discussion. After a few meetings, the Operator and Processor can describe the Visionary's modus operandi in painful detail:

- They are more likely to show up for meetings where they have the chair, or have control of the meeting.
- When they do show up, they will be garrulous and engaged, at least at the outset.
- Their engagement will dwindle as the discussion moves away from their personal input.
- They will frequently unhook from formal meetings before they have ended, or wander in and out as other things get their attention.

- If the meeting is such that the Visionary has to stay throughout (or if the Visionary does not have enough status to come and go as they please), they will tend to dominate, hyperlinking the discussion through topics that matter to *them*, and these interactions will often end without anything substantive being agreed or acted on.
- They prefer spontaneous, informal meetings to scheduled, formal ones—so they'll often grab passersby and hold an informal, impromptu meeting that may at best ignore and at worst undermine the formal work of the group.

HOW THE OPERATOR SHOWS UP

Operators have a more binary approach to meetings than Visionaries. They try hard not to be there at all (because they have so much to do elsewhere), but when they do turn up, they treat it like any other task on their list, staying engaged and seeing it through.

Once there, the Operator will interact in fits and starts, more engaged when the discussion revolves around the practical, less so when it is purely theoretical:

- Operators contribute when they have something specific to say. While not sparse with their opinions, they do restrict them to their accepted area of expertise, unlike the Visionary, who will weigh in on most everything.
- When not directly contributing, the Operator will often be multitasking—it's hard to resist all those other tasks they can get done during a meeting!
- It's second nature for the Operator to push discussions out of the theoretical into the practical, so when they do contribute, they'll often conclude with a call to action.
- Because they are likely to be tasked with implementing them, the Operator is alert to impractical suggestions (even when multitasking) and will interject if they think something unfeasible is about to be proposed.
- It's rare for an Operator to perform well in back-to-back meetings. Their need to get out and *do* something makes the effort of working through a series of meetings over a prolonged period a strain.

- The easiest time to lose an Operator is during a break, when the irresistible urge to grab their cell phone and find an emergency to fix takes over. (It's easy to spot the Operators at workshops and seminars—they're the ones still lingering in the hallways on their phone ten minutes after the session has restarted.)
- Operators are usually strong networkers—they view their network as a resource to help them get things done—and will often use the breaks and downtimes in meetings to lobby the other participants one-on-one for what they would like to see happen.

HOW THE PROCESSOR SHOWS UP

Easily the most reliable of the three natural styles, the Processor's commitment to order and process means that if they are slated to appear at a meeting, they'll be there—on time.

Once there, the Processor will exhibit predictable tendencies:

- They have a tight schedule to maintain, so they become agitated (though often don't show it outwardly) when the meeting doesn't start on time—usually because everyone is waiting for the Visionary to arrive.
- Their respect for process means that they like to work their way through the agenda sequentially, and they don't react well to sudden lurches off topic.
- Processors tend not to speak in a meeting unless asked a direct question, or if they see or hear something so egregious they feel they must speak up.
- Because they contribute infrequently, what they do say tends to be viewed as important, or at least worthy of serious discussion.
- The infrequency of their contribution is often misinterpreted by the Visionary and Operator as sullenness or disapproval. Later, when relationships between the Visionary, Operator, and Processor begin to fray, the Processor's lengthy periods of silence can begin to seem judgmental.
- Processors like to build their case, logically and sequentially. It is important for them to lay things out step by step, including any relevant history or chronology, and they will do so even if everyone else in the meeting already knows all the relevant data. If interrupted or asked to speed things along, they will often go back to the beginning of their case and start again.

- Like the Operator, Processors are uncomfortable with interactions that don't yield an actionable result, but unlike the Operator, that result doesn't have to be in the form of a frontline task—it can just as easily be a report, a memo, or a new policy.

HOW FORMAL MEETINGS GRIDLOCK

Once the V-O-P team has met on a number of occasions, three things become apparent.

1. There is no V-O-P "team," just individuals in a group setting.

Successful teams operate like a group of crack surgeons performing a complex operation—they gather around an issue, dissect it, hold it up to the light, swap information and opinion, all the while searching for the best solution for the enterprise or organization. The V-O-P team doesn't do this. In fact, the Visionary, Operator, and Processor don't operate as a team at all, but as individuals in a group environment—a very different thing.

Because of the fundamental differences in how they behave in meetings, their natural tendency with any issue is to pass it from one to the other and back again, each doing their V, O, or P thing in turn, with little or no genuine pooling of knowledge, experience, or skill.

2. The group is rarely, if at all, in "the zone."

This is a state best described by Mihaly Csikszentmihalyi in his book *Flow: The Psychology of Optimal Experience*. Csikszentmihalyi describes a place reached by individuals when they are in a state of peak performance—everything is moving along smoothly and we're knocking down our goals one by one. We're enjoying what we are doing, having fun and being productive at the same time.

Teams can reach this same state of flow, and when they do, they accomplish their goals with (relative) ease, without tension or stress, and with disagreement expressed in a positive, supportive way (more about this in Part III).

Because the Visionary, Operator, and Processor have incompatible goals and motivations, and act so differently in meetings, the V-O-P team rarely, if ever, reaches this stage of flow. Instead, the opposite of flow happens. As the spotlight moves from Visionary to Operator, Operator to Processor, and back again, the discussion and interaction are staccato and brittle. Tensions grow, leading to increasingly frequent curt and unproductive disagreements. Little of value is achieved and everyone leaves the meeting tired and unfulfilled.

3. Trust is undermined.

Turning up for a meeting and leaving some time later feeling frustrated and dissatisfied happens to all of us once in a while. For the V-O-P team, after it happens two or three times, that frustration rapidly turns into mistrust. Why? Well, once it becomes clear that no matter how often they meet, they can't produce anything of value, it's natural to look for a common thread, to try to identify an underlying reason for the team's dysfunction. And (as we all do) the Visionary, Operator, and Processor each start by assuming the other is at fault: "How could she go on and on about that crackpot idea of hers when it was obvious that the rest of us weren't buying it?" "Why doesn't he just get his diary out, write down the date of our meetings, then turn up?" "If I have to listen to another 35-page presentation on why our receivables are up by 0.2 days, I'll shoot myself."

No one likes to have their time wasted by others, certainly not willfully and repeatedly. Yet to the Visionary, Operator, and Processor that's exactly what it feels like—that when they meet, the others are, in their own V, O, or P way, wasting everyone's time. So, after leaving a few unprofitable meetings, watching the same (to them) irritating behaviors repeat again and again, the Visionary, Operator, and Processor begin to lose trust in one another. After all, they think, "it's *my* time they're wasting, and if they're this cavalier about my time, how can I trust them with anything else?"

Once the V-O-P team meetings become clumsy, unsatisfying, and unprofitable, and the Visionary, Operator, and Processor lose trust in each other, then the participants, not surprisingly, start looking for ways to avoid them. Existing meetings are postponed or frequently rescheduled, and no-shows by the Visionary or Operator become more prevalent.

The group, nonetheless, still has its mandate to fulfill: a business to run, a problem to solve, a recommendation to make. The Visionary, Operator, and Processor can't just abandon ship. They must find other ways, apart from (or in addition to) fruitless meetings, to get the team to the point of making effective decisions together.

PHASE 2: INFORMAL COMMUNICATIONS

Now that the V-O-P team has discovered that their formal meetings are ineffective, they move into the second phase of development: they begin to rely increasingly on informal communications, outside of formal meetings, to bridge the gap.

This search for some other way to communicate as a team is not done jointly or in a structured manner. After all, the very reason that the team is looking for alternative methods of communication is precisely because of their failure to work collegially. Instead, the Visionary, Operator, and Processor resort to the particular communication alternatives that each believes will be most effective.

HOW THE VISIONARY COMMUNICATES INFORMALLY

For the Visionary, this means doing more of what they do best: inspiring and motivating people. As we've seen, Visionaries excel at informal communications and become easily bored or distracted in formal meetings. They are therefore usually the first to attempt to move the group away from structured meetings into less formal interactions.

And when it comes to informal communications, no one improvises better than the Visionary. Unannounced drop-ins, spontaneous discussions, off-the-cuff meetings are their stock-in-trade, so when it becomes clear that the formal team meetings are yielding little in the way of positive results, Vs simply up the volume and do more of what they love doing. Wandering into the Processor's office unannounced, they'll put their feet up on the coffee table and try to bond with their colleague, hoping a direct appeal to the heart and a frank discussion of the issues will resolve the impasse.

This shift of focus to informal communications frees Visionaries from the restrictions of the formal meeting and enables them to behave in an even more Visionary way than before. This feels good (of course) to them, but doesn't make things easier for the Operator and Processor, who now have to battle a whole new set of Visionary foibles:

- The Visionary's informal communications are mostly spontaneous and unplanned (i.e., they'll either just walk in on you or call you out of the blue), so the "interruption factor" is exceptionally high.
- When they move into "phase 2" informal interactions, they do so with vigor. Expect them to "pop in" frequently, and at a high energy level each time.

- They bring little in the way of preparation or supporting documentation, so the one-on-one interaction is usually unfocused and without a clear goal.

- While a one-on-one "discussion" with a Visionary can be dazzling and inspiring, it's rarely a genuine dialog—usually the Visionary leaves the interaction more convinced of its positive effect than the recipient.

- The outcome is usually amorphous—few specific decisions ensue from an informal interaction with a Visionary. Often the Visionary is satisfied with a vague sense that "things will be better" as a result of the discussion.

- Where specific decisions are made, they're rarely translated into action. There is little follow-up or accountability on the Visionary's part to ensure that decisions have been implemented, and in their next interaction they may never refer to whatever was decided previously.

For the Operator and Processor, being on the other end of the Visionary's shift from formal meetings to informal communications can feel like they've been swept into a maelstrom that's half charm initiative, half flame-thrower. Well intentioned as the Visionary's newly ubiquitous pop-in, pop-up approach is, it merely exhausts the Processor, who retires hermitlike to his or her domain, trying to stay out of the Visionary's way, and drives the Operator out to the relative peace of the front line.

HOW THE PROCESSOR COMMUNICATES INFORMALLY

For the Processor, the alternative to the dysfunctional team meeting is simple: "Let's trade data—emails, analysis, and reports. If we can't communicate face to face, then we *can* communicate through documents." To the Processor at least, this method of communication is infinitely more preferable: no messy emotion getting in the way, no sloppy meetings deviating from the agenda—just an exchange of the most important thing of all: objective data. So this shift from formal team meetings to the distribution of information starts out as a great relief to the Processor. However, for the recipients—the Visionary and Operator—it feels very different:

- Because Processors prefer to put things in writing (it allows them to be precise, and to say only what they want to say), they have a huge stack of stuff ready to go, so there's no "ramp-up time"—the information starts flowing thick and fast, right away.

- Processors like to keep an audit trail, so their documentation is voluminous. They also don't like to précis information (in case something is missed or left out), so their written communication with the Visionary and Operator is exhaustive, as they send everything they have on a given topic, rather than just the highlights.

- Processors like to communicate on a schedule—it doesn't come naturally to a Processor to call an ad hoc meeting or to dash off a quick note—so their information distribution tends to come in large chunks (after or before other meetings they participate in, or at the end of the month when reports are run, for example). Therefore, the Visionary and Operator aren't just getting a lot of information, they're getting a lot of it all at once.

- Because of their bias toward objectivity, Processors rarely express opinions unless asked (and sometimes not even then). As a result, most of what they send out is raw data, which they assume the Visionary and Operator will interpret for themselves. (Of course the Visionary and Operator have neither the time nor the inclination to study and interpret the data, which they believe to be the Processor's job.)

- The voluminous, unprocessed information that the Processor sends is usually accompanied by extensive caveats, which the Processor views as both reasonable and necessary for an understanding of the data, but which to the Visionary and Operator drain the information of any real use.

So when the shift of focus first begins to move from stagnant V-O-P team meetings to informal, non-meeting communications, the Processor is not only well positioned to respond, but happy to do so. Problem is, their communication turns out to be resolutely one-way—when the Visionary and Operator receive the Processor's well-intentioned flood of new reports, memos, and emails, their reaction is similar: what do I do with all of this?

With the Visionary unwilling to read this avalanche of detailed information and the Operator having no time to do so (even if they wanted to, which they don't), their response to the Processor's enthusiastic outreach is… nothing. Silence. Or maybe a few short replies, revealing little, other than that

the recipients haven't read what was sent to them. Receiving little or no acknowledgment, and certainly no substantive responses, the Processor becomes bewildered and disillusioned, until eventually, feeling that the entire exercise is a
futile one, they disengage from phase 2, turn off the spigot, and revert to their
normal day-to-day routine.

HOW THE OPERATOR COMMUNICATES INFORMALLY

For the Operator, the shift from formal meetings to informal communications
brings little change. The breakdown of the V-O-P team meetings is no surprise to them—it only confirms their view that most meetings are a waste of
time—and the subsequent response of the Visionary and the Processor is (in
the Operator's view) even less useful.

Unlike the Visionary and the Processor, the Operator feels no need to
become proactive in the vacuum left by the stalled meetings. After all, they
were a distraction from getting on with their own tasks in the first place, so now
it has become clear the meetings aren't working, the Operator can get back to
what they were doing before—their real job.

This response—accepting that the formal meetings aren't working but not
racing to substitute anything else, and instead, just getting back to work—is
in keeping with the Operator's natural style, but it causes real problems for the
Visionary and the Processor.

- What to the Operator is merely a return to business as usual—getting
  back to their day job—looks, to the Visionary and Processor, like the
  Operator is withdrawing from the V-O-P team, or at least deprioritiz-
  ing it.
- This is, in fact, partially true—the Operator has decoupled, to the extent
  that they don't feel the need to "fix" the V-O-P dysfunction, and will
  wait passively to see what happens next, if anything.
- Most communication with the Operator now needs to be by phone or
  email (because they're now "back out on the job"), and while this suits the
  Processor, it frustrates the Visionary, who prefers face-to-face contact.
- Because of their now-partial detachment from the V-O-P interaction,
  the Operator's benign neglect of the Processor's flood of information will
  be higher than even that of the Visionary, and may extend to ignoring
  "non-optional" information—information the Processor is circulating

not in an attempt to be helpful, but as part of the organization's critical decision-making process.

So, stuck between the V's outreach phone calls and the P's rising flood of information, the Operator retreats to focus on existing tasks and leaves the Visionary and Processor feeling that the Operator has flown the coop.

WHY INFORMAL COMMUNICATIONS FAIL

The Visionary, Operator, and Processor have each responded to the stagnant team meetings in their natural way: the Visionary reaches out in person, seeking to motivate and encourage; the Processor floods the team with data and analysis; the Operator stoically returns to the front line, trying to evade them both. How does this pan out?

As we've seen, the seeds for success are glaringly absent. The Visionary, Operator, and Processor have such different communication styles that the way in which they each respond to the gridlocked team produces something worse than gridlock: hostility and/or withdrawal.

The reason for such a viscerally negative response is twofold.

1. Infringement on personal space.

Up to this point the V-O-P team has been working on neutral ground, as it were: their interactions took place within the somewhat artificial, depersonalized environment of a meeting. The stylized routine, the neutral location, and multiple participants working together provide a buffer between the Visionary, Operator, and Processor. If they irritate or frustrate one another, at least it is in the relatively neutral group context.

Once the V-O-P team moves into the second phase—focusing on informal communications—the protective padding of the meeting environment is removed. Most of the now informal interactions are one-on-one, and so the ensuing frustrations and irritation take on a much more personalized form. In a meeting a participant may watch a Visionary, Operator, or Processor in action and think, somewhat abstractedly, "Boy, that's annoying"; in a one-on-one environment, the much more personal response is "Boy, *I'm* annoyed."

Part of the reason for this is physical. The informal interaction is out of the meeting room environment and now in the personal working environment of the V, O, or P. The V's pop-ins or disruptive phone calls intrude into the recipient's personal space. Even the P's stream of emails and memos are coming directly into the V's and O's physical and electronic in-boxes, and feel much more intrusive than when presented as part of a meeting's information packet. As this intrusion into physical space continues, the Visionary, Operator, and Processor develop a subliminal sense of personal infringement.

2. Misinterpretation of intent.

To the Visionary, popping in to see a Processor without prearrangement or an agenda and with the vaguely defined notion of talking things over is a positive, benign interaction. The V's aim is simple: to find a point of interpersonal contact that will bridge the obvious gap that appears between them in formal meetings.

To the Processor, this unannounced disruption to their schedule by a Visionary with too much time on their hands and little idea of what they want to talk about seems thoughtless by the most generous interpretation, and at worst openly manipulative.

Similarly, the Visionary's side discussions with the Operator are (in the V's view) intended to help build rapport and develop a shared understanding of how best to interact with the Processor. But to the Operator, the out-of-the-blue calls and unannounced chats are unneeded distractions from getting work done, and at worst make the Visionary look like they are unduly preoccupied with office politics.

To the Processor, once it becomes clear that the formal meetings are not producing anything of value, sending out helpful information seems an eminently sensible and logical step, one that allows everyone the opportunity to make sensible decisions based on unemotional data, unaffected by the tensions arising from being in the same room together.

But to the Visionary, the Processor's reams of data seem passive-aggressively self-serving, constantly making the data-driven case without any apparent appreciation of the wider issues involved. To the Operator, the mass of information sent by the Processor seems naive and unnecessary, something that could only be produced by someone who has no clue what it's really like to work on the front line. Even setting motive aside, on a purely practical level the Processor's firestorm of written communication is simply too much volume for either the Visionary or the Operator to read, let alone process.

The result? Eventually, in retrospect, those fruitless V-O-P team meetings begin to look like a walk in the park. The second phase of informal communications has, far from resolving the impasse, proved just as non-productive, and has introduced a degree of personal conflict not previously experienced.

Not surprisingly, the Visionary, Operator, and Processor all begin to look for a way out of this even more frustrating and irritating second phase, away from the debilitating informal communication, and back to something more sustainable and, above all, more contained.

PHASE 3: CONSTRICTED DECISION-MAKING

The third phase of the breakdown of the V-O-P team is a return to something more formalized, but less unwieldy: a shorter meeting, (theoretically) devoted solely to making pressing decisions.

This pendulum swing away from informal communications and back to a meeting format happens for two reasons: urgency and reaction. *Urgency* because during phase 2 very few decisions get made, if any (for the reasons detailed above), leading to a pressing "decision backlog" that now needs to be cleared up; and *reaction* because the discomfort everyone felt during phase 2's informal one-on-one communications makes the prospect of meeting in a group almost attractive in comparison.

So the team reconvenes (usually at the behest of the Visionary, who more than the others, is prepared to try something new), but with an important change in the rules of engagement: little debate, no unnecessary discussion, no detailed analysis; let's just sit down and work through the key decisions that need to be made.

The rationale behind this constriction is that during phase 1 the team meetings became so dysfunctional that decisions were rarely made, and if they were, they were of poor quality because everyone was so fraught from the underlying tensions. The alternative informal meetings of phase 2 didn't work either. So, let's try short meetings focused solely on making decisions, and stay as close to a yes-or-no vote as possible.

The problem of course is that the traits that hobbled the team earlier are still inherent in the individuals, and once they gather as a group, they can no more *not* exhibit them than fly to the moon. Regardless of their well-meaning intent, once they assemble for the newly foreshortened meeting, the same old dynamics kick into place. Perhaps one or two successful micromeetings take place and some decisions get made, but after a short time the natural styles reappear: the Visionary can't help launching into one more creative, brainstorming side-trip, the Processor cannot help but respond with detailed questioning and lengthy analysis, and the Operator can't help but start looking for ways to get out of the next meeting.

Eventually, inevitably, even the abridged "let's-just-make-decisions" meeting fails to produce results.

This third, shortened-meetings phase is usually short-lived. Recognizing that they cannot work effectively as a team, however constricted the meeting goals are, and having proved that working around or outside of the formal meeting environment doesn't work either, the team is once more effectively gridlocked.

PHASE 4: GRIDLOCK, COMPROMISE, OR COLLAPSE

At this point, one of five things can happen, four of which are common and negative, one of which is rare and positive.

Option 1: Gridlock continues indefinitely.

In a large organization that can afford the drain on resources, the team may continue to meet for the foreseeable future, gridlocked and achieving little. The participants lower their expectations, both of each other and of the team as a whole, and together they eke out an accommodation that allows the meetings to continue even though everyone knows that little will actually be achieved.

This is often the endgame in the public sector and larger not-for-profit institutions, where meetings are frequently viewed as sacrosanct and important in and of themselves, and the idea of substantially changing, let alone disbanding, them is anathema. When this happens, the team meetings begin to resemble standing committees, meeting regularly and stoically plowing through insubstantial matters, achieving little if anything of import.

Option 2: The team disbands.

In small or high-growth businesses with a constraint on resources, the gridlocked team cannot be allowed to continue; the organization simply doesn't have the time, energy, or money to allow it. Here, in a smaller, more transparent organization, the inability of the team to gel is evident to others, and at some point it becomes clear that unless something changes soon, senior management will call a halt to the whole process.

Now while in the public sector and in many not-for-profits such as academic institutions, the V-O-P team members may enjoy tenure (or something akin to it, whereby the security of their position in the organization isn't directly connected to their performance in teams and groups), this is not so in the private sector, where prominent failure in leading a team can often have a negative effect on job security. So in this situation the Visionary, Operator, and Processor will often make every effort to avoid disbanding, usually by taking options 3 or 4, even though, as it turns out, both of these merely delay the inevitable.

Option 3: A compromise is negotiated.

Anxious not to be seen to fail, and weary from the frustrations and tensions of working together, a V-O-P team often ends up negotiating an *implied compromise* (implied, because such a compromise is rarely negotiated openly—in fact, the participants may not be consciously aware that they have done any such thing).

The compromise arises from the team's need to show results in the form of actionable decisions, however reached. Having clearly established that they are unable to reach decisions on a true team basis (jointly, coequally, in a spirit of sharing and cooperation), an understanding emerges that certain specific team members have the lead—a casting vote in essence—in those areas of the team's purview about which they have most knowledge or involvement.

This is essentially an abrogation of team ownership to individuals. Paul makes the decisions about product line A because he's the shift supervisor there, while Rihanna, his counterpart on shift B, makes the decisions about product line B. Carey takes the lead on anything to do with marketing because that's his background, and Wanda, the senior v-p of manufacturing, is the lead in decisions to do with production.

This isn't entirely a retreat to blatant rubber-stamping. The rest of the team members continue to play their part, asking occasional questions, making the odd recommendation, but everyone knows how and by whom the issue will ultimately be resolved, and there is little incentive to rock the boat and return to full-blown (and ultimately futile) V-O-P debate.

This option is more effective than the continuation of gridlock—at least here some decisions are being made—but it is still, in essence, a failure of the team. Personal fiefdoms have replaced genuine teamwork, losing all of the benefit of having a team in the first place.

Option 4: Outside help is sought.

The final option for the dysfunctional team is to reach outside the group for help. Perhaps a facilitator is brought in to improve the quality of team meetings, or the group is sent off en masse to a workshop or conference, or given a book to read and told to absorb its lessons. Often the team will try this approach multiple times, reaching for outside help as each of the phases fails to produce results.

Whatever the vehicle, the use of outside help, although well meaning (as with so much of the V-O-P interaction), is ultimately futile. As we have already seen, such an intervention works only with the *effects* of group dysfunction such as distrust, poor communication, and fear of change, for example, and not with the *root cause*: the Visionary, Operator, and Processor styles and their inherent incompatibility.

FINDING THE KEY, UNLOCKING THE DOOR TO SUCCESS: THE FIFTH OPTION

It would seem from much of this chapter that the V-O-P team is doomed to failure from the start. In essence, that is true: the team *is* doomed to failure for all the reasons we have explored so far.

And yet, successful groups and teams are everywhere, in organizations large and small. There are people who have found themselves trapped in the destructive cycle described in this chapter and yet they have succeeded in the end. There are teams that have managed to transcend the inherent incompatibilities of the Visionary, Operator, and Processor.

How did they do it? If a V-O-P team is unstable, how can we make it stable? That's the fifth option in the endgame, and the subject of the rest of this book.

The answer is both simple and logical. If V-O-P teams are doomed to failure, then stop being a V-O-P team.

Option 5: A fourth style develops within the group.

If the V-O-P team is unstable, how can we make it stable? The answer is by add-ing a fourth—learned—style to the team, and thereby turning it into *more* than a V-O-P team.

If, as we've seen, left to their own devices the Visionary, Operator, and Processor are incompatible and dysfunctional, then *let's not leave them to their own devices.* Instead, like a car without gas, let's add what's needed to make it work.

Successful teams do this intuitively. Whether or not they use, or are even aware of, the Visionary, Operator, and Processor vocabulary, they grasp their way to an understanding that the mix is unstable. By trial and error they learn that the only way to make it stable is to introduce a fourth, learned style, one that pulls the Visionary, Operator, and Processor together into a coherent, highly functional, successful team.

Teams that get there by trial and error do so painfully over time, losing and bruising people along the way, never entirely sure why what they are doing is working, and hopeful that what *is* working will continue to work.

Your transition doesn't need to be one of trial and error. In the rest of this book, I will show you precisely what this fourth style, which I call the Synergist, is, how it is developed, what it does, and how it changes the unstable team into a stable, successful V-O-P-S (Visionary, Operator, Processor, Synergist) team.

CHAPTER SUMMARY

Left to their own devices, the V-O-P (Visionary, Operator, Processor) team is inherently unstable and will descend into gridlock relatively quickly.

The V-O-P team usually goes through four phases:

1. Meeting formally. In this phase the Visionary, Operator, and Processor first realize that they cannot, jointly, make consistently good decisions, mostly because their way of "showing up" in meetings is different and incompatible.

2. Communicating informally. In phase 2 the Visionary, Operator, and Processor try communicating one-on-one outside of the formal meeting structure. They soon discover that this too is ultimately futile, as the same incompatible differences still exist between them.

3. In fact, the pain caused by trying to communicate informally turns out to be even greater than that caused during the formal meetings, and so the Visionary, Operator, and Processor turn to the third phase: attempting shorter meetings, more focused on getting decisions made and restricting the V-O-P interaction.

4. However, even in these constrained meetings the Visionary, Operator, and Processor cannot but help let their natural styles emerge, and it's not long before the team moves into the fourth phase, the endgame.

For most teams, the endgame involves one or more of four options: reducing expectations of the team and the participants and simply continuing, even though no one now expects anything of value to emerge from the process; disbanding; obtaining outside help (which ultimately doesn't work, thus only postponing the inevitable); or negotiating an implied compromise.

There is a fifth option, which many high-performing teams discover by trial and error, and without using the vocabulary or methodology outlined in this book: introducing a fourth, learned style, called the Synergist. Introducing this fourth style to the group changes the dynamic of the guaranteed-to-fail V-O-P team to something new, a V-O-P-S (Visionary, Operator, Processor, Synergist) team—one which has considerable chance of success.

 Scan this QR code to be taken to a web page containing case studies and examples specific to this chapter, or point your web browser to http://PredictableSuccess.com/syn-ch06.

7

FROM TRIANGLE TO PYRAMID

Adding a New Dimension to the Group Dynamic

THE VISIONARY, OPERATOR, AND PROCESSOR are like the epidermis of an organization—prick them, and as we've seen in Part I of this book, they bleed, in predictable ways. The reactions of the Visionary, Operator, and Processor are so ingrained, their natural styles so much a part of who they are, that the V-O-P team reaches a standoff, with the participants trapped in their own V-, O-, or P-driven agenda. Viewed abstractly, such a team looks like a triangle, with the V, O, and P each positioned at a corner.

Unfortunately the two-dimensional triangle formed by the Visionary, Operator, and Processor is just that: two-dimensional. It's almost a caricature of what a team should be, with no depth, lacking the ability to go deep on any topic, unable to mine each other's knowledge, skills, and experience for the benefit of the organization as a whole.

In order to become a true team, the triangle needs to find a way not just to coexist but to thrive and blossom in each other's company, a way to bring the best out in each other in a manner that's (relatively) free of tension and that engenders mutual respect and support.

So if the Visionary, Operator, and Processor are not going to change their natural styles and we cannot remove them from the team, there is logically only one way to substantively change the existing team dynamics, and that is to *add* something: a fourth style, one which, when introduced into the team, will transform it from a flat, two-dimensional triangle into a fully realized, three-dimensional pyramid; a team with depth, freed from dysfunction and released into productivity and high performance.

WHAT SUCCESSFUL TEAMS DO

Over decades of watching teams form, then fail or gridlock, from time to time I would see a group break through the standoff and become a high-performing, successful team. Very occasionally I'd witness a team being successful right out of the blocks. When I analyzed what was happening in these groups, the difference between them and a gridlocked team was subtle, but massively impactful.

In the high-performing teams, not only did the Visionary, Operator, and Processor show up, but from time to time a fourth, unnamed style appeared in the team's interaction. At first, I had no context for this fourth style. I didn't know what it was or where it came from. All I could tell initially was that it wasn't one of the Visionary, Operator, or Processor styles; it was something on its own, separate, apart.

As I tracked how these high-performing teams interacted, some characteristics of the fourth style began to emerge. Most striking at first was what the fourth style was *not*.

- It was not a replacement for any of the three natural styles—the Visionary, Operator, and Processor were still there, present and active.
- It wasn't persistent: the fourth style wasn't always in the room like the Visionary, Operator, and Processor—sometimes it appeared, sometimes it didn't; sometimes it would appear briefly then quietly disappear.
- It wasn't intrusive. The fourth style rarely seemed to dominate or command the others—it seemed more to instruct and inform the other styles rather than lead them.
- It wasn't necessarily natural. Although in later years I would find out that some people do naturally exhibit the fourth style, what became clear from the beginning was that the Visionary, Operator, and Processor could (and did) learn it, and use it effectively.

In due course I termed this fourth, learned style "the Synergist," because in my observations that's essentially what it did. When the Synergist style appeared, the gridlocked, personal-agenda-driven team would be transformed into a powerful, results-oriented V-O-P-S team—one in which the Visionary, Operator, and Processor were all free to be themselves, but in a way which enabled them to work together fruitfully and which brought out the best in each other.

Eventually, after watching hundreds of V-O-P interactions made successful by the addition of the Synergist, I was able to more clearly define what the Synergist style is and what it does.

WHAT IS A SYNERGIST?

The Synergist is the missing link that transforms the two-dimensional V-O-P group into a truly three-dimensional team. It does this by enriching and transforming the interaction between the Visionary, Operator, and Processor in ways we'll examine momentarily. But before we look at what a Synergist *does*, let's take a closer look at what the Synergist *is*.

AN (OPTIONAL) FOURTH STYLE

At root, the Synergist is simply a fourth style, but one which doesn't always show up. Just as the Visionary, Operator, and Processor are the three natural styles that always appear in a group environment, so the Synergist is one that *may* emerge in that environment.

PRIMARY FOCUS ON THE ENTERPRISE

The key defining characteristic of the Synergist style is that unlike the Visionary, Operator, and Processor styles—which focus primarily on the desires and preferences of the individuals themselves in ways we've examined—the Synergist is focused primarily on what is best for the enterprise (the organization, department, division, project, group, or team).

This detached perspective—not focusing reflexively on their own concerns—gives the Synergist a high-level perspective of the team's activities. If, as we've seen, the Visionary, Operator, and Processor can be seen as the epidermis of the organization, each reacting reflexively and predictably, the Synergist can be compared to the neocortex, collecting information and signals from the rest of the body, processing them, and outputting instructions that enable the team or group to perform productively.

The Synergist's viewpoint is similar to what Ron Heifitz in his excellent book *Leadership on the Line* calls "going to the balcony." It's as if the Synergist observes the V-O-P interactions from an elevated level, watching their interactions on the dance floor below, choosing to engage only when an intervention is necessary to move the team process forward.

A LEARNED STYLE

While natural Synergists exist (we'll discuss them shortly), they are rare. If they were common, most teams of any size would be statistically likely to include a Synergist from the outset, thus avoiding the V-O-P gridlock.

The good news is that the Synergist is a style that anyone can emulate irrespective of their natural style. Any Visionary, Operator, or Processor can (and should) learn to also be a Synergist. Although as we'll see later, some natural styles find it easier than others to do so, the most effective team is one in which all of the members have learned how to be a Synergist when necessary.

Learning how to be a Synergist does not abrogate or dilute an individual's natural style. A Visionary who learns to be a Synergist doesn't stop being a Visionary or have their Visionary wings clipped. An Operator who has learned the Synergist style isn't diluted into an Operator-lite, and a Processor-Synergist isn't an emasculated Processor. Instead, a V, O, or P who has learned the Synergist style has an additional set of tools and techniques to use within the team environment. Think of it as a car with a powerful overdrive button that can be engaged or disengaged as needed.

EMERGES IN THE V-O-P ENVIRONMENT

Because they are natural styles, it's not hard to spot a Visionary, Operator, or Processor outside of the group environment. Their attitudes, communication styles, even their physical work surroundings are filled with telltale giveaways.

The Synergist style, on the other hand, is only necessary—and therefore only appears—within a group environment. While the Processor will still process and the Visionary will continue to think creatively and strategically in their day-to-day activities, and the Operator will continue to crunch through tasks regardless of the surroundings, the Synergist has little to do—no raison d'être—outside the group environment. This is one of the reasons why natural Synergists are rare; where they do exist, they are unfulfilled when on their own and feel valuable or useful only when in a group.

The reason the Synergist style emerges is essentially Darwinian—as we've seen, the V-O-P styles are on their own incapable of generating fruitful interactions, and so a fourth style *must* emerge in order for this to happen. The Synergist style is called into being by the need for the Visionary, Operator, and Processor to connect and harmonize in order for the team to move forward.

WHAT SYNERGISTS DO

So how does this happen? In practical terms, what is it that the Synergist does that breaks the gridlock of the V-O-P team and releases it to perform effectively?

REGULATE

Most of the conflict that appears in the V-O-P team occurs when one or more members operate at the extreme of their natural tendencies.

Visionaries acting within normal bounds are exciting, creative, engaging people to be around. It's when they stray to the edges of the shiny-blue-ball syndrome, or fall into a rabbit hole of infinite hyperlinking, that they become impossible to deal with. Operators simply getting on with the job are a great asset to any group, but when they become obsessive about task completion at the expense of everything else, then the team suffers. When they're simply doing their job, Processors bring structure and control to the team's efforts. Only when they insist on overanalyzing everything does life become unbearable for the others.

The Synergist's first, and arguably most important, job is to regulate the range of those characteristics within which the Visionary, Operator, and Processor operate, allowing them to flourish in their roles without straying into the red zone of unhelpful extremes of behavior.

RESOLVE

As we've seen repeatedly, many of the goals, aspirations, and motivations of the Visionary, Operator, and Processor are, in their raw form, incompatible. This is not to say that they are irreconcilable, simply that while the Visionary, Operator, and Processor remain locked into their V-, O-, and P-based agendas no resolution is possible.

With the Synergist on the scene, this dynamic changes. With a fourth perspective available—one based primarily on the good of the organization as a whole—what was previously insoluble becomes resolvable. Resolution is made possible by unshackling the three from their style-driven agendas. The role of the Synergist is to bring that fourth perspective, and use it to resolve differences among the Visionary, Operator, and Processor.

INTERPRET

Many of the difficulties in the Visionary-Operator-Processor interactions are due to misunderstandings in communication. The vocabulary that the three styles use, the different meanings they give to certain words and phrases, and differences in the use of metaphor, descriptors, and hyperbole all combine to produce a communications landscape dotted with land mines.

Within this environment, Synergists act as minesweepers, scanning for potential communication hazards on the horizon and defusing them where possible. They interpret the Visionary's, Operator's, and Processor's languages, and clear up misunderstandings when they do occur.

ELEVATE

Another key role of the Synergist is somewhat self-referential: to invoke the Synergist style in the Visionary, Operator, and Processor and, when necessary, to elevate them from their dominant V, O, or P thinking to take a Synergistic view of the issues being discussed or worked on.

This isn't a persistent state. The group wouldn't produce anything of value if all its members were operating permanently in the Synergist style. Every team needs different perspectives and personalities to function most of the time. But at key moments—we'll see specifically which key moments in the next chapter— it is equally important that all of the team, including the Visionary, Operator, and Processor, rise above the immediate work at hand and share the Synergistic view from the balcony.

SEQUENCE AND CHOREOGRAPHY

Like a group of people dropped on a dance floor and asked to samba without any prior instruction, the Visionary, Operator, and Processor stumble frequently because of the lack of basic choreography. Not knowing where and when to turn or step, inevitably they stand on each other's toes, bump into each other, and generally get in each other's way.

From their elevated position on the balcony, the Synergist is perfectly placed to help the Visionary, Operator, and Processor choreograph their interactions for best effect. Seeing when a Processor needs to make a valid interjection and when to hold back, perceiving when the Visionary needs to bring the brainstorming to an end, and knowing how and when the Operator should lead the discussion to some actionable conclusion—all are more easily spotted by the Synergist from that unique perspective, but almost impossible for the Visionary, Operator, and Processor to see at ground level.

In chapter 8 we'll examine in detail precisely how the Synergist intervenes at key stages to bring harmony and flow to the team's interactions.

CONNECT

Once the Visionary, Operator, and Processor have had their excesses regulated, their misunderstandings explained, and learned some basic choreography, the scene is set for the group to become a real team—to connect the disparate knowledge, skills, and experience of the team members and to produce something larger than the individual parts.

This act of connecting—the ability of the Visionary, Operator, and Processor to sit together and extract from one another the needed insights, suggestions, prompts, and everything else that is required to sculpt the best solution to a specific issue—is almost impossible for the V-O-P team to do alone because of their very different natural styles.

The Synergist is the vital missing piece that enables this phase in the interaction. Because they are focused primarily on what's best for the enterprise as a whole, the Synergist can act more as an interested observer and less as an invested participant. They can draw out what is needed from each participant in an agenda-neutral manner, without reigniting any of the conflicts that would arise if the V-O-P team tried to do so alone.

HARMONIZE

Really a part of connecting but worth emphasizing is the Synergist's ability to harmonize the contributions of the Visionary, Operator, and Processor into a cohesive whole.

One roadblock the V-O-P team hits frequently is their inability to agree on the content or form in which to communicate the output from their interactions. While they are unlikely to use the V-O-P terminology, complaints to the effect that "this isn't Visionary enough," or "this is too Processor-ish" can result in endless rewriting or, at worst, total stalemate, as each person jostles to massage the end result into something reflecting their own primary style.

The Synergist alone is able to facilitate a conflation of the Visionary, Operator, and Processor ideas into one harmonized whole. This does not mean that the Synergist becomes the team's copywriter—they aren't taking dictation from the Visionary, Operator, and Processor, nor are they personally responsible for the production of the team's output. Rather, as we'll see in the next chapter, the Synergist style emerges throughout the team at this stage in the interaction, informing and directing their actions in a way that produces a unified, harmonized result.

MOVING FORWARD

A key stage in the team's interactions is when they have finished one thing and are moving on to something new. The conclusion of one project and the start of a new one resets the V-O-P interactions to their initial state—it's like a mini version of forming the team from scratch—and as such, opens up the opportunity for the default, dysfunctional patterns to reemerge.

In high-performing teams the Synergist style comes to the fore in endings and beginnings. Just as the Synergist's enterprise-wide perspective is invaluable in harmonizing the work of the Visionary, Operator, and Processor at the conclusion of one thing, as we'll see in chapter 8, so that same perspective is invaluable in settling on goals and setting the ground rules when starting something new.

WHERE SYNERGISTS COME FROM

Where does a team find its Synergist? The answer is, from a surprisingly wide variety of sources.

Unlike the naturally occurring Visionary, Operator, and Processor styles that each of us exhibits to one degree or another, anyone can learn (albeit with varying degrees of difficulty) to be a Synergist in *addition* to his or her own natural style. There are also some people who are natural Synergists. They possess an intuitive, inherent understanding of the Synergist mindset and respond reflexively to situations in a Synergist manner. They are as much Synergists by default as the Visionary, Operator, and Processor are Vs, Os and Ps.

Think of it in terms of say, tennis players. Anyone can, in theory, take tennis lessons and become proficient to some degree. Even the least proficient player can learn the rules and be able to at least hit the ball back over the net in the right circumstances. Similarly, any Visionary, Operator, or Processor can learn to act as a Synergist at a basic level. Some people, on the other hand, will as a result of their tennis tuition become highly proficient players—and some Visionaries, Operators, and Processors learn to be highly proficient, master Synergists. Most people develop to a point somewhere between the two extremes—Visionaries, Operators, and Processors who, with the right guidance, become reasonably competent Synergists.

There is one other group, however—those few who, when they first get a tennis racket in their hands, whether at age six or sixteen, realize that they have a natural aptitude for the game. Their hand-eye coordination, spatial awareness, ability to focus, and natural athleticism combine to make them "naturals," less in need of instruction than they are of simple practice. So it is with the few born Synergists—those who naturally take the enterprise view, have a dispassionate, agenda-neutral perspective, and for whom the group or team environment is where they are most comfortable.

Let's look first at the development of the Synergist style alongside the three natural V-O-P styles, and then a little closer at the natural Synergist.

THE V-O-P+SYNERGIST

How can a Visionary, Operator, or Processor also become a Synergist? Well, to continue the sports analogy, much in the same way as a golfer can also be a tennis player—they simply learn to be so.

Obviously, there is no "learning" required to be a Visionary, Operator, or Processor—as we've seen, these are natural, innate styles—so there is no fear that by adding a second, learned style, the individual's natural style will be in any way jeopardized. Informed, yes, but not endangered.

Learning the Synergist style is rather like packing a raincoat for a trip when unseasonable weather is predicted—if and when you need it, you can pull it out of the bag and use it—and when it isn't needed, it can be set aside and you can wear what you originally planned to wear.

Many Visionaries, Operators, and Processors develop a Synergist style over time simply by trial and error. Watching their V-O-P teams gridlock regularly, they try things out to see what might change the pattern. By adopting a moderated tone here, suppressing a reflexive response there, or by stepping back to take a wider view, they slowly learn what works and what doesn't work in guiding a team forward to success.

What the Synergist does isn't rocket science. Most of what I discuss in Part III is little more than informed common sense—but it's common sense that's almost impossible for the Visionary, Operator, and Processor to see unaided because of the filters imposed on their thinking by innate mindsets.

As a result, this organic, trial-and-error way of developing a Synergist style can be a long and tortuous process, with many false starts and cul-de-sacs. Despite this, some Visionaries, Operators, and Processors persist and succeed, becoming highly adept Synergists with the added advantage of having learned the Synergist style the hard way, and therefore indelibly.

For others, they may attend courses or workshops or read books that provide glimpses of what a Synergist does and how they might modulate their typical behaviors for the benefit of the team as a whole. (Because the Synergist isn't something dreamed up or invented, but rather just a name I have given to something that evolves in all successful teams, there are echoes and shadows of the work of the Synergist—even if that term is never used—in every good team-building resource.)

Yet others benefit from having good role models: watching peers, colleagues, or mentors who are either natural Synergists themselves or who have learned to be so. Being mentored by a successful Synergist is a great accelerant to developing the Synergist style. Even though they may not use the V-O-P-S terminology, or perhaps not be able to lucidly explain precisely what happens when they move into Synergist mode, hearing someone describe what they are trying to achieve when they lead a team—and even better, seeing it in action— is an invaluable learning experience.

And finally, there are those who read this book. Simply by recognizing the patterns laid out in Part I, and understanding the importance of developing the Synergist mindset discussed here, you will already be most of the way on the path to becoming a V-O-P+Synergist—someone who adds the Synergist style to their natural one. And, as we'll see in Part III, learning the mechanics of being a Synergist is not complicated—in fact, it's considerably easier than recognizing the need for it in the first place.

THE VISIONARY+SYNERGIST

Of the three natural styles, Visionaries are the most likely to instinctively recognize the need for (and the importance of) the Synergist role and, although they face significant challenges in doing so, will often be the first to adopt it.

The reason for this lies in the Visionary's naturally creative thought process coupled with their willingness to try new things. Unlike the Operator, who will, with relish, give the team up for dead when it gridlocks (so they can get back to doing things), and the Processor, who when faced with gridlock is more likely to repeatedly try to make the existing structure work, the Visionary will actively seek out alternatives.

The starting point for the Visionary's transition to Visionary+Synergist is usually in an abstraction to first principles. Faced with the seemingly insoluble puzzle of how to get the team to gel, the Visionary's natural tendency is to go back and up: back to the team's inception, by asking, "What is it we're here to do? What's our essential purpose?"—and up to the strategic level by asking, "What is the best way for us to achieve those goals? How can we best, together, reach our objective as a team?"

This move back and up in the Visionary's thinking is the nearest the Visionary, Operator, or Processor gets to thinking like a Synergist while still operating in natural mode. When thinking this way—about essential goals at a strategic level—the Visionary is very close to the Synergist's enterprise-focused, from-the-balcony perspective.

The key difference, of course, is that the Visionary is taking this view through the V lens and is highly likely to exhibit classic Visionary responses: look for an answer that is new and exciting, lose interest if nothing like that appears relatively quickly, and move on to another challenge once it does. The key insight that can start the transition from Visionary to Visionary+Synergist is to see that it's not the *answers* that are important, but the *questions*: that the very act of "going to the balcony" and rising above the detail of the team interaction is what's needed. Once Visionaries see the value of lifting themselves out of the Visionary box and up to a higher plane, the organic development of the Synergist style can begin.

The primary reason Visionaries often fail to make the transition to Visionary+Synergist is their lack of disciplined focus coupled with their inability to be dispassionate. Visionaries are so easily distracted that it doesn't take much to knock them out of the Synergist style back into full V mode.

THE PROCESSOR+SYNERGIST

The second most likely V-O-P team member to add the Synergist style organically is the Processor, albeit from a very different starting point than the Visionary.

The Processor's starting point for becoming a Processor+Synergist lies in the very strengths that the Visionary lacks: disciplined focus and the ability to be dispassionate. As we've seen, these two key strengths are what give the Processor the ability to gather and analyze data, and to design and maintain high-quality systems and processes. Coincidentally, they are also the very strengths of perspective the Synergist brings.

So the doorway for the Processor to start the transition to becoming a Processor+Synergist usually appears at a point when the Processor's discipline and dispassionateness has yielded a substantive win for the team (say, crunching data that produced a highly valuable a-ha moment, or putting in place a system that greatly enhances productivity). If at this point the Processor, like the Visionary, realizes that it isn't so much the *answer* that was important but the way in which they arrived at the answer (through dispassionate, disciplined focus), then the organic development of the Synergist style may begin.

Again, if like the Visionary, Processors realize they have the end of a ball of string that may hold the key to unlocking the gridlocked team, a step-by-step process of discovery and exploration down the road to becoming a Processor+Synergist can start.

What is likely to derail their development are characteristics often missing in the Processor: the natural ability to think strategically and a willingness to improvise. For a true Synergist, strategic thinking is the natural starting point— what is best for the enterprise overall? Processors tend more naturally to think tactically: how do I implement this or that? The Processor also finds it easiest to think inside the box, replicating what they did previously with few changes, while Synergists innovate, experiment, and improvise all the time, knowing they need to do so in order to connect and harmonize the V-O-P team.

THE OPERATOR+SYNERGIST

Of the three natural styles, the Operator has the least in common with the Synergist and is the least likely to develop the Synergist style unaided.

The reason for this is straightforward: the Operator places little value on the group environment as an effective way to make decisions and views most meetings as a distraction from the real task of getting things done. So, as we've seen, when the team gridlocks, the Operator feels little compulsion to do anything about it.

As a result, few windows of opportunity exist for the Operator to glimpse the value of the Synergist style. Indeed, the Operator may go so far as to repudiate the value of the Synergist style when it *does* turn up, viewing it as just another pointless waste of time trying to keep alive what seems an already discredited V-O-P team.

This isn't to say that Operators cannot learn and use the Synergist style— they can and do. The point is that they rarely do so *unaided.* The Operator is unlikely to begin the journey to becoming an Operator+Synergist on their own initiative, and they may reject the idea of the Synergist style altogether when first presented with it. But Operators are above all else practical, and if they see something that works, they will be the first to adopt it.

The key, then, is to first let the Operator see the success of the Synergist style in unlocking the team. After either the Visionary or Processor has developed the Synergist style, or after the team has identified a natural Synergist, then, faced with the clear evidence of success, the Operator will be more likely to begin the process of developing the Synergist style.

This means, of course, being patient with the Operator, taking time to show and explain the benefits of being able to move in and out of the Synergist style, clearly linking those benefits to observable, positive changes in the way the team interacts. Once the Operator is convinced that the Synergist style does indeed work, and that by developing the skill themselves they can help radically transform the previously sterile team interactions, they will move toward becoming an Operator+Synergist just as fast as the Visionary and Processor.

THE NATURAL SYNERGIST

An alternative way for a team to tap into the Synergist style is to graft in—or discover that they already have in their midst—a natural Synergist.

Although such people are rare, they do exist, and they are surprisingly easy to spot. Natural Synergists don't fit easily into any of the V, O, or P molds, nor do they exhibit primarily V, O, or P characteristics. Instead, they manifest characteristics entirely of their own:

- They are more comfortable in group environments than otherwise and blossom in the company of others.
- They have a high degree of emotional intelligence (EI) and are skilled at relating to people and building strong relationships.
- They are equally skilled at understanding and managing the dynamics of group interactions. Not only do they read individuals well; Synergists also read groups well.
- They are persuasive without being manipulative.
- They are focused primarily on the good of the enterprise overall, not on their personal agenda.
- They are typically good long-term and strategic thinkers, an attribute they share with the Visionary, which gives them the basis for building a relationship with Visionaries on the team.
- They often have an affinity for systems and processes, understanding their importance for the long-term development of the organization as a whole, which provides a platform for them to develop relationships with the Processors on the team.

Natural Synergists are often found in those parts of an organization that require good networking and group communication skills, such as marketing, public relations, training and development, human relations, and corporate communications. They can also be found lurking in areas where good negotiation skills are required, for example, in some parts of the legal department and in corporate merger and acquisition teams.

THE V-O-P-S CODE

Whichever way the Synergist arrives on the scene (whether a natural one emerges or one or more of the team develop the style), the presence of a Synergist is not in itself enough to transform the gridlocked group into a high-performance V-O-P-S team. Two additional things need to happen before this will be the case:

1. The rest of the team needs to develop a minimal level of the Synergist style.

For clarity we have assumed thus far that everyone exhibits one of the three—now, four—styles: Visionary, Operator, Processor, or Synergist. In reality, of course, most people have a strong *primary* style (their dominant tendency), but will also exhibit elements of the other styles, usually with a strong second suit, plus vestiges of one or both of the others. But to transform into a V-O-P-S team, it's not enough for there to be merely one or more people on the team who are primarily Synergists. *All* team members need to develop at least a minimal degree of the Synergist style. The next chapter shows in detail why this is, and how it happens.

2. The group must tap into the Synergist style and be guided by it at crucial times.

Obviously, there's no point in having the Synergist style in a team if it doesn't have a role in the team interactions. But nor does the transition of a gridlocked team into a high-performing V-O-P-S team imply that once there, the Synergist style somehow takes control and manages everything from that point. Just as the Visionary, Operator, and Processor styles have their place in the team interaction—and cause the team to become dysfunctional when overused or overexposed—so the Synergist style has its place and needs to be used appropriately.

Part III of this book details precisely when the Synergist role works best in the high-performance team, and where use of the Synergist style can go wrong.

CHAPTER SUMMARY

The Synergist is a fourth, learned style that complements the Visionary, Operator, and Processor styles, turning the gridlocked V-O-P team into a high-performing V-O-P-S team.

Any of the V-O-P team can learn to become a Synergist—in addition to retaining their own Visionary, Operator, or Processor style.

There are some natural Synergists—people who have an innate Synergist disposition. These are rare, however, and most teams form without a natural Synergist on board.

Visionaries are the most likely of the three natural styles to learn how to be a Synergist, followed by the Processor.

Operators find it hard to develop into Synergists, but once they see a successful Synergist make a real difference to the gridlocked V-O-P team, they will develop a respect for the style and will adopt it for themselves.

The Synergist works in the V-O-P team at key moments to resolve conflict; choreograph the Visionary, Operator, and Processor's interactions; harmonize their output; and move them effectively on to their next topic or project.

The Synergist style isn't persistent: it appears intermittently as needed by the V-O-P team.

 Scan this QR code to be taken to a web page containing case studies and examples specific to this chapter, or point your web browser to http://PredictableSuccess.com/syn-ch07.

8

THE SYNERGIST'S TOOLKIT

How the Synergist Releases Group Cohesion and Flow

IN THE LAST CHAPTER we explored *what* the Synergist does. In this chapter we look at *how* the Synergist does it. In particular, we examine the specific skills the Synergist brings to the team to help transform the dysfunctional dynamic among the Visionary, Operator, and Processor into a high-performing group.

First, a couple of quick points to bear in mind.

THE NATURAL VERSUS LEARNED SYNERGIST

As we've seen, a key feature of the Synergist style is that it is primarily a learned style. Although natural Synergists do exist, they are rare, so in most teams the Synergist input comes from Visionaries, Operators, and Processors who have learned to emulate the Synergist style.

The learning requires commitment. Synergism doesn't happen overnight—it's not like flicking a light switch. It's more like developing a new habit—but anyone can master the basics relatively quickly by following the principles laid out below.

TOO MANY SYNERGISTS?

Should everyone aspire to being a Synergist? Well, there's no reason for anyone not to master the Synergist style, and the more people in any group who can act as Synergists, the better. So, yes, everyone should aspire to learning at least the basics of the Synergist style.

An additional reason to encourage widespread adoption of the Synergist style is to avoid an overabundance of Visionary+Synergists. As we saw in the last chapter, Visionaries tend to grasp and adopt the Synergist style most easily (followed by Processors and Operators respectively). While a team with one early-adopter Visionary+Synergist is better than a team with no Synergist at all, the more of the other members who learn to act and think like Synergists, the more balanced the team will be—and with concomitantly higher performance.

Finally, widespread adoption of the Synergist style brings benefits for the enterprise as a whole, beyond the confines of formal team activities. By encouraging a comprehensive adoption of the Synergist style, the *entire organization* benefits from systemically improved interaction between everyone—Visionaries, Operators, and Processors—at all times, and in all parts of the organization, not just in teams and groups.

THE RULE OF ONE-THIRD

A word about the adoption rate of the Synergist style: although it may seem a daunting task to encourage the organization-wide development of Synergists, it has been my observation that a pivotal point is reached when around one-third of the employees in any group or team actively use the Synergist style. At that stage, the degree of demonstrable positive change in group interactions (specifically the reduced amount of tension, conflict, and dysfunction) has a snowball effect on the adoption of the Synergist style by the rest of the team.

This quickened rate of adoption is only to be expected—some people will hold back at first from adopting the Synergist style because they don't quite understand it; some because while they understand it, they don't believe it will make any real difference; and others will be outright cynical. Encouraging the early adopters to move ahead with learning and implementing the Synergist style provides a real-life case study that helps the rest of the team understand how the Synergist works in practice, and provides visible proof for the doubters.

MULTIPLE SYNERGISTS ON THE SAME TEAM

When there are multiple Synergists on the same team, does it become confusing if a number of people are switching in and out of Synergist mode and trying to do all that's outlined in the rest of this chapter? Not really—certainly no more than if (as is usually the case) there is more than one Visionary, Operator, or Processor on the team.

Quite the opposite happens in fact—although one person *can* do all that's required of a Synergist, it's physically and mentally tiring, and it's considerably easier for the team as a whole when there is more than one person able to move into Synergist mode.

THE SYNERGIST'S TOOLKIT: NINE SKILLS AND A COMMITMENT

Now that we've examined some caveats, what is it that the Synergist actually *does* to release cohesion and flow in the previously gridlocked or compromised group?

The Synergist's toolkit is nothing mysterious or magical—it's essentially a set of nine learned skills that anyone can develop. None of the nine skills individually will be new to anyone who has worked in an organization for any length of time, and most people will have already developed at least some of these skills already.

But there is one piece of "magic" that transforms these nine relatively mundane skills into something very special—the secret sauce of Synergism, if you will, and it's a *personal commitment* on the part of the Synergist that governs and informs the use of the nine skills.

THE ENTERPRISE COMMITMENT

The specific commitment that the Synergist makes is a simple one: *"When working in a team or group environment, to place the interests of the enterprise above my personal interests."*

In other words, the Synergist commits to what I term "the enterprise commitment"—to keep the goal or objective of the *group* foremost in the group's interaction.

This may seem blindingly obvious, and it is. So much so that the enterprise commitment is how natural Synergists think by default. The fact that for them the enterprise commitment comes hardwired is what makes them natural Synergists to begin with.

It is not the natural Synergist who has problems with the enterprise commitment; it's the Visionary, Operator, and Processor. But even for them, their difficulty is not with the commitment in and of itself. Most Vs, Os, and Ps when asked will accept that it's perfectly reasonable that they should place the interests of the enterprise above their personal interests when working in a team or group environment. Their problem lies not with the enterprise commitment but with its unavoidable consequence: that to place the interests of the enterprise above their personal interests, they will often by necessity be required to *subjugate their instinctive Visionary, Operator, and Processor tendencies.*

And this, as we've now seen repeatedly, is extremely difficult for the V, O, and P to do.

COMMITMENT, MEET TOOLKIT. TOOLKIT, MEET COMMITMENT.

Given the myriad ways we've seen in which the Visionary, Operator, and Processor cannot help but react negatively when working together, subjugating their instinctive responses to meet the enterprise commitment may seem insurmountable, but it is actually remarkably easy to change.

The reason it's easy to fix lies in the existence of the ability to switch into the Synergist mode. This simple fact—that the Visionary, Operator, and Processor for the first time have an alternative mode of interaction—transforms the team landscape by dramatically broadening the canvas on which the V, O, and P operate.

Think of it this way. It's not as if previously the Visionary, Operator, and Processor were locked into their identities because of stupidity or intransigence. Most people in non-Synergistic teams are intelligent people who, even without knowing any of the terms in this book, understand that they are engaging in patterns of dysfunctional interaction that would be good to overcome. The problem is that, at that point, they have no options, no other way to act. None of them can, or wants to, become like the others (which would be of no use anyway—a team of all Vs, Os, or Ps has even bigger problems, as we'll see in the next chapter), and the only version of a fourth, alternative style is usually a vague resolution that "we all need to be a bit more adult about this."

Now something vital has changed. Now for the first time there is a clear alternative: switching into Synergist mode.

There is a virtual circle here. The enterprise commitment is what puts the Synergistic magic into the toolkit, and in turn, the existence of the Synergist toolkit gives the Visionary, Operator, and Processor what they need to make the enterprise commitment work.

REMEMBERING THE ENTERPRISE COMMITMENT

The enterprise commitment is the doorway to the Synergist's toolkit. It's only when they are acting in the light of the enterprise commitment that the Visionary+Synergist, Operator+Synergist, or Processor+Synergist will reach for the skills we are about to discuss.

So, for the Visionary, Operator, or Processor learning the Synergist style, there is one mechanical yet simple problem to be overcome from the get-go: to remember the enterprise commitment.

After perhaps years of operating in V, O, or P mode, it can be difficult for team members to break old habits when they first start to learn the Synergist style. A hot-button topic, an unfortunate use of terminology, a rolling of the eyes—almost anything can cause their default V-O-P synapses to trigger and override a more appropriate response.

As with any old habits, the easiest way to break them is to replace them with new ones. For a V, O, or P learning the Synergist style, the single most important new habit to cultivate is *simply to recall the enterprise commitment regularly and consistently*.

For that reason, it's useful to start the journey to becoming a Synergist by taking whatever literal, physical steps are necessary to keep the enterprise commitment before you at all times, and to do so for long enough that it becomes second nature.

Here are a few suggestions for how to build a permanent awareness of the enterprise commitment. Find one that works for you:

- Print it on a card and set it in front of you in every meeting.
- Read it out loud at the start of meetings.
- Write it out by hand at the top of each new page of notes you take.
- Set an automatic reminder on your cell phone, tablet, or laptop to pop up a discreet text reminder every 15 minutes during meetings.
- Make a note of specific hot buttons that push you back into your V, O, or P style at times when it would have been more constructive to remain in Synergist mode. Try to identify patterns you can anticipate and avoid in the future.

THE SYNERGIST TOOLKIT

Every Synergist is an individual, of course, each with different strengths, weaknesses, and ways of doing things. Nonetheless, as with every Visionary,

Table 8.1   The nine Synergist skills

Personal Productivity	Teamwork
Time management	Conflict management
Priority management	Difficult conversations
Crisis management	Communication skills
Delegation	Inclusiveness
	Accountability

Operator, and Processor, Synergists also share enough common characteristics to be instantly recognizable by a set of core skills that they use.

All of these skills are teachable—none depend on inherent ability, so no one is excluded from becoming a Synergist. As we'll see, some of the skills will come more easily to Visionaries, others will be more readily adopted by Operators, and some will seem more intuitive to Processors, but all can be learned and deployed to some extent by anyone.

The nine skills fit into two categories. One of the categories is obvious, given all that we've learned so far, and can be placed under the general heading of teamwork. The other, less obvious category I have termed personal productivity.

PERSONAL PRODUCTIVITY

It's obvious that the key role of the Synergist is to facilitate positive interaction in the group or team, and so the skills listed in the teamwork category seem self-evidently necessary—but why is it important that the Synergist also develop skills in the area of personal productivity?

There are two reasons, both essential for the development of an effective Synergist: *pressure* and *presence*.

1. Pressure. When under pressure, all Visionaries, Operators, and Processors retreat to their natural styles. Watch a Visionary perform under a tight deadline, and they become even more V-like. Load up an Operator with even more tasks than they currently have, and they will exhibit even more compulsion to get work done. Drop Processors into a crisis, and they exert even more control and depend even more on systems and procedures than before.

If Vs, Os, and Ps are not in control of their own working environments—if they have poor time management skills, or they don't manage crises well, or if they cannot prioritize tasks, or don't delegate effectively to others—if, in short, they show up to the group disorganized, distracted, and overcommitted, then one thing is certain: rather than being cognizant of the enterprise imperative and operating when necessary as a Synergist, they will, under the pressure of their own inefficiencies, revert to their natural styles simply in order to cope.

An in-control, self-managed V, O, or P can move into Synergist mode with ease and flow; someone who is overwhelmed cannot.

2. Presence. Operating effectively in Synergist mode requires a sense of presence—a concentration and focus—that is impossible to maintain if the individual is mentally distracted by pressing issues. So even if poorly self-managed Visionaries, Operators, or Processors should overcome the pressures to remain in their natural styles, they will operate as brittle and ineffectual Synergists.

Watching the nuances of the rest of the team's interactions, deciding on the right intervention, managing hot buttons, and avoiding potential stumbling blocks—all the moment-by-moment activities of the Synergist—are hard to focus on if your cell phone is vibrating incessantly, emails are building up in an overloaded in-box, and you're already 20 minutes late for your next appointment.

So for these two reasons—pressure and presence—the first step on the road to becoming a Synergist is to gain reasonable control of your personal productivity.

Note that word "reasonable." It is not the case that everyone who wants to become a Synergist must become a productivity ninja—the Synergist is not a superhero who excels at everything and has no weaknesses. It is simply that those wanting to learn and use the Synergist style need to master the following five skills to at least a level that permits them to turn up at a meeting undistracted and able to focus on the matters at hand.

It's outside the scope of this book to teach each of these nine skills individually—there is already a library of information available on each one.

We have, however, put together a comprehensive list of recommended resources for each skill at The Synergist website, together with a self-assessment you can use to identify the skills you most need to work on. Use the resources link at the end of this chapter to access these tools.

TIME MANAGEMENT

The lack of personal time management skills is the single most common reason that people become overcommitted and disorganized. To put it simply, without minimal time management skills it is very difficult for a Visionary, Operator, or Processor to have the equilibrium required to function as a Synergist.

   The prospective Synergist's challenge is to be on top of their own time management to the extent that they can engage with their team or group without feeling distracted or overwhelmed by their other commitments. The minimum set of time management behaviors needed to operate effectively as a Synergist is in the table below—how do you score?

Table 8.2   Time management behaviors

	Never→Sometimes→Always				
Has a clear daily / weekly / monthly activity plan					
Fulfills commitments made to others (regarding meetings, calls, reports, etc.)					
Accurately estimates time required for activities					
Engages fully in the matter at hand (not distracted by other commitments)					
Is able to quickly respond to urgent unplanned demands without abandoning existing goals and objectives					

   As is the case for all of the skills in the Synergist toolkit discussed in this chapter, a detailed list of resources to help build your personal time management abilities is available at the URL in the summary at the end of this chapter, together with a more detailed self-assessment that will help you identify which parts of the Synergist's toolkit you need to work on most.

PRIORITY MANAGEMENT

Time management skills, however good they may be, will not on their own deliver the foundation of personal productivity that a leader requires in order to move in and out of Synergist mode with ease.

A week spent on project B—however well managed that week might be—is a week lost if in fact you should have been working on project C. Doing all the right time management things—planning, listing, categorizing, delegating, recording, following up—is all for naught if focused on the *wrong priorities*. Too often, even those with strong time management skills become overwhelmed because they consistently mis-prioritize where they are putting their time and energy.

The Synergist's challenge: Even if you are doing things right, are you doing the right things?

Here are the minimum priority management behaviors expected of an effective Synergist:

Table 8.3 Priority management behaviors

	Never→Sometimes→Always				
Has a clear understanding of the organization's primary goals and objectives					
Has a clear understanding of his or her own primary goals and objectives					
Has a reasonable understanding of the primary goals and objectives of each of his or her team members					
Is focused primarily on achieving high-priority goals and objectives					
Manages lower-priority activities appropriately and without distracting from the achievement of high-priority items					

CRISIS MANAGEMENT

The Visionary, Operator, or Processor's equilibrium can often be derailed at any time by one thing: a crisis. And crises cannot always be avoided; often they are outside of our control. So the key issue is not the crisis itself, but the way in which it is handled. Any V, O, or P who reacts disproportionately will find it hard to maintain a Synergistic state of mind should the group or team hit a severely rough patch—which is precisely when the Synergist style is most needed.

The Synergist's challenge: To be like water and react appropriately to crises: Are the ripples you create in response to a crisis no bigger and no smaller than they need to be?

Here are the minimum crisis management behaviors required of an effective Synergist. How do you score?

Table 8.4 Crisis management behaviors

	Never→Sometimes→Always				
Remains calm and focused in an emergency					
Seeks to minimize the disruption caused by emergencies and problems					
Moves quickly to resolve and move on from emergencies and problems					
Puts systems and processes in place to prevent unnecessary repetition of emergencies and problems					
Empowers others to solve problems, rather than acting as a firefighter to personally fix every problem					

DELEGATION

The last skill needed in the category of personal productivity is delegation, the ability to hand off tasks better done by others, releasing you to do what only you can do best.

Note that this skill differs from the preceding three in that while everyone can develop and utilize time-, priority-, and crisis-management skills, not everyone has someone they can delegate to. Nonetheless, all teamwork involves what might be called *intra*-delegation—the delegation of tasks among the team members themselves. So, individual contributors who don't have direct subordinates or assistants to whom they can normally delegate still need to develop this skill for use *within* the team environment.

Even the most effective individuals will achieve less than optimum results if they try to do everything themselves. Furthermore, the key reason for putting a team together in the first place—to get the best from each team member—is lost if everyone is buried under a mountain of minutiae and not focused on those areas at which they are most skilled.

The Synergist's challenge: To consistently delegate tasks where possible, leaving you free to do what you do best.

Here are the minimum delegation behaviors expected of an effective Synergist.

(Note that these are written from the perspective of the individual's outside-of-the-team, day-to-day activities—because it's by delegating *there* that they can come to the team environment with a fresh mind, untrammeled by overcommitment. Each of these behaviors can then be repeated within the team environment itself by substituting the phrase "team assignment" for "job description" and "team member" for "direct report." Individual contributors with no direct reports to whom they can delegate will use only this second version.)

How do you score?

Table 8.5   Delegation behaviors

	Never→Sometimes→Always				
Understands those aspects of their job description that only they can deliver on					
Identifies those aspects of their job description that can be delegated to others					
Delegates those tasks to subordinates or assistants within their areas of responsibility					
Allocates delegated tasks in a way that will challenge and develop the individuals they are delegated to					
Follows up on delegated tasks in a timely manner, without micromanaging					

TEAMWORK

The personal productivity category of skills ensures that the Visionary, Operator, and Processor come to the team with the mental equilibrium required to shift seamlessly into Synergist mode. The second category of skills, teamwork, is about what they then *do*.

Although all leaders will bring their own personalities and differences of approach when they switch into Synergist mode, there are five core skills needed by every Synergist when engaged with the team: conflict management, difficult conversations, communication skills, inclusiveness, and accountability.

CONFLICT MANAGEMENT

Dealing with conflict in a team is usually a matter of extremes—the Visionary, Operator, and Processor are often either too ruthlessly confrontational or too conflict-averse. The result is either an overcompetitive, testosterone-driven environment or the slow buildup of passive-aggressive resentments (or, on occasion, both).

Synergists do not overreact to conflict—nor do they needlessly create it or, worse, avoid it. Instead, they manage conflict positively, always in the light of the enterprise commitment, seeking the best outcome for the organization as a whole.

The Synergist's stance can best be summarized as being ruthlessly constructive—a firm but supportive embrace of conflict being a necessary part of the team process—while always seeking to drain conflict of unnecessarily negative or personal attacks.

The Synergist's challenge: To turn conflict from a bruising reassertion of needs into a positive force for improving the team's outputs.

Table 8.6 shows the minimum conflict management behaviors expected of an effective Synergist—how do you score?

DIFFICULT CONVERSATIONS

Not all of the team's problems are caused by outright conflict. Much of it simmers beneath the surface, caused by the misunderstandings and differences in style and approach that we saw earlier in Part I. To recall a few examples: the Visionary's frustration with the Processor's seemingly infinite obsession with detail; the Processor's annoyance at the Visionary's apparent glibness and hyperbole; the Operator's disbelief at how little the Visionary and Processor

Table 8.6   Conflict management behaviors

	Never→Sometimes→Always				
Openly addresses possible areas of conflict as they appear					
Encourages the airing of all sides of an issue					
Does not show favoritism					
Encourages those in conflict to resolve issues rather than ignore them					
Acts as a mediator where necessary					
Adopts a win-win approach rather than a "I win, you lose" approach					

appear to understand how the real world works. None of these (mis)percep-tions might ever explode into actual conflict, but unless they are addressed, the team will remain gridlocked or in passive-aggressive compromise.

At the center of the Synergist's toolkit is a readiness (and the skill) to draw out painful, difficult, or negative issues as they arise and not to let them fester or grow. By forcing to the surface the presuppositions and predispositions that the Visionary, Operator, and Processor have toward one another, the Synergist builds understanding, breaks down barriers, and develops unity in the team.

The Synergist's challenge: To uncover painful, difficult, or negative issues arising from the individual styles and facilitate their resolution by exploration and understanding.

Table 8.7 shows the minimum behaviors expected of a Synergist to enable difficult conversations between group members. How do you score?

COMMUNICATION SKILLS

At the core of the Synergist's toolkit is a skill we have seen the need for through-out this book—facilitating effective communications.

The Synergist's role here is not so much about their own communication skills as their ability to facilitate effective communication among the others. As we have seen repeatedly, even if the Visionary, Operator, and Processor

Table 8.7   Enabling difficult conversations

	Never→Sometimes→Always				
Addresses difficult, painful, or negative issues when they arise					
Is graceful and diplomatic in addressing such issues					
Is clear and unambiguous regarding the issue at hand					
Ensures there are no hidden agendas when discussing difficult or negative issues					
Is open and nondefensive when dealing with difficult or negative situations					

individually possess great communication skills, their actions and preconceptions about each other preclude their ability to be heard.

It's the Synergist's role to bridge that gap by helping everyone understand how best to communicate in a way that will ensure they are heard and understood.

The Synergist's challenge: To remove barriers that prevent the Visionary, Operator, and Processor from communicating effectively with each other.

Table 8.8 shows the minimum behaviors expected of a Synergist to enable effective communications in the V-O-P team.

INCLUSIVENESS

On their own, we know that the Visionary, Operator, and Processor will end up in their corners working less as a team and more like three independent entities, only occasionally pooling their efforts.

The Synergist's role is to break down the brittle independence of individuals by ensuring that everyone on the team is jointly engaged in all aspects of the team's interactions, not just those in which they feel most comfortable.

The Synergist's challenge: To break the cycle of V-then-O-then-P, V-then-O-then-P interaction and substitute fully inclusive interactions.

Note that this does not mean the Synergist will laboriously insist that every person on the team expounds at length on every point on the agenda, or on everything that comes up. Inclusiveness is about engagement, not participation.

Table 8.8 Enabling effective communication

	Never→Sometimes→Always				
Encourages others to communicate clearly and unambiguously					
Models and encourages active listening to others					
Identifies and shares communication styles and methods that have a negative effect on other team members					
Translates vocabulary and terminology that are causing misperceptions or misunderstanding					
Orchestrates team communications to ensure that all team members contribute appropriately					

A team member can be fully engaged without always feeling the need to actively participate in the discussion.

Here are the minimum behaviors expected of a Synergist to ensure inclusiveness in the team or group. How do you score?

Table 8.9 Ensuring inclusiveness

	Never→Sometimes→Always				
Encourages all members of the team to engage in all stages of the team's interactions					
Varies the lead role in the team's interactions from time to time to ensure everyone's sense of ownership					
Remains alert to situations in which team members have zoned out, identifies why, and reengages the team member					
Solicits feedback and summaries from team members at the end of an interaction to gauge the degree of inclusion					

ACCOUNTABILITY

Finally, an effective Synergist will ensure that the team holds itself accountable to do those things it commits to doing.

This is not to say that the Synergist takes personal responsibility to be accountable for the team as a whole—that's an untenable position for any one team member. Rather, the Synergist is best positioned to prod the team to adopt a position of mutual accountability.

The Synergist's challenge: To build an interdependency that ensures the team delivers on its promises.

Here are the minimum accountability behaviors expected of an effective Synergist—how do you score?

Table 8.10   Accountability behaviors

	Never→Sometimes→Always				
Ensures there is clear, unambiguous ownership of delegated tasks and responsibilities					
Encourages the setting of realistic achievement milestones for delegated tasks and responsibilities					
Ensures that team members report regularly on progress with delegated tasks and responsibilities					
Encourages the team to identify reasons for missed milestones and uncompleted tasks					
Prompts a realistic reassessment of milestones when necessary					

THE V-O-P+ CHALLENGE

Laid out below is a general guide to those skills in the Synergist's toolkit that each of the Visionary, Operator, and Processor find easiest and hardest to adopt. But don't forget: what follows is a broad generalization, and we've provided an online assessment on the website accompanying this book (see the link at the end of this chapter) that will help you identify which of the nine skills you personally are strongest at and those you may need to work on more.

THE VISIONARY

Here are the three areas where Visionaries most often excel, and the three at which they are most often challenged, when making the transition to Visionary/Synergist.

Table 8.11   Rating the Visionary

Personal Productivity	Teamwork
	✗ Conflict management
✗ Priority management	
✓ Crisis management	✓ Communication skills
	✓ Inclusiveness
	✗ Accountability

Visionary strengths

Crisis management: Visionaries operate at full commitment mode during a crisis—they're focused, alert, and up for the challenge. Their decisiveness and risk-taking come to the fore, and they can engender high levels of loyalty in their team at times of great pressure.

Communication skills: Most Visionaries are natural communicators and enjoy any opportunity to motivate and encourage others.

Inclusiveness: Reaching out to a wider group of people and making them feel included is a natural trait for the Visionary. They like to have people around to share their ideas with (and to debate with). When Visionaries decide to include you in their clique, they can be charming and persuasive.

Visionary weaknesses

Priority management: Because of their addiction to the shiny-blue-ball syndrome, Visionaries find it very hard to stay consistently focused on one set of priorities.

Conflict management: In a strange dichotomy, Visionaries are often very good at having difficult conversations with people but poor at conflict management. Due to their strong egos, they will often deal with conflict either by avoiding it (for fear of their egos being hurt) or by going over the top, bordering on abusiveness (because their egos are so strong).

Accountability: Visionaries don't like to be tied down, and accountability is a version of precisely that.

As with the Operator and Processor, this is not to say that the Visionary cannot learn these three skills—just that they will likely require more work and commitment than the others.

THE OPERATOR

Here are the three areas where Operators are most often challenged, and the three at which they often excel, in making the transition to Operator/Synergist.

Table 8.12   Rating the Operator

Personal Productivity	*Teamwork*
✗ Time management	
✓ Priority management	
✓ Crisis management	
✗ Delegation	✗ Inclusiveness
	✓ Accountability

Operator strengths

Priority management: When it comes to sticking to agreed-on priorities, the Operator is probably the most focused member of any team—provided they have had input into the process that set the priorities in the first place. Once an Operator has determined those priorities, it's very hard to shake them.

Crisis management: Like Visionaries, Operators shine in a crisis. Unlike Visionaries, they do so not by coming up with innovative solutions but by working long hours, soaking up pressure without complaint, and being prepared to improvise and take risks.

Accountability: Operators have a love-hate relationship with accountability. If they feel that they are being forced into accountability for something over which they don't have responsibility, they'll shake it off like a dog with fleas. But, as with setting priorities, when they are actively involved in the process and see a direct connection between their task list and what they're being held account-able for, they embrace it with relish.

Operator weaknesses

Time management: Operators overcommit. Period.

Delegation: Because they're task-focused, Operators find it hard to give tasks away. As we've seen, Operators are good dumpers—they'll pass off those things they really don't want to do (like filling in forms), but true delegation is a stretch.

Inclusiveness: Operators have an innate preference for working either alone or with a small team that they control. An extreme Operator will be an out-and-out maverick, disconnected from the rest of the organization. Wherever they are on the independence scale, working inclusively with the rest of the team will always be a challenge.

THE PROCESSOR

Here are the three areas where Processors are most often challenged, and the three at which they often excel, in making the transition to Processor/Synergist.

Table 8.13 Rating the Processor

Personal Productivity	Teamwork
✓ Time management	✗ Conflict management
	✗ Difficult conversations
✗ Crisis management	
	✓ Inclusiveness
	✓ Accountability

Operator strengths

Time management: Most Processors have a high need for order, and this extends to time management. They guard their schedules carefully and over-commit much less than Operators.

Inclusiveness: Although not usually gregarious by nature, Processors are collegiate and have no problem being part of a wider team and ensuring others feel included and welcome.

Accountability: Setting, achieving, and reporting back on milestones is second nature to a Processor. They not only have a high sense of accountability to others, but their self-accountability is high also. Missing a deadline is not something they enjoy.

Operator weaknesses

Crisis management: Processors tend to work at a steady pace, irrespective of the surrounding environment. When a crisis hits, they often either continue on just as before—despite the need for an appropriate change of pace—or absent themselves altogether.

Conflict management and difficult conversations: The risk-averse nature of most Processors together with their distrust of emotion means that they tend to shy away from both these areas.

CHAPTER SUMMARY

Anyone can learn to be a Synergist.

The more people on a team who can switch into Synergist mode, the better.

As many people as possible in the organization should learn to use the Synergist style.

Once around a third of the people in an organization learn to use the Synergist style, the rate of adoption increases significantly.

The Synergist's toolkit consists of nine key skills, plus an overarching commitment.

The overarching commitment, known as The Enterprise Commitment, is this: "*When working in a team or group environment, to place the interests of the enterprise above their personal interests.*"

The nine key skills fall into two categories—personal productivity and teamwork.

The personal productivity skills are necessary to ensure the equilibrium of mind necessary for a Visionary, Operator or Processor to switch into Synergist mode. They are time management, priority management, crisis management and delegation.

The teamwork skills are used to interrupt the default pattern of VOP dysfunction and take the team out of gridlock and compromise. They are conflict management, difficult conversations, communication skills, inclusiveness and accountability.

Each of the Visionary, Operator and Processor are naturally better at some of the nine skills and more challenged by others.

 Scan this QR code to be taken to a web page containing case studies and examples specific to this chapter (including an Y assessment to discover how you rate in each of the nine skills in the Synergist Toolkit), or point your web browser to http:// PredictableSuccess.com/syn-ch08.

9

STARTING FAST, FINISHING STRONG

The Life Cycle of a Highly Successful Group

BEFORE WE MOVE ON TO EXPLORE the now-Synergistic team's new way of interacting, let's look briefly at the choreography of the Visionary, Operator, Processor, and Synergist—how they come together in a group or team for maximum effect.

ORGANIC AND CONSTRUCTED TEAMS

There are essentially two types of teams: first, what we might call an *organic team*, a group of people who come together of their own volition (for example, to start a business or solve a community problem); and second, what we can term a *constructed team*, one put together by selection, such as a project group or a subcommittee.

The differences between organic and constructed teams hold important lessons, particularly for the success of constructed teams.

WIN/LOSE VS. MEH

In terms of the results they achieve, it's easy to see that the first type, the organic team, is subject to Darwinian laws. When people come together voluntarily to start something (a new business, say, or a presidential campaign), the outcome is binary. If the team is good enough, it may achieve its goals, but if the team is not good enough, the new venture will perish.

The second type, the constructed team, typically operates in a less primal environment. As we saw in chapter 6, it can often underperform for some time without immediate consequence, and if it is disbanded or reconstructed, the core of the enterprise is rarely at stake (it is on occasion, but not usually).

SELECTION VS. SELF-SELECTION

Besides the nature of failure, organic and constructed teams also differ, by definition, in choreography—the sequence in which the Visionary, Operator, Processor, and Synergist show up.

The constructed team's composition is usually decided at the outset, and the selection process is based on factors such as functional knowledge, availability, and willingness to get involved. This has two consequences: the disposition of Vs, Os, Ps, and Ss is essentially random (hence the built-in dysfunction inherent in most constructed teams); and after it has been set up, the composition of the constructed team alters only rarely.

The organic team is different. Just as evolution has over time equipped species with what they need to survive, so successful organic teams learn to adapt their team composition over time in order to reach their goal (a successful new business, say, or election to the presidency).

This process of adaptation which happens in every successful organic team follows a predictable pattern, one that is based entirely, albeit subliminally, on ensuring the optimum sequencing of the roles of Visionary, Operator, Processor, and Synergist.

HOW ORGANIC TEAMS ADAPT TO ACHIEVE PREDICTABLE SUCCESS

Although the pattern applies to any group of two or more people pursuing common goals, this inherent adaptability of the organic team is most easily explained in the context of a new business venture.

In my previous book, *Predictable Success: Getting Your Organization on the Growth Track—and Keeping It There*, I demonstrated how every new venture proceeds invariably through seven stages of growth. It is precisely the need to transition from one of these seven stages to the next in order to survive that

Figure 9.1 The Predictable Success® Growth Cycle

causes the organic team to adapt in a way that builds, over time, the V-O-P-S team.

To see how this happens, first look at Figure 9.1. Don't worry about understanding the terms on the diagram—we'll get to those shortly. You can see that Predictable Success is one of the seven stages of growth through which every organization progresses.

Predictable Success is the apex of the growth curve. The three stages before Predictable Success (Early Struggle, Fun, and Whitewater) are growth stages. The stages after Predictable Success (Treadmill, The Big Rut, and Death Rattle) are decline stages.

Before we see how the V-O-P-S team develops organically as the organization moves through this life cycle, note these three important factors.

1. Organizations cannot jump a stage. For example, it's not possible to move into Predictable Success directly from Fun, bypassing Whitewater, any more than it's possible to jump from childhood to adulthood and bypass puberty. Every organization trying to get to Predictable Success will move through each of Early Struggle, Fun, and Whitewater at some point. However, by taking the right steps—essentially, ensuring the organic team is rightly composed—it is possible to minimize the time spent in a specific stage.

For more information and a detailed study of each of the seven stages of growth, see *Predictable Success: Getting Your Organization on the Growth Track—and Keeping It There.*

A free extract is available at http://PredictableSuccess.com/book.

2. Organizations can move back as well as forward in the growth cycle. For example, it is possible (and quite common) for an organization to cycle in and out of Whitewater and Fun a number of times. As we'll see, this is the fate of most organizations that fail to understand the key role of the Synergist.

3. It is possible for an organization to remain in Predictable Success indefinitely. Once the organic team has fully evolved, there is no theoretical reason the organization should not stay in Predictable Success indefinitely. As we'll see, in practice the team can often misstep, causing a decline either back into Whitewater or forward into Treadmill.

While every organization will proceed sequentially through the growth curve, starting in Early Struggle, not every organization makes it through all seven stages—some organizations stop at one or more stages, some make it to one stage, then drop back to the previous stage or stages, and some organizations fail at a certain stage. The goal of a successful organization is to get to Predictable Success—and to stay there for as long as possible.

Here's an overview of each of the seven stages in the Predictable Success life cycle. If you have been involved in any size of an organization for any reasonable length of time, you will likely discover you have developed an intuitive understanding of each stage in the cycle, and that although the terms used may be new to you, the concepts most probably are not.

Most importantly, notice how in order to progress from one stage to the next the organic team must adapt its composition—the mix of Visionary, Operator, Processor, and Synergist—each step of the way.

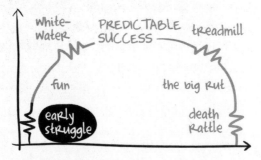

Figure 9.1a

EARLY STRUGGLE
What's happening with the business

It feels like you're hacking through the jungle as you fight to keep your newly born organization alive. The two main challenges are (1) making sure there is enough cash to keep going, until (2) you've clearly established that there is a profitable, sustainable market for your product or service.

The mortality rate of organizations is high in this stage—over two-thirds of all organizations don't make it out of Early Struggle. You're fighting for your new venture's very existence.

What's happening with the team

Team components: Visionary

 By the very nature of entrepreneurship, most new ventures are started by Visionaries. It's their vision, whether doodled out at 4 A.M. on a kitchen table or gestated for many years, that gives birth to the new venture in the first place.

Because it's *their* vision that they're pursuing, the Visionary can find the passion and reserves of strength necessary to hack through the jungle in search of a profitable, sustainable market, and the resilience to cope with the many setbacks the new business will face—including the constant search for additional sources of funding to keep the business alive.

FUN
What's happening with the business

You've broken through the Early Struggle. You've identified a profitable, sustainable market and replaced dependence on external funding with cash from customers. It's time to have Fun! Now you're free to concentrate on getting your product or service into the market, so the key focus moves from cash to sales, from *finding* the market to *mining* the market.

This is the time when the organization's myths and legends are built, and the Big Dogs emerge—those loyal high producers who build the business exponentially in this time of rapid early-stage growth.

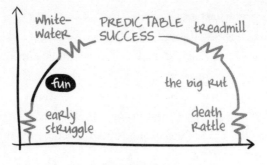

Figure 9.1b

What's happening with the team

Team components: Visionary + Operator

 While Visionaries have all the traits needed to launch a new business, they're less skilled at the minutiae involved in actually running it. Once there is any real detail to be attended to (which can be right from Day One), they need an Operator on board. In fact, it is almost impossible for a business to move from Early Struggle into Fun without at least one Operator working alongside the Visionary to look after the day-to-day activities involved.

This combination of Visionary and Operator is extremely powerful, as the Visionary's breadth of vision, enthusiasm, risk-taking, and creativity melds with the Operator's relentless task-focused attention to detail to produce a highly flexible, responsive, effective team. While most mom-and-pop businesses comprise this team of Visionary and Operator, so also do many very much larger businesses that have Vs and Os in the CEO/COO positions.

WHITEWATER
What's happening with the business
The very success that you reaped in the Fun stage brings with it the seeds of Whitewater. Your rapidly growing organization becomes larger and more complex, and you start to drop the ball with alarming frequency—essentially

Figure 9.1c

because the simple systems and processes you put in place in Fun cannot cope with the complexities of scale.

As you eat the cost of expensive errors, the key emphasis shifts once more, this time from sales to profitability. Achieving sustained profitable growth requires you to put in place more sophisticated procedures, policies, and systems.

Unfortunately, putting those systems in place proves harder than you expected. Making the right decisions seems easy, but implementing them and making them stick is incredibly difficult. The organization seems to be going through an identity crisis, and you may even doubt your leadership and management skills.

What's happening with the team

Team components: Visionary + Operator + Processor

 As the business grows and becomes more complex, the organic team for the first time recognizes the need to add the Processor style at a senior level. Although systems and processes may have had some place during Fun, now, in Whitewater, the need for them is paramount.

In response, the Visionary and Operator add a Processor to the team—often a CFO/CPA or a general manager, sometimes a human relations manager and/or an information technology chief—roles that previously had secondary importance in the organization.

At this point, all of the V-O-P conflicts and tensions discussed in Part I of this book emerge, and the team moves into gridlock or compromise. When this happens, the Processor is usually blamed, for two reasons: (1) they don't share the sweat equity that the Operator and Visionary developed together during the Fun stage, so their job security is tenuous, and (2) as they're the newest arrival on the scene, it's natural to blame them for the increase in tension and dysfunction.

As the V-O-P gridlock intensifies, often the Visionary and Operator will marginalize or fire the Processor in frustration, believing that the P's removal will take the business back to the Fun stage—which, in fact, it does. However, this relief from Whitewater is only short-lived. The first thing the business does once it returns to Fun is begin to grow again—quickly pushing it back into Whitewater and resurrecting the need for a P to put in place more sophisticated systems and procedures.

Chastened, the Visionary and Operator work harder this time at finding a Processor who "gets it"—someone who is more in tune with the organization's freewheeling culture and more likely to fit in than the previous one.

Unfortunately, as we've seen repeatedly, once they hire a Processor, nothing can prevent the V-O-P dysfunctional triangle from re-forming, and the team is left with three choices:

1. Cycle repeatedly in and out of Fun and Whitewater as it continues to search for a compatible Processor.
2. Return permanently to Fun, eschewing additional growth (essentially choosing to remain a mom-and-pop business of limited size) in order to avoid the pain of Whitewater.
3. Somehow discover, either consciously, subliminally, or by trial and error, the key to breaking the V-O-P deadlock—the Synergist role.

PREDICTABLE SUCCESS
What's happening with the business

You've developed a team that has successfully navigated your organization through Whitewater—congratulations! You have reached the prime stage in your organization's growth—what I call Predictable Success.

Figure 9.1d

Here, you benefit from two considerable competitive advantages. First, you can set (and consistently achieve) your goals with a predictable degree of success. Second, because you have the right systems and processes in place, you can grow your business to whatever size the industry will allow.

Unlike Fun (when you were growing, but weren't quite sure how or why), in Predictable Success you know *why* you are successful, and you can use that information to sustain growth over the long term.

What's happening with the team

Team components: Visionary + Operator + Processor + Synergist

In order to break through to Predictable Success the organic team has adapted to its prime state—a Synergistic team working in a state of flow with all four styles represented and active.

Most organizations arrive at this stage through a protracted, painful process of trial and error, with many of the participants bruised—in fact, during the transition through Whitewater they may well have lost some top performers along the way.

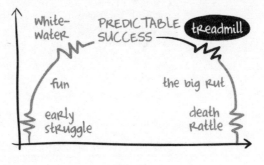

Figure 9.1e

TREADMILL
What's happening with the business

In theory, there is no reason for any organization to decline from the position of Predictable Success. In practice, many organizations swing too far toward dependence on process and policies. Creativity, risk-taking, and initiative decline in response, and the organization becomes increasingly formulaic and arthritic.

Working for the organization at this stage in its development can feel like being on a treadmill—a lot of energy is being expended, but there's little sense of forward momentum. There's an overemphasis on data instead of action, and form takes precedence over content. Good people begin to leave, many of whom have been with the organization for some time.

What's happening with the team

Team components: Operator + Processor + Synergist

Although the business (and team) can in theory remain in Predictable Success indefinitely, in reality what happens most often is that, having suffered through the turmoil of bringing the Processor on board and installing the systems and procedures necessary to tame Whitewater, the team does what we all do—it over-eggs the pudding.

Having seen the benefit of systems and processes, the team assumes that if x is good, then 2x (more systems and processes) must be even better. In order to install and manage the now increasingly ubiquitous systems and procedures, the Processor role takes on a position of even greater prominence in the organization. New hires are either outright Ps or have a high Processor element in their makeup. Compliance is increasingly rewarded (rather than creativity or initiative), and noncompliance is punished.

Not surprisingly, the Visionary, who started the business in the first place out of a desire for autonomy and freedom, increasingly loathes this new environment. The constriction and claustrophobia a V feels from having to comply with so many systems and processes drain their engagement and enthusiasm.

This is the point in many organizations' development when the original founder will leave—and with them the Visionary element of the team.

THE BIG RUT
What's happening with the business

Treadmill is a dangerous stage in the organization's development. If it is checked in time, creativity, risk-taking, and flexibility can be reinjected, taking the organization back to Predictable Success. Left unchecked, however, the organization will decline further into The Big Rut.

In The Big Rut, process and administration have become more important than action and results. Worse, the organization loses its ability to be self-aware, unable to diagnose its own sickness and decline. In fact, everyone is in a comfort zone of bureaucratic calm, and no one really wants the situation to change. When an organization reaches The Big Rut, it can stay there for a long time, on a very gradual, slow decline.

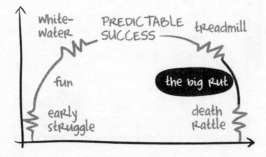

Figure 9.1f

What's happening with the team

Team components: Processor + Synergist

 Once the Visionary has gone, the organization accelerates into bureaucracy, and it is only a matter of time before the Operators leave. This happens for two reasons. (In fact, Visionaries and Operators often leave together, as a team, to go do something new together.)

1. Operators have a symbiotic relationship with Visionaries. Each needs the other: the Visionary to provide the overarching strategy for the Operator to implement, and the Operator to turn the Visionary's ideas into action.

2. In The Big Rut, the Operator loses the ability to "move the needle"—to make a real difference in the organization. Given increasingly pointless or bureaucratic tasks to perform, they lose interest and begin to look elsewhere for more gratifying employment.

DEATH RATTLE
What's happening with the business

Eventually, for all bureaucracies, there is a last, final attempt to resuscitate the organization, whether by the appointment of bankruptcy practitioners or by being acquired in part or in whole. Someone may make a bid for the

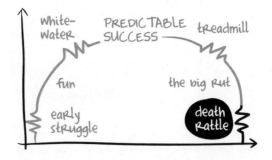

Figure 9.1g

organization's assets, or its name, or its customer list. Whichever happens, the organization will not survive in its present form.

After a brief death rattle (when illusory signs of life may be seen as a result of acquisition negotiations), the organization dies.

What's happening with the team

Team components: Processor

 With the Visionary and Operator now gone, the Synergist no longer has a role to play, and so eventually, only the Processor is left, administering the death rites of the organization.

LESSONS FOR THE ORGANIC TEAM

What are the lessons for the organic team from this brief tour of the Predictable Success life cycle? By its very nature the organic team alters dynamically to meet its needs, so there isn't a lot it needs to learn. But there are two key transitions it should be particularly aware of:

1. Plan the transition from Whitewater to Predictable Success

Most organic teams stumble painfully through Whitewater, losing momentum and morale, while searching for a resolution to the V-O-P conflict. By understanding the key role of the Synergist and following the principles in this book, the transition from Whitewater into Predictable Success can be accelerated and the pain threshold greatly reduced.

2. Avoid the decline into The Big Rut

For an organization to slip briefly into Treadmill is not unusual. In fact, it's impossible to stay firmly in the middle of Predictable Success. Most organizations oscillate between Whitewater's boundary with Predictable Success and the fringes of Treadmill—a pointer showing the organization's position on the life cycle would look more like a dancing rev counter than a steady compass point.

This oscillation happens because every organization's reliance on systems and processes increases and decreases from day to day in reaction to internal and external changes. De-emphasizing adherence to systems and processes (for example, to facilitate a flexible, entrepreneurial response to a market opportunity) will take the organization back toward Whitewater for a while. Then, as systems and processes catch up, it will reemerge into Predictable Success.

Strengthening systems and processes (for example, in response to a drop in product quality) will cause the organization to edge forward into Treadmill. Then, as stability is reestablished and the systems and processes are relaxed, it will return once more to Predictable Success.

This natural oscillation becomes problematic only when the organization stays too long in Treadmill. The longer it stays there, the more it risks becoming numb to the effects of oversystemization, thus losing the ability to self-diagnose and causing it to fall into The Big Rut—from where there is no recovery.

The simplest way to prevent this slide through Treadmill into The Big Rut from happening is to *depersonalize* the Visionary role.

Why depersonalize? Well, think of it this way. By the time the business has hit Predictable Success (in fact, usually long before), there will be many Operators and Processors scattered throughout the organization. Although there may be one or more uber-Os or uber-Ps at the senior executive level—those who play the Operator and Processor role in the senior team—there are also many more Os and Ps working at all levels throughout the organization, carrying out tasks and maintaining systems on a day-to-day basis. As a result, the organization is not dependent on any one person for its O-ness or P-ness. Although the loss of the uber-O or uber-P would be as painful as the loss of any other top executive, if it does happen, the organization still has a working Operator or Processor infrastructure which another uber-O or -P can be hired or promoted to manage.

Not so with the Visionary. At this stage in the organization's development—in Predictable Success, just before the slide into Treadmill—the Visionary role is most often still personified in one or two key individuals (usually, though not always, the founder and/or owner).

When the organization hits Treadmill, should the Visionary become frustrated and decide to leave or sell out (a common event at this stage), because—unlike the O and P role—there is no V infrastructure, the organization is left without an effective Visionary component. Indeed, the history of business is littered with highly visionary organizations that lost their mojo once the Visionary founder left.

INSTITUTIONALIZING THE V ROLE

To prevent this happening, once the organization hits Predictable Success, the Visionary should begin the process of institutionalizing his or her Visionary role—in essence, building a V infrastructure.

Starting with the hiring process, and extending to training, mentoring, and coaching, astute Visionaries (particularly if they are the founder, owner, or CEO) will take responsibility for ensuring that the Visionary style is engendered throughout the organization by developing Vs in every major division, department, geographical location, and project.

Why is this important, and how does it prevent the slide into The Big Rut?

First, the Visionary and Processor styles are mutual bulwarks that, when balanced correctly, keep each other in check. Systems and processes keep the Visionary operating within reasonable boundaries, and the Visionaries' creativity, risk-taking, and intuitive decision-making prevent systems and processes from taking over. Without a Visionary infrastructure throughout the organization to balance the growing tribe of Processors, the organization will begin to oversystematize and atrophy from the bottom up.

Second, it's vital for the continued quality of the organization's outputs—whatever it makes or delivers for customers and clients—that the Visionary role permeates the company. Previously, when the organization was small, one or two people could play the Visionary role precisely *because* of the company's size; the founder and/or owners could be involved in all or most of what was going on. In the larger, more complex business, the Visionary is increasingly isolated from most of what the business does—and so the Visionary input into product or service quality is lost.

Think of the simple example of a restaurant founded by an Operator/chef and a Visionary front-of-house maître-d'. With one restaurant, or even two, the Visionary can ensure customers and staff are happy and that everyone has a great experience. If, with success, the two restaurants grow to a chain of 10, the founder/owner can no longer give every restaurant her personal attention every evening—she has to build a V infrastructure of front-of-house managers to do so. The same principle applies equally to multibillion-dollar businesses.

LESSONS FOR THE CONSTRUCTED TEAM

What of the constructed team—what can it (or more precisely, those who select the participants for the constructed team) learn from the organic team's development through the life cycle?

Quite a bit, as it turns out. If you're putting together a constructed team, here are four main principles to learn from how the organic team develops.

DON'T ALWAYS START WITH A FULL V-O-P-S TEAM

It isn't always necessary for a constructed team to try to emulate an organic team that has reached Predictable Success. In other words, you don't always need to ensure there is a perfect V-O-P-S balance in the team right from the start.

In fact, at the very beginning of a project, you might not need a team at all. Those organizations, for example, that want to design and launch a new product or service may find it substantially more effective to simply give a Visionary some resources and let that individual emulate the organic team's development—adding an Operator to begin with and growing from there—rather than starting with a fully fledged project team from the outset.

DON'T START WITH A V-O-P MIX

By now it goes without saying that putting together a constructed team composed of Visionaries, Operators, and Processors without a Synergist, or who have had no Synergist training, is effectively preordaining the team to gridlock and compromise.

Starting with a V-O-P mix—even though this is the most common configuration of constructed teams—is the organic team's equivalent of jumping right into Whitewater. A simple way to avoid this is to use the assessment included with the web-based resources associated with this book (see the Appendix) to identify the V-O-P-S mix of a proposed constructed team and make adjustments accordingly.

MATCH THE VISIONARY AND THE GOAL

In tracing the development of the organic team, we've seen how important the Visionary is in the beginning, because they bring the passion and resilience needed to cope with early setbacks. In a constructed team, it's important to tap into this by ensuring that at least one of the Vs on the team has a passion for the team's ultimate goal.

Visionaries aren't good mercenaries—they're at their best when working toward a goal they truly believe in. If dropped into a team whose ultimate purpose is of limited interest to them, they disengage quickly. So make sure that you seed the constructed team not just with a V, but with a V who strongly believes in the team's ultimate objective.

CONSIDER USING SUBGROUPS TO MAXIMIZE COMPLEMENTARINESS

Just as various combinations of the full V-O-P-S team emerge at different stages in the organic team's development, so it is worth considering the use of sub-groups of the constructed team at different stages in what *it* is doing.

Even though the V-O-P combination is innately dysfunctional, four of the other possible combinations are not, and they can work together very well, albeit within constricted horizons.

Use the Visionary and Synergist to brainstorm

Because they both have a medium- to long-term focus and share a preference for the big picture over operational detail, the Visionary and the natural Synergist are a great subgroup to put together for brainstorming purposes.

Not everything they come up with will be actionable—far from it. But unin-hibited by the Operator's and Processor's tendency to run everything through a "yes, but will it work in the real world" filter, they will produce a lot of great ideas.

Use the Operator and Processor to translate into action

Once the Visionary and Synergist have completed their brainstorming work, consider putting the Operator and Processor together in a subgroup to stress-test those ideas against operational realities and to turn them into an imple-mentable action plan.

This works well because, of the four styles, it's the O and P who are the most pragmatic, and who are less likely than the V and S to be seduced by a clever or elegant, but impractical, idea. Also, because the three-way V-O-P tension is removed due to the absence of the Visionary, typically (so long as it is not for an overly protracted period that would threaten the Operator's patience), the O and P can coexist cooperatively.

Use the Visionary and Operator to implement

Once the battle plan has been developed by the O and P from the V's and S's strategy, the subgroup that can best implement the plan is the Visionary and Operator working together.

We already know that the Operator is naturally disposed to implementation by default, and the symbiotic relationship with the Visionary makes the pair a highly effective team to work together at the front line—similar to the Fun stage for the organic team, where the V-O combination takes the business through rapid early-stage growth.

Use the Processor and Synergist to maintain and autopsy

Finally, the Processor and Synergist form a perfect subgroup to work behind the scenes, installing and maintaining the systems and processes needed to support the V and O while they are out in the front line implementing the plan.

Similarly, if an autopsy is required to analyze what worked well and what didn't, the Processor and Synergist are more likely to produce high-quality, objective information, untarnished by the V's and O's predilection for anecdote and subjective analysis.

Of course, not every team, or team activity, will yield itself to being broken down into such neat subgroups. But, if you are putting together a constructed team that will go through each of the stages above (phases of teamwork that Bruce Tuchman famously characterized as "Forming, Storming, Norming, Performing, and Transforming"), then such an approach may work for you.

Two combinations to use sparingly

Note that there are two combinations to use sparingly or not at all (in addition to the V-O-P triangle): the Operator and Synergist, and the Visionary and Processor.

In both cases, there is not enough in common in their worldviews and personal styles to generate a strong working relationship (which is one of the reasons why in the development of the organic team neither combination ever appears together without one or the other styles also being present). Putting the O and S, or the V and P together won't cause sparks or gridlock like the V-O-P mix—quite the opposite. They'll simply never gel and their output will be anemic.

CHAPTER SUMMARY

There are two types of teams—organic teams and constructed teams.

Organic teams comprise a group of people who come together of their own volition (for example, to start a business or solve a community problem).

A constructed team is one put together by selection, such as a project group or a subcommittee.

Organic teams have a binary, win/lose success profile—if the team fails, so does the entire enterprise. Constructed teams work in a less primal environment and can underperform for some time without immediate consequence.

A constructed team is usually selected at the outset, and only rarely changes thereafter. An organic team changes over time to ensure it meets its goals.

A constructed team may or may not have an optimal V-O-P-S mix—usually not. A successful organic team will develop over time, in Darwinian fashion, into a V-O-P-S mix.

The driving factor in shaping the changes that the organic team makes to its composition is its need to move the enterprise through seven growth stages: Early Struggle, Fun, Whitewater, Predictable Success, Treadmill, The Big Rut, and Death Rattle.

When the enterprise is at its peak—in the stage called Predictable Success— the organic team will have evolved into a V-O-P-S combination.

Organic teams can accelerate their move into Predictable Success by recognizing the crucial role of the Synergist and using the precepts in this book.

Constructed teams can learn from watching the way in which the organic team develops over time, and where appropriate, mimicking that adaptive approach.

 Scan this QR code to be taken to a web page containing case studies and examples specific to this chapter, or point your web browser to http://PredictableSuccess.com/syn-ch09.

Part III

BECOMING A LEADER OF LEADERS

10

INSIDE THE SECRET GARDEN

Discovering the Synergistic Team's Hidden Pattern of Success

SYNERGISTS ESSENTIALLY DO TWO THINGS: they put the previously gridlocked V-O-P team back on track by removing conflict and tension, and they create an entirely new environment that allows the team to perform at the highest level. In this chapter you will see what that high-performance environment is and how the Synergistic team operates within it.

BEHIND THE WALL

Every successful team or group works to the same hidden pattern: a predictable cadence in their interactions that produces flow, engenders cooperation among team members, and results in high-quality decisions. Only by accessing the Synergist style can a group or team access this pattern. Even in those rare occasions when the V-O-P team breaks through with a brief spurt of productivity, they do so because one or more of the team members is subconsciously operating in the Synergist role. Most importantly, only the Synergistic team can consistently operate within the pattern.

The pattern is a natural one, a subliminal rhythm that all successful teams fall into. Natural Synergists understand the rhythm intuitively. A team blessed with a natural Synergist will find itself subconsciously following this new pattern because the Synergist team member will prod it to do so. Conversely, the Visionary, Operator, and Processor do not "naturally" understand this pattern of successful team interaction—in fact, the V, O, and P tendencies that we've seen in earlier chapters fight against it, pulling the team's interaction *away* from the new pattern and into failure.

THE RHYTHM OF SUCCESS

All groups and teams are formed for the same basic purpose. Whether it's the executive committee of a Fortune 100 company or an ad hoc group designing a new employee orientation program, the reason for putting people together in a team is always the same: to pool the knowledge, experience, and skills of each individual member in order that they may *together* produce high-quality decisions on behalf of the enterprise as a whole.

Because all groups and teams are put together for this same underlying reason, all *successful* groups and teams, irrespective of their specific goals, follow a similar route or pattern in their interactions—the pattern of high-quality decision-making.

At the 30,000-foot level, this pattern of high-quality, team-based decision-making looks like this:

$$\text{Investigation} \rightarrow \text{Interpretation} \rightarrow \text{Implementation}$$

For the group to deliver a high-quality decision, it must move through these three sequential stages, which I call a "3-I" pattern. First, *Investigation:* the group has to collect the information it needs in order to make a good decision. Second, *Interpretation:* the information and data have to be interpreted, from which comes the actual decision. Third, *Implementation:* the group must determine what needs to happen in order for the decision to be implemented (either by themselves or by others).

This 3-I pattern of successful team decision-making has two characteristics:

1. It may be used by the team often (repeatability)

Depending on its overall mandate, the team may cycle through this pattern of Investigation, Interpretation, Implementation only once or, more likely, repeat it many times, often in the course of a single meeting.

For example, a team whose mandate is to select a supplier for a key raw material or component might move through the 3-I pattern just once,

gathering bids (Investigation), assessing them (Interpretation), and informing the purchasing department of their choice (Implementation). Most
other groups and teams, particularly those with broad responsibilities
(like an executive management team), will cycle through the 3-I pattern
repeatedly.

2. Each of the three stages can vary in length and complexity (flexibility)

Not all three stages are of equal intensity or duration. Depending on the topic
under consideration, a particular stage may be short-lived or extensive. For
example, the Investigation stage for a team tasked with proposing a new enterprise-wide IT system will be substantially lengthier and more complex than that
for a management team considering a vice president's request for sick leave. In
the latter case, the Investigation might amount to little more than ensuring that
everyone on the team has copies of both the v-p's request and company leave
policy in hand.

Similarly, the Interpretation stage of, for example, a hiring committee will
vary in complexity and length depending on the short list of candidates. If there's
a clear front runner, the decision will likely be reached much more quickly than
if there are three equally compelling candidates.

Nonetheless, whether a stage is lengthy and complex or short and simple
(even to the extent that the team may move through it almost instantaneously),
all three stages together form the universal 3-I pattern of successful, team-based
decision-making.

STUMBLING IN THE FOOTHILLS

From the 30,000-foot level the 3-I pattern doesn't look too daunting. Surely the
Visionary, Operator, and Processor can master this relatively simple sequence?
Is the Synergist really necessary to ensure that the team follows what is, after all,
a seemingly logical process?

The reason that the Visionary, Operator, and Processor are unable to work
the 3-I pattern lies in the detail. If we come down from the 30,000-foot level and
look at each of the three stages more closely, we can see that each stage in itself
comprises three sub-elements—making in total nine imperatives for success. It
is the nature of these nine imperatives that causes the Visionary, Operator, and
Processor to stumble and gridlock.

Here are the nine imperatives, three for each 3-I stage:

Table 10.1   The nine imperatives of high-quality, team-based decision-making

Investigation	Interpretation	Implementation
Intellectual rigor	Stamina	Consensuality
Embracing change	Discipline	Communication
Financial understanding	Objectivity	Accountability

From what we've already covered in Parts I and II, you can probably already identify from this table some of the imperatives that will trip up each of the Visionary, Operator, and Processor, even from just these short descriptions.

Stage 1: Investigation

The first stage in effective team-based decision-making is for the group to collect the information it needs in order to make a good decision.

As we've already seen, the Investigation stage of the 3-I pattern (as with all three stages) can be short and simple, or long and complex, depending on the issue under consideration—a management team meeting regularly may require little more than reading a supplied document or listening to someone make a proposal.

Conversely, a single-topic project team—like the example given earlier of a team tasked with recommending a new enterprise-wide IT system—may spend months, even years, in the Investigation stage.

Either way, whether the process is simple or complex, successful teams—those with strong Synergistic input—consistently address three imperatives at the Investigation stage: intellectual rigor, embracing change, and financial understanding.

To be clear: depending on the issue under consideration, there may be additional imperatives at play during the Investigation stage, but these three cause the most trouble for the V-O-P team.

INTELLECTUAL RIGOR

In the context of high-quality, team-based decision-making, we can define intellectual rigor as: *The commitment to ask as many questions as are necessary to uncover all the material information required to make any needed decision.* Three important factors into this are:

1. It's a *commitment* by the team—not a whim, or a maybe-we-will, maybe-we-won't option, but an inviolable commitment made by all participants at the start of each team interaction.
2. It involves asking as many questions as are necessary—which might be two questions or 102, depending on the issue.
3. It relates to only *material* information, not every iota of information that could possibly be uncovered.

Right away you can see how, left to the V-O-P natural styles, dysfunction will kick in. The Visionary is unlikely to be thrilled at the idea of following such a rote process every time (they'd rather reach for a spark of genius from time to time), and their attention span in asking all the questions necessary will be severely strained; the Processor will likely find more questions to ask than either the Visionary or Operator is comfortable with, and will interpret "material information" very broadly; and the Operator will quickly become frustrated at all the questions and the apparent lack of action.

At this vital first step in the 3-I cycle, the Synergist's role is critical. By keeping the team focused on the importance of intellectual rigor and simultaneously blunting the extremes of possible reactions, the Synergist takes the team into

Table 10.2 Behaviors that develop intellectual rigor

Intellectual Rigor	Never→Sometimes→Always				
We go beyond an initial information exchange					
We do not rush to judgment					
We do not instantly accept any one team member's analysis of a situation					
We ask detailed questions to uncover key facts					
We clearly distinguish emotion from information					

flow right from the start. As a result, the Visionary, Operator, and Processor begin building the muscle of productive interaction.

Table 10.2 shows five behaviors I see Synergists coax from their team to deliver intellectual rigor, together with a brief explanation of each. (Use the table to score how your team does—you can download copies of all the mini-assessments in this chapter from the website using the link in the chapter summary.)

We go beyond an initial information exchange

Many V-O-P teams restrict the first Investigation stage to a single, initial exchange of information and then move quickly to Interpretation. This often happens when there is a strong Visionary-Operator combination on the team. The Visionary wants to start brainstorming solutions right away, and the Operator supports this because it takes the team one step closer to decision-making. With their tendency to fast decision-making, both the Visionary and the Operator are typically reluctant to ask (and wait for) more information; they prefer to get to a decision on the basis of the available—even if inadequate—data.

The Synergist's role is to ensure that time is spent bringing just enough of the right information to the table in order to make a good decision. They achieve this by modeling and encouraging the next four behaviors, and by encouraging a reversal of the usual choreography of V-O-P interaction. By actively involving the Processor right from the start, intellectual rigor is more likely to be applied.

We do not rush to judgment

One of the Synergist's key roles is to *appropriately* slow down the team's interactions—not unduly or irrelevantly (as the Visionary and Operator often fear the Processor is doing), but enough to ensure that the decisions the team makes are considered ones.

Think of it like this. If a golfer is consistently spraying the ball left or right, and rarely hits it down the middle of the fairway, the first thing a golf coach will tell the golfer is to slow down their swing. By slowing their swing, the transition through each component part—backswing, point of impact, follow-through—is smoother, and with a better result—the ball goes where the golfer wants it to.

Similarly, the Synergist slows down the team's interaction so that the three component parts—Investigation, Interpretation, Implementation—combine seamlessly to produce consistently high-quality decisions. That process of slowing down starts right at the outset, by preventing the default V-O-P dynamic of an early rush to judgment based usually on insufficient information.

This early rush to judgment in the Investigation stage typically happens when one of two things happens—either the Visionary believes they see a universal pattern in a small sample of data ("Sales of product X always go down when we discount product Y, so one must be cannibalizing the other"), or the Operator equates anecdotal coincidence with a trend ("Customer A just told me that their product arrived with a crack in the front left side, customer B told me the same thing last week, so we must have a problem in manufacturing").

Highly successful teams take hypotheses reached by such leaps of logic and have the Processor analyze them for veracity. By encouraging this to happen, the Synergist ensures intellectual rigor is being applied. And, coincidentally, this helps train the Visionary and Operator to think more Synergistically—once they know that their leaps of logic won't be accepted at face value and will instead be subject to analysis, they are less likely to throw something out there simply in the hope that it will push the team closer to decision-making.

We do not instantly accept any one team member's analysis of a situation

As we've seen, one of the coping dynamics that often emerges is that to avoid conflict, the participants cede certain topics, agenda items, or areas of opinion to specific individuals.

For example, if everyone becomes wearily familiar with the fact that the Operator rarely concedes anything about pricing (because it's the Operators who actually have to sell the product to customers), then the others may balk at arguing about pricing. Or, if a Processor has gone to the wall frequently on the impossibility of delivering product to the retail stores more quickly (because they know the delivery system is tapped out and cannot be reengineered), then the others may cede any discussion of the delivery process to the Processor.

While this may work as a coping system for reducing stress in the dysfunctional team, once the Synergist is involved, it can be—and needs to be—removed as a barrier to intellectual rigor. The Synergist can reopen discussion on the ceded topics by posing appropriate questions.

We ask detailed questions to uncover key facts

Central to pushing past a cursory initial information exchange into intellectual rigor is a commitment to constructive inquiry, asking just enough detailed questions to uncover the key facts needed for a high-quality decision.

Left to their own devices, however, the Visionary, Operator, and Processor are unlikely to engage in a cooperative Q&A session during the Investigation stage.

The Synergist changes this dynamic by:

- *encouraging* the Visionary to ask creative, probing questions, showing how constructive inquiry can be a creative process in and of itself and not just a means to an end;
- *corralling* Processors to keep their questions focused only on those areas that are of material importance to the matter under consideration;
- *coaching* the Operator to use the questioning behavior to find out what worked and didn't work in the past (thus ensuring that hard, real-world data is brought forward to the Interpretation stage—something the Operator values highly).

With the Synergist's input, all the participants can learn the value of constructive inquiry and learn to contribute positively to the experience rather than rush past it for fear of conflict and tension.

We clearly distinguish emotion from information

The tensions caused by the differing natural styles often raise the emotional level of the V-O-P team's discussions. In the Investigation stage, this clouds the issue as each of the Visionary, Operator, and Processor gets into defensive positions, justifying their information rather than treating it as objective data available to the entire team. The team then tries to avoid this by keeping its discussions short and to the point—but of course, this foreshortening has the highly negative effect of precluding intellectual rigor.

Here the Synergist must act as a lightning rod, grounding the discussions by pointing out unnecessary conflict caused by emotion, and returning the team to an objective consideration of the underlying data.

Over time, the Synergist will learn the foibles and hot buttons of each team member and, if working with the same group of Visionaries, Operators, and Processors for any reasonable period, will soon be able to head off most of the overly emotional discussions by nipping them in the bud at the outset.

EMBRACING CHANGE

The second imperative in the Investigation stage is to embrace change. In this context, we can define embracing change as: *the commitment to identify, assess, and embrace positive change agents, and to identify, assess, and account for unavoidable negative change agents.*

For the team to make high-quality decisions, it is important that in the Investigation stage the members not only review existing, accepted facts (internal documents, spreadsheets, historic data), but that they also consider "what they don't know that they don't know"—external changes that may impact their decision such as industry best practices, demographic shifts, and technological innovations.

Embracing change in this way is problematic for the Visionary, Operator, and Processor. As with intellectual rigor, it arises from the communication difficulties they encounter. Put simply, the tension and conflict generated when they discuss already-known facts is so high that the prospect of extending their discussion into the unknown—investigating beyond existing data, if you will—is too daunting to contemplate.

As a result, discussions at the Investigation stage are often brittle and restricted to what is already known, which allows less room for heated debate than discussing the unknown. It is the Synergist's role to encourage and model behaviors that break this dynamic, like those shown below in Table 10.3.

Not all of these specific behaviors will be necessary in every cycle through the Investigation stage, but their underlying thrust—to actively consider the possible impact of external change—is universally important.

How does your team or group fare?

Table 10.3   Behaviors that encourage acceptance of change

Embracing Change	Never→Sometimes→Always				
We explore industry trends outside of our organization					
We are in close contact with our customer base					
We read and research outside industry sources					
We challenge fundamental assumptions					
We work outside our comfort zone					

We explore industry trends outside of our organization

The first place to look for probable change is in what is happening in the industry as a whole outside of the organization. By encouraging simple information-sharing—the pooling of information gleaned from attending industry conferences, reading industry literature, and talking to peers in other organizations, for example—the Synergist can provide a tension-free environment to begin the process of identifying and embracing change.

A conflict-free discussion of what each is seeing in the way of likely future changes in the industry is one that yields truly synergistic results for the team. The Visionary, Operator, and Processor will each, by preference, be looking at different aspects of potential industry changes. Taken together, this makes for a rich discussion when facilitated by the Synergist.

We are in close contact with our customer base

The second obvious source of information about external changes in the enterprise's operating environment lies in its customer base. Most organizations exist to meet their customer needs, and yet those needs are often ignored entirely during the Investigation stage.

Not every decision faced by a team is going to have an impact on external customers, but there is always an *internal* customer—the people in the organization who have to implement, or work with the impact of, the team's decision. During the Investigation stage an effective Synergist will prod the team to actively identify the internal and/or external customer(s) most impacted by the team's deliberations, and will reach out to them to explore their needs and desires, specifically looking for anything that has changed.

We read and research outside industry sources

Effective teams are intellectually curious. They identify patterns, best practices, and trends outside their industry that will (or could) have a material impact on the business. Industry leaders know that it is from here that true competitive advantage comes. While many organizations can emulate best practices from *within* an industry, it's the true innovator who identifies, converts, and monetizes trends happening *outside* their industry.

In the safer environment engendered by the Synergist, this discussion can now take place, with the Visionary, Operator, and Processor trading observations and opinions on what they see happening outside their industry.

We challenge fundamental assumptions

Without input from the Synergist, V-O-P teams tend to be amplifiers of the past. An unhealthy bias toward the status quo develops when the team routinely accepts as valid the assumptions that may, in fact, have been overcome by events.

With Synergist facilitation, it is easier for the team to explore the assumptions underlying the information gathered in the Investigation stage.

We work outside our comfort zone

Finally, the Synergist can help fulfill the imperative to embrace change by encouraging the team to step farther and more frequently outside its comfort zone.

This is not to say that the team will never again experience conflict or have arguments, but with input from the Synergist they will, over time, be able to have those arguments without threatening the overall cohesion of the team. And, as a direct result, team members will more readily push the boundaries of their discussions when in the Investigation stage.

FINANCIAL UNDERSTANDING

Not everything that is important is exciting, and the third imperative in the Investigation stage is definitely in that boring-but-crucial category. In this context, we can define financial understanding as: *The ability to read and*

understand the basics of an Income Statement, a Balance Sheet, and a Cash Flow
Projection.

One of the most notable characteristics of teams operating without a
Synergist is how frequently their outputs are financially naïve. They often either
ignore the financial implications of their decisions or make sweeping assumptions that don't hold up in the real world.

There are two reasons why this happens:

1. There is no one among the Visionaries, Operators, or Processors on the
   team who has enough of a financial understanding to inform the team's
   deliberations, and the dysfunction among the existing team members is
   such that the thought of adding yet another person to the team to help
   out with this is daunting; or

2. There *is* someone on the team who does have enough financial understanding to inform the team's deliberations, but the noncollaborative
   nature of the V-O-P interaction precludes this from happening. As
   a result, the financially literate team member is sidelined or elects to
   remain mute rather than ride into battle with their observations.

An effective Synergist will ensure that this gap in financial understanding
is filled, either by coopting someone onto the team (even temporarily) who
can help or by providing those team members who do possess an understanding of how the numbers work with a safe environment in which to share their
knowledge.

Table 10.4 Behaviors that indicate financial understanding

Financial Understanding	*Never→Sometimes→Always*				
We can read and understand basic financial statements					
We request the financial data underpinning the decisions we make					
We understand the financial impact of our decisions					
We have a balanced focus on revenue, profits, and cash					

Table 10.4 shows the four behaviors which indicate that a group is meeting the imperative of financial understanding. How does your group rate?

We can read and understand basic financial statements

The team should be able to read and understand basic financial statements. This doesn't mean that each member of the team needs to become a mini-CPA, just that they can together work out the import of basic financial documents.

For the Synergist, the key role here is to ensure that the team doesn't become overly dependent on any one person to do the number-crunching for the group. Often when one person in a group has detailed financial knowledge (usually a Processor), everyone else in the group will look to that individual to interpret any financial information.

For effective, team-based decision-making, it's important that this doesn't happen. Instead of acting as subject-matter experts and having this aspect of the team's activities in essence outsourced to them, those who understand financial statements, facilitated by the Synergist, must *coach* those who don't, allowing the team to come to a considered, joint understanding of the financial implications of their decisions.

We request the financial data underpinning the decisions we make

Reading and learning to understand basic financial information is for most people a tiresome exercise, however important it may be. So, not surprisingly, many groups develop a blind spot when it comes to the need for it. Put simply, many teams fail to request necessary financial information because they don't want to go through the mental exercise of analyzing it. This is particularly true of the Visionary and the Operator, neither of whom naturally possesses the commitment to detail that is required.

Recognizing this, the Synergist will work—often with the Processor—to identify the financial data the group requires and to make it available when it is needed.

We understand the financial impact of our decisions

The group's ability to read and understand basic financial statements is important not only for the input side of the team's deliberations but also for the output side, that is, for the financial impact of their decisions. When financial impact is an explicit part of a team's deliberations, then even a V-O-P team will incorporate the financial impact into their outputs. But with a Synergist on board, the team should be able to assess the financial impact of its decisions in *any* material circumstance and to communicate it to the relevant stakeholders.

We have a balanced focus on revenue, profits, and cash

Visionaries, Operators, and Processors each have an affinity for different ways of measuring financial return. Visionaries like the grandness of big revenue numbers, as do Operators (particularly if they are in sales). Founder-Visionaries have an acute understanding of the importance of profit. Processors are attracted to return on investment because it measures efficiency, which they understand.

The Synergist ensures that the team takes a balanced approach when examining the financial implications of data, ensuring everyone gets heard, and not allowing any one measurement of success to dominate the others.

CHAPTER SUMMARY

All teams are formed for the same underlying reason: to pool the knowledge, experience, and skills of each individual member in order that they may together produce high-quality decisions on behalf of the enterprise as a whole.

There is a pattern—a rhythm of success—that all successful teams adhere to. It is the pattern of successful team-based decision-making.

That pattern consists of three stages every team goes through—the 3-I pattern:

Investigation → Interpretation → Implementation

Each of the three stages in turn comprises three imperatives—nine attributes in all, none of which the V-O-P team can develop without the involvement of the Synergist.

The imperatives of the Investigation stage are:

- Intellectual Rigor;
- Embracing Change; and
- Financial Understanding

The next chapter details the imperatives in the Interpretation stage, and chapter 12 examines the Implementation stage, along with the Synergist's role in the teamwork.

 Scan this QR code to be taken to a web page containing case studies and examples specific to this chapter, or point your web browser to http://PredictableSuccess.com/syn-ch10.

11

PULLING THE TRIGGER

Evaluation and Decision-Making

THE EVALUATION AND DECISION-MAKING PROCESS is difficult in any organization—either everyone wants to chime in, or as with the V-O-P team, the group gridlocks. The 3-I process simplifies this by giving guidelines for *how* decisions are made. The second I of the process, Interpretation, identifies three Synergistic imperatives that, taken together, ensure the team makes a high-quality decision.

INTERPRETATION

The Interpretation stage involves working through the information that was gathered in the Investigation stage with the goal of making a high-quality decision based on that information—tempered by the team members' experience and knowledge.

Table 11.1 The nine imperatives of high-quality, team-based decision-making

Investigation	*Interpretation*	*Implementation*
Intellectual rigor	Stamina	Consensuality
Embracing change	Discipline	Communication
Financial understanding	Objectivity	Accountability

The three Synergistic imperatives in this stage—stamina, discipline, and objectivity—not surprisingly echo the three main missing factors in the non-Synergistic V-O-P team's deliberations. Previously, the inherent tensions in the team made the interactions between the Visionary, Operator, and Processor so fraught that it would quickly drain the participants of all three imperatives.

Now, with those tensions banished or greatly reduced, rather like going to the gym after a long absence, the Synergistic team must learn to rebuild the muscles of stamina, discipline, and objectivity in order to stay focused and engaged during the Interpretation stage.

As we look at each imperative in turn, bear in mind that while the team will not be required to exhibit a high level of all three on every occasion—sometimes the Interpretation stage can be short and relatively simple—an effective Synergistic team *will* need to be able to draw on each one of them regularly and often.

STAMINA

The first imperative—stamina—is needed because the Synergistic team typically spends more time together in the Interpretation stage than in any other. (Although there may be a higher volume of work to do in the Investigation stage, the bulk of investigative work is usually done by individuals or subgroups outside of the team environment).

The Interpretation stage is also when each individual team member's energies are drained most quickly, because it is here, in the cockpit of actual decision-making, that everyone's opinion and personal preferences come to the fore. As a result, there is frequently more for the Synergist to do in the Interpretation stage than in any other. All in all, once the team moves into the Interpretation stage and starts the process of decision-making, a high level of stamina is required to ensure that the end result is in keeping with the enterprise commitment. Here's the stamina imperative:

We have the mental, physical, and emotional strength to concentrate for prolonged periods on the detail of both decision-making and implementation.

Notice that this isn't only about physical stamina—mental and emotional stamina are just as important. We'll see why in just a moment. Notice too that although the stamina imperative first shows up in the Interpretation stage, it continues into the Implementation stage—as we'll see in the next chapter, the

Visionary and Operator in particular often fight to remain focused when the team transitions into Implementation.

Here are the minimum stamina behaviors the Synergist will want to ensure are exhibited by the team.

Table 11.2 Behaviors indicating stamina

	Never→Sometimes→Always				
We stay physically engaged for reasonable periods of time					
We stay mentally engaged for reasonable periods of time					
We stay emotionally engaged for reasonable periods of time					
We are all equally engaged in all parts of our interaction					
We remain equally engaged in every mode of interaction, whether Visionary, Operator, or Processor					

We stay physically engaged for reasonable periods of time

The inability of members to stay alert during team interactions is self-evidently problematic in building a high-performance team, and yet you'd be surprised— or perhaps from your own experience you wouldn't—at how many groups underperform for this very reason.

Fatigue, at least, and exhaustion, at worst, lead to stress and disengagement even in the Synergistic team, and can stem from one (or both) of two sources: individual team members failing to look after themselves properly, or the team failing to schedule its work effectively.

Minimal physical fitness: Obviously, team members aren't required to run a marathon at the drop of a hat. But an inability to think clearly first thing in the morning without 12 cups of coffee or consistently nodding off in the afternoon thanks to a lunchtime carb overdose (and I've seen both, often) constitutes a basic inability to perform at the level needed for high-performance teamwork.

While gym coaching is clearly beyond the duties of the Synergist, it is important to spot when an individual team member's physical and mental fitness is getting in the way of quality teamwork, and then to use the difficult-conversations skill from the toolkit to address it.

Sensible scheduling: Many organizations run permanently on meeting overload—scheduling too many meetings and overscheduling the agendas for those meetings. It's no wonder that team participants are so often exhausted—and disengaged—by the middle of the week. The Synergist will look for ways to give the team meetings air—room for the participants to work at a steady pace but without feeling constantly under pressure. Here are a few ways to do this:

- See if meetings can be scheduled less frequently without causing problems in hitting milestones (a simple fix, often viewed as anathema in large organizations).
- Scan for items to take off the agenda, rather than adding more.
- Include frequent short breaks for team members to regroup and reenergize.
- Change location and working style (standing, sitting, break-out groups, dyads) frequently to help reinvigorate the team.

We stay mentally engaged for reasonable periods of time

Of course, there's a degree to which mental stamina is directly connected to physical stamina—tired body, tired mind, and all that. But the Synergistic team battles another, much more debilitating attack on its intellectual stamina, and it (as always) stems from the differences in people's natural styles.

The Visionary's, Operator's, and Processor's mental reserves drain at different rates, depending on what the group is engaged in at any one time. A Visionary's mental stamina, for example, will drain much faster when everyone is poring over a spreadsheet than it will during a brainstorming session. A Processor's mental stamina will drop more quickly while engaging in a robust debate than it will during a PowerPoint presentation. Spend too long in any one activity and, like a laptop running a processor-heavy peripheral, the team's "brain battery" will quickly drop to critical levels.

The challenge for the Synergist is to be aware of their colleagues' battery levels, and to be alert for those who are (metaphorically) flashing an orange light. Usually a change of topic or pace, or even a simple break, will be enough to allow the "blinking" participant to recharge.

We stay emotionally engaged for reasonable periods of time

Emotional engagement is a tricky thing to monitor, but incredibly important to manage. In this context, "emotionally engaged" means not going to either end of the spectrum—neither withdrawing emotionally from a particular aspect of the team interaction (either out of disinterest or as a passive-aggressive response to something someone else has said or done), nor blowing up emotionally.

Thankfully, as we've seen, a high percentage of the causes of emotional disengagement among the Visionary, Operator, and Processor can be avoided or diluted by moving into Synergist mode. But even then, it is unrealistic to expect that emotional tiredness and consequent disengagement will never happen— after all, the team members are only human.

The Synergist's role here is the same as for mental disengagement—to remain alert, watch for signs of it happening, and if possible, switch what the team is engaged on or take a break to allow folks to recharge. Signs of emotional disengagement include:

- Negative body language (folded arms, leaning back, standing up and walking to the side of the room, leaving!).
- Shutting down—apparently staying engaged but essentially withdrawing from participation in the team's interaction.
- Continuing to participate, but in a monotone or in terse sentences.
- Continuing to participate, but using overly emotional language.

We are all equally engaged in all parts of our interaction

You will recall that one of the coping mechanisms developed by the dysfunctional, non-Synergistic team is to effectively cede certain parts of the team's interactions to one or the other of the Visionary, Operator, and Processor, turning the rhythm of the group's deliberations into a series of individually dominated interactions (in which discussion of each agenda is the domain of either the V, O, or P) rather than a series of true group interactions (in which all participate on each topic).

It's the Synergist's role to stay alert to such recidivism, and when it happens to bring the whole team back into the interaction. The good news is that for a consciously Synergistic team (i.e., one that has learned the use of both the enterprise commitment and the Synergist's toolkit) this is a remarkably easy behavior to correct—on most occasions, simply pointing it out is enough to shake the team out of their torpor and back into collegial interaction. This may need to happen a number of times before the old behavior is fully eradicated.

We remain equally engaged in every mode of interaction, whether Visionary, Operator, or Processor

Finally, it's important for the Synergist to remember that even if every member of their team has transitioned into a Visionary+Synergist, Operator+Synergist, or Processor+Synergist, they still each retain their natural preferences.

No magic switch has been thrown that suddenly makes the Visionary wildly enthusiastic about detailed minutiae, the Operator ecstatic about more systems, the Processor a hyperbole-slinging iconoclast. Even though tension and conflict is largely gone, the old preferences remain, and the natural tendency of the V, O, and P will still be to zone out when the team is working in one of the other modes.

This behavior is as easy to spot—and fix—as the withdrawal behavior discussed above. Just as it's not hard to notice when the group as a whole has effectively ceded control to one individual, so in any reasonable-sized team it's just as less obvious when one subgroup is finding it hard to stay engaged. Signs to watch for include:

- An outbreak of multitasking.
- Side discussions between subgroups.
- Individuals zoning out of the interaction.
- Attempts to take the interaction back or forward to a different phase, particularly if expressed with frustration.

The fix is simple: point out the return of the old behavior and reengage the subgroup that has zoned out. After a few interventions, the team will become self-aware of the issue, and although it may never disappear entirely, the instances of it happening will dramatically decrease.

DISCIPLINE

Discipline is different from stamina. As we've just seen, stamina means the ability to stay engaged over a prolonged period of time. Discipline is about staying engaged on the *right things*.

Think of it this way—I send my son out to the garden one bright Saturday afternoon with instructions to cut down an old blighted tree. He comes back some hours later, clearly exhausted. My tour of the garden indicates that while he did in fact make a start on the tree, it's still standing. For whatever reason—his attention had wandered, or he didn't enjoy tree-chopping—most of his considerable efforts had instead gone into weeding the flower beds. My son has shown stamina, but not discipline.

Teams are the same. They can exhibit considerable stamina—working long hours, getting through prodigious amounts of information—all the while occupied with the wrong issues.

Here's how the imperative of discipline can be defined in the Interpretation stage: *We maintain focus on and commitment to a course of action until it is completed.*

Here are the minimal behaviors a Synergist should be looking for the team to exhibit to meet the discipline imperative:

Table 11.3   Behaviors indicating discipline

	Never→Sometimes→Always				
We stay focused on the topic at hand					
We do not use analysis as work avoidance					
We work through problems rather than switching topics					
We don't swing for the fences					

We stay focused on the topic at hand

"Well, duh," you're thinking—that's a no-brainer, surely? But in fact, this behavior is a tricky one for the newly Synergistic team—and for a counterintuitive reason.

Think back to the previously dysfunctional team—gridlocked, compromised, no real ability to interact positively. Now envisage the newly Synergistic team—in the flow, operating from a place of safety, able to communicate richly and effectively. Guess what they want to do now? That's right—communicate. A lot. They want to bond, to make up for lost time and recover old ground.

As a result, the team begins to hopscotch around from topic to topic—but for the opposite reason from why they did so before. Previously they topic-hopped because of their *lack* of ability to communicate effectively; now they're doing the same thing because their communications are rich and enjoyable, and, like kids in a playground, they want to explore the new landscape as much as possible.

The Synergist's role here is a nuanced one. It's important to allow the team the ability to exercise their new collegiality, but it's equally important that they stay focused, particularly in this crucial Interpretation stage.

The best fix is to use a simple time mechanism. Start by allowing five or ten minutes of diversion before pulling the team back to topic, and over a series of interactions gradually reduce the time allowed to the point that the team gets the message: Let's finish what we've started. Instead of floating off topic during their deliberations, encourage the team to use break times to wander into other areas of interest.

We do not use analysis as work avoidance

Oh, the siren song of further analysis when a difficult decision looms! We've all experienced the temptation of procrastinating rather than doing the hard work of making decisions, and the Synergistic team is no different.

As we know, this particular form of procrastination—analyzing information even further, or better yet, finding a reason to collect even more data—is primarily a Processor trait, and at its worst, it leads the team into paralysis by analysis.

In its first few interactions together, the newly Synergistic team is not exempt from this behavior, and for a simple reason: the V and O still trust the P to know more about data analysis than they do, and with the old conflict and tension now gone, they no longer get as frustrated with the Processor as they did previously. Net result: the Processor (initially) gets *more* leeway to overanalyze in the Synergistic team than during the V-O-P dysfunction.

This is essentially a problem of discipline—the overanalysis is being used by the team as work avoidance, an excuse to put off the tough job of actual decision-making. An effective Synergist will do two things:

1. **Recognize the work avoidance and call it.** It's usually not hard to get a Synergistic team to recognize when it is avoiding making hard

decisions—as we'll see throughout the 3-I process, once the Synergist has called a negative behavior a few times, the team will typically become quite adept at self-policing itself in the future.

2. **Revisit the financial understanding imperative from the Investigation stage.** The more all members of the team learn and understand how to analyze data, the less likely the Visionary and Operator are to be overdependent on the Processor. If the team is regularly sliding into overanalysis as a form of procrastination, then it's likely the financial understanding imperative from stage 1 hasn't yet been fully met.

We work through problems rather than switching topics

As has been said earlier, the Synergistic team is not a group of invincible superheroes. Although the dysfunctions of the unstable V-O-P triangle are gone, there are other ways that the transformed team can underperform if it isn't vigilant. The most common way is by fudging problems that come up, deferring or avoiding issues that threaten to return the group to tension and conflict.

But doesn't the enterprise commitment and the Synergist role remove the old V-O-P gridlock?

Well, yes, it does—but V-, O-, and P-related issues aren't the only reason why team members might disagree. Now that everyone can move *beyond* their natural instincts, a whole new world of potential conflict opens up: *real* disagreement, based not on personal styles but on the objective interpretation of data.

This type of disagreement—a difference in interpretation of objective fact not related to the team members' natural styles—is obviously something that can happen to any group. For the team members, however, it feels like all the old dysfunction is creeping back in—here we are, fighting all over again, as dysfunctional as ever! They feel deflated, as if nothing has changed.

Of course, none of this is the case. It's simply that by removing one debilitating cause of disagreement (V-O-P dysfunction) the team has been freed up to have normal, healthy disagreements.

When this first happens, it is a vital moment for the Synergist. As the Visionary, Operator, and Processor freeze, fearful that the old V-O-P problems are returning, they will understandably, though wrongly, try to defer or ignore the problematic issue and move on to something else . It's crucial for the

Synergist at this point to ensure that the group stays disciplined and focused on the issue at hand, for two reasons:

1. **Doing otherwise opens the door to a dysfunctional pattern.** Once the team fudges a problematic decision for the first time, the likelihood that they will do so again rises considerably. It only takes the team to repeat this behavior three or four times for it to become synaptic—a "grooved," natural response when faced with difficult decisions.

2. **It prevents the team from developing their conflict management skills.** You may recall from chapter 8 that one of the key Synergistic skills is conflict management—precisely because the Synergistic, team is not free from conflict. When the team faces its first (and subsequent) difficult decisions, the Synergist must remind the group that this is a natural occurrence, and that it's important for the team to work through it, not to defer or ignore it.

Over time the Synergistic team members will realize that the conflict they now face occasionally is perfectly healthy, that they can manage it just fine, and that it is not a harbinger of a return to the old dysfunction.

We don't swing for the fences

There is one remaining piece of residual muscle memory from the old V-O-P dynamic team for the Synergist to deal with the Visionary's tendency to (over-) reach for creative, big-picture solutions.

This continues to be an issue for the Synergistic team for a couple of reasons:

1. **The Visionary often has seniority in the team.** Usually the Visionary in a team is either part of the founder/owner group, or if in a larger organization, a longtime employee at a senior level.

    Why is this important? Because their seniority gives the Visionary greater facility to retain idiosyncratic or preferred behaviors than the others, and this specific behavior—coming up with sweeping, "swing for the fences" solutions—is the last one they will willingly yield.

2. **Because the Visionary is, well, the visionary.** Neither the Operator nor the Processor is naturally drawn to highly creative thinking—so when it comes to finding a creative solution to the issue under consideration, why not let the Visionary take the lead?

The problem, of course, is that the Visionary's swing for the fences may be unnecessarily risky, when a simpler, more straightforward solution is within reach if the team would only remain focused on the matter at hand. Furthermore, allowing this behavior—to swing for the fences—to take hold is another route back to the suboptimal pre-Synergist choreography of alternating control among the three natural styles.

For the Synergist, this is essentially a discipline issue. There's nothing wrong with the Visionary throwing their ideas in along with everyone else's, but it must be *subjected to the same intellectual rigor*.

This can be particularly difficult because the Synergist may have less seniority than the Visionary. Often the more senior Visionary will shut down debate on their out-of-the-park idea by delivering it with a tone of finality, or by transitioning the team immediately to discussing its implementation, or by physically bringing the discussion to an end. Much of this is subconscious—another example of recidivist old-style muscle memory in action. But what's a less senior Synergist to do? Here are a few suggestions:

- This is a good time to suggest a break, if possible, to slow the Visionary's momentum toward closure.
- Expose the Visionary's idea to the wider group in the light of the enterprise commitment. Does it really represent what's best for the organization as a whole, or is it solely scratching the Visionary's itch?
- Ask the Visionary to switch into Synergist mode and to debrief their own idea.
- Over time, encourage the Operator and Processor to build their own brainstorming and critical analysis skills so that they can participate with the Visionary during the idea-formation stage, rather than yielding the floor to them.

OBJECTIVITY

We've learned that in the Interpretation stage the Synergistic team needs to stay fully engaged (stamina), and to stay focused on the right things (discipline). All of what has been achieved so far will be for naught, if at the end of the process the team fails to make a truly objective decision.

Here's the definition of objectivity in the context of the Synergistic team: *the commitment to base decisions solely on the appraisal of the relevant facts, and without undue consideration of personal prejudices.*

As with some of the earlier behaviors in this stage, this has nothing to do with prejudices based on V-O-P styles—as Synergists we've learned to tame those—but is due to personal preferences that are entirely individual and unconnected to our V, O, or P natures.

For instance, team member A might have a loathing for direct-mail marketing campaigns rooted in a hatred of junk mail. Team member B might *love* direct-mail marketing campaigns because they hit the ball out of the park with one a few years ago. If this team discusses adding a direct-mail marketing campaign to the marketing strategy, A's and B's biases will have an impact, even though they are unrelated to their V, O, or P styles. They're just personal preferences, pure and simple.

The Synergistic team is not free from the potential impact of such personal preferences. To guard against this, here are the minimum behaviors a Synergist will look for to ensure objectivity in their team.

Table 11.4   Behaviors indicating objectivity

	Never→Sometimes→Always				
We don't bring personal agendas to the decision-making process					
We clearly separate anecdote from data					
Where possible we seek outside corroboration for our decisions					
We reality-check and stress-test our decisions					

We don't bring personal agendas to the decision-making process

This behavior is essentially an explicit statement of the enterprise commitment, and although it may seem like a tough challenge—*no* personal agendas?—it's perhaps the easiest behavior in the 3-I pattern for the team to develop.

The easiest way to do so is at the point when the team moves into decision-making mode, when analysis is over and it's time to decide on a course of action. At that point, the Synergist should ensure the team does do two things.

First, formally reintroduce the enterprise commitment. If it feels inappropriate for your team, have everyone read it quietly for a few minutes. Second, on the basis that self-reflection is the best teaching, go around the team and ask each member to reflect on what personal agenda items they think they *might* have with regard to the subject at hand, and which they'd like the team's help to guard against.

I've found that, while awkward at first, when done consistently, this practice quickly turns into a highly profitable time of self-reflection for the team.

We clearly separate anecdote from data

When the team moves into final decision-making mode, one of the ways that objectivity disappears is through a failure at that point to distinguish between anecdote and data.

This issue is frequently driven by the Operator, and understandably so. After all, the Operator is the person most out on the front line, interfacing with people, and so they come to the team with a lot of anecdotally based evidence—for example, an unhappy customer or two who have received damaged product, and from which the Operator has deduced that there must be a problem in the shipping department.

For the Synergist, this is a challenge similar to the Visionary's desire to swing for the fences. Just because someone has reached a conclusion based on anecdotal evidence doesn't in itself mean that the evidence (or the conclusion) is *wrong*—just that there cannot be a presumption that it's automatically right.

If the team's decision on the matter is not to be flawed, dealing with this issue requires a break in the flow of decision-making to snap the team out its underlying presumptive acceptance that the given anecdote is equivalent to data.

The Synergist should either halt the discussion and have the anecdotal evidence removed from consideration, or, if the team feels strongly that the anecdotal evidence *should* be considered, then move the team back into the Investigation stage to gather enough additional, objective evidence to prove or disprove the anecdotal presumption.

Where possible we seek outside corroboration for our decisions

Too often teams conclude the decision-making process without checking how their decision stacks up against what others have done elsewhere. This decision-making in a vacuum leaves the team vulnerable to blind spots—built-in, hidden biases that the team, without outside comparisons, has become inured to.

These taken-for-granted, unspoken assumptions lurking behind an important decision—like "We always buy those components from China," or, "The admin department has to be in Chicago, where our head office is"—are assumptions that the team wouldn't think of questioning while in its own fishbowl, but which are more likely to be questioned when confronted with examples of how other teams (and other organizations) dealt with similar issues.

There are two points to remember here:

1. Although the dysfunctional V-O-P team had enough problems working together internally that the idea of looking *outside* the group environment likely never occurred to any of them, the Synergistic team can—and should—pull off this external corroboration with ease. Benchmarking is such a powerful but simple tool that it's a shame to leave it unused.

2. Sequencing is important. This benchmarking or looking for best practices elsewhere is not a substitute for the team doing its own work. Lazy teams benchmark with other organizations as a replacement for original thinking. High-performance teams use benchmarking as a corroborative process, *after* they've done their own thinking first.

We reality-check and stress-test our decisions

On the few occasions a dysfunctional V-O-P team actually reaches a decision, it's obvious that they will be in no hurry to reconvene later to see whether or not their decision is working out in practice. As a result, innate biases that have made it through to the final decision never get corrected. And it shows—the end users who have to work with a V-O-P team's decisions can often identify who the dominant contributor was by the bias in the solution: overly systematized, the Processor; overly sweeping, the Visionary; overly simplistic, the Operator.

The Synergistic team knows not to assume that their decisions are perfect, throwing them over the transom then moving on to the next item. Rather, they beta test their decisions: they let them operate provisionally for a week, a month, a quarter, whatever is appropriate, then reconvene, study the results, and revise them as necessary in the light of the feedback they receive.

CHAPTER SUMMARY

The second step in the 3-I process is the Interpretation stage, in which the data that has been gathered in stage 1, Investigation, is evaluated and a final decision is made.

The three imperatives during the Interpretation stage are Stamina, Discipline, and Objectivity.

The stamina imperative implies that the team has the mental, physical, and emotional strength to concentrate for prolonged periods on the detail of both decision-making and implementation.

The discipline imperative implies that the team can maintain focus on and commitment to a course of action until it is completed.

The objectivity imperative implies that the team will base its decisions solely on the appraisal of the relevant facts, without undue consideration of personal prejudices.

The third stage in the 3-I process, Implementation, is discussed in the next chapter.

 Scan this QR code to be taken to a web page containing case studies and examples specific to this chapter, or point your web browser to http://PredictableSuccess.com/syn-ch11.

12

MAKING IT WORK
The Final Stage—Implementation

WE'RE REACHING THE END of our examination of the 3-I pattern, the hidden rhythm of successful, team-based decision-making that the Synergistic team, freed from the V-O-P dysfunctions, is able to attain.

In the previous two chapters we looked at the first two stages of team decision-making, Investigation and Interpretation. In this chapter we'll examine the last of the three stages in the pattern, Implementation, in which the team must determine what needs to happen for their decision to be implemented.

You will recall that each stage carries with it three imperatives for the team to meet in order to successfully navigate each stage. Let's take a look at what the team is seeking to achieve in the Implementation stage, then at each of this stage's three imperatives in turn.

Table 12.1 The nine imperatives of high-quality, team-based decision-making

Investigation	Interpretation	Implementation
Intellectual rigor	Stamina	Consensuality
Embracing change	Discipline	Communication
Financial understanding	Objectivity	Accountability

IMPLEMENTATION

For the old, dysfunctional V-O-P team, the Implementation stage is usually abrupt; once a decision is made, it is released into the wild and left to fend for itself. It's therefore not surprising that the implementation rate of V-O-P team decisions is typically low. Without guidance and help from the team that came up with the decision in the first place, there are simply too many ways in which it can be derailed or sandbagged.

For the Synergistic team, there is no reason for this to be so—with the team in flow, the extra time invested to ensure a smooth handover from making a decision to successfully implementing it is time well spent.

Unfortunately, even many Synergistic teams fail to make this investment, either because of other time pressures on team members or simply from a lack of appreciation of its importance. When they allow this to happen, the Synergistic team is in danger of nullifying everything accomplished in the Investigation and Interpretation stages, and sabotaging its chances of success just as surely as the dysfunctional team did. Irrespective of the reason, whether it's a dysfunctional V-O-P team that simply cannot do it or a Synergistic team working out of ignorance, if a team does not adequately plan to shepherd its decisions from idea into reality, the probability of that reality ever happening is low.

Think of it this way. While a team is gestating an idea, it is rare that everyone else in the organization is waiting with bated breath to adopt the results of their deliberations. Unless the organization is teetering on the brink of disaster and the team is tasked with its survival, everyone else has a million other things to do and barely notices the arrival of the team's decision. So, once the team hands it off to the disinterested onlookers, it's only a matter of time before, starved of attention, it quietly expires.

In essence, the Synergistic team must act as its own midwife—not just birthing the decision but tending and caring for it in the first stages of implementation until it has reached the point where its survival is assured. Achieving the requires that the team meets three imperatives: *consensuality, communication,* and *accountability*. Let's look at each in turn.

CONSENSUALITY

First admission: I made this word up. "Consensual" is an adjective, but not a noun (though it should be). What I mean by consensuality is that at the point of implementation, the team's decision should arrive in the wider organization without any sense of imposition.

In fact, the opposite should be the case. Any key individuals involved in implementation who are *not* on the team—those on the receiving end of the organization—should, by the time the decision arrives with them, feel that they have played an integral role in formulating the decision, that their role in the implementation process is a consensual one right from the start.

Consensuality can be achieved by the team making this commitment: *We commit to early, frequent, and congruent consultation with key individuals, specifically with those holding authority, responsibility, and/or influence over the implementation or outcome of key decisions.*

The second part of the consensuality commitment identifies those with whom we want to build consensus, and the first part states how we will do it—through frequent consultation with the key implementers, ahead of time. Note that the commitment to consensuality also requires that those communications be *congruent,* and we'll see shortly what is meant by that and why it is important.

Here are the minimum behaviors required for a team to meet the consensuality imperative.

Table 12.2   Behaviors indicating consensuality

	Never→Sometimes→Always				
We consult with those who have the authority, responsibility, and influence needed to implement the decisions we make					
We implement with cabinet responsibility					
We implement through one voice					
We implement with porous borders					
We view end users as co-implementers					

We consult with those who have the authority, responsibility, and influence needed to implement the decisions we make

The core reason why consensuality is important—and why so many otherwise excellent team-based decisions fail at the point of implementation—is that there are people (often, many people) *outside* of the team who have considerable impact on whether or not the team's decision will actually make it to the point of adoption.

An effective Synergist will help the team identify and reach out to three groups in particular:

- Those with *authority* to implement the decision. If the team is recommending, say, switching the sourcing of a component from one country to another for cost-saving reasons, then the CFO may have the ultimate authority to make the decision.
- Those with *responsibility* to implement the decision. In our example, though the CFO may have the authority to approve the change, it will be the purchasing department that will have to implement it.
- Those who can *influence* the adoption of the decision. In this case, the quality control team may have neither the ultimate authority in making a decision to switch supplier nor any responsibility for making the change, but they *are* likely to have considerable influence over whether or not it actually happens.

We implement with cabinet responsibility

It's hard to build consensus with the rest of the organization if some members of the team itself feel the decision has been imposed upon *them*.

Remember, even a Synergistic team carries with it no guarantee of unanimity. As we saw in the previous chapter, people differ for reasons that go beyond their V-O-P style, and the Synergistic team is as subject to those differences as any group. So, if a decision has been reached through the Interpretation stage that they don't agree with, some team members may be feeling decidedly nonconsensual.

How can the team move beyond their internal differences so that they can reach out to the wider organization in unanimity? The answer lies in the concept of cabinet responsibility.

Cabinet responsibility is part of the British parliamentary system which states that members of the highest executive team in the land (the Cabinet, which comprises the prime minister, ministry heads, and secretaries of state) must publicly support all governmental decisions made in Cabinet, even if they do not privately agree with them.

In other words, when, after a full and honest debate, the team reaches a majority decision, the other members of the team accept that decision. And, most importantly, they do not work behind the scenes to undermine the decision or those who supported it.

Implementing with cabinet responsibility is one of the highest callings of the Synergistic team, and is a public embodiment of the enterprise commitment.

We implement through one voice

Even when unanimity is established and each member of the team, bound by cabinet responsibility, is fully supportive of the team's decision, there is still a way in which consensus can be lost—and that's by a hydra-headed implementation strategy.

Allowing multiple team members to speak for the team may seem like a good democratic principle, and low risk as long as cabinet responsibility is at work. But in practice, however tight the team is, messages will get garbled, causing ambiguity and confusion, and thereby diluting consensuality.

This is not to say that just one person from the team must take responsibility for every aspect of implementing the team's decisions—except in the simplest of cases, that would be impractical. Rather, for each major element of the implementation, one person should clearly be seen as the main conduit to the rest of the organization.

Thankfully for the Synergist, this goal—to have each team member adhere to agreed, specific, and limited implementation roles, and not to wander into other team members' sandboxes—is rarely a hard sell. By appealing to everyone's busyness, it's usually easy to gain the team members' assent to limiting their activities in the Implementation stage.

(This is particularly so for the Operator and Processor. Curtailing the Visionary's natural loquaciousness and their belief that at some level all good ideas belong to them can be a challenging task. We'll see later in the accountability imperative how best to overcome this.)

We implement with porous borders

The single most powerful way to build consensuality is to operate the team with porous borders, particularly in the Interpretation and Implementation stages.

Most teams operate behind high fences. They work in a closed environment and rarely engage with others from outside of the team until their decision is made, at which point it is tossed over the fence to be implemented.

For a team wishing to build external consensus, this is the very opposite of what needs to happen. Instead of retreating behind fences, the Synergistic team breaks down the boundaries between it and those who will ultimately be responsible for implementing their decisions, involving them, formally and informally, in the decision-making process.

Here are some of the practical ways to do that.

- Invite authority-, responsibility-, and influence-holders to sit in on team meetings when issues affecting them will be discussed.
- Solicit friends-of-the-court-type submissions from those who will be materially impacted by the team's deliberations.
- If appropriate, meet occasionally as a team in the physical environment in which authority-, responsibility-, and influence-holders work, in order to gain a better understanding of how the team's decisions will affect them.
- Publish and circulate minutes of each meeting to all the main authority-, responsibility-, and influence-holders and ask for their feedback.

We view end users as co-implementers

Finally, in building consensuality, the Synergistic team blurs the line between the end users and the implementers. In the example given earlier in the chapter, feedback should be solicited not only from the CFO, the purchasing department, and the quality control team, but also from the shift supervisors of the production line which must install the new components, and the customers who use the end product.

We are by now well aware of the reasons the dysfunctional V-O-P team fails to get this far in implementation. We've all seen (and perhaps fallen prey to) initiatives that arrive with the final end user fraught with impracticalities and flaws—and which are in any case such a surprise to the end user that any chance of consensual implementation is slim. For the energized, fully functional Synergistic team, reaching out to the end user is an integral part of the entire 3-I process (not just in implementation), thus dramatically increasing the likelihood of successful adoption.

COMMUNICATION

As we've probably all experienced, even the best implementation plan can be derailed by poor communications. And even the most consensual of decisions can arrive DOA if no one knows what on earth is going on.

The difference between consensuality and communication is important. Through consensuality the team ensures that no-one feels they're having the implementation of a decision forced on them against their will; and by communication we explain clearly what it is we expect their role to be in the implementation process.

Consensuality and communication are symbiotic: without good communication, consensuality will only result in frustration, and without consensuality, even the best communications will be received grudgingly and acted on with less than alacrity.

Here's the definition of communication in this context: *The commitment to fully explain, to as many stakeholders as possible, as often, and in as much detail as is required, the key implementation steps for all major decisions.*

Table 12.3 shows the minimum behaviors required for the Synergist team to be sure it is communicating effectively in the Implementation stage.

Table 12.3 Behaviors indicating communication

	Never→Sometimes→Always				
We identify the main stakeholders in all major decisions we make					
We develop an implementation communication plan					
We engage in two-way communication throughout the implementation process					
We provide fast response to action-based communications					

We identify the main stakeholders in all major decisions we make

We've already identified some of those who are stakeholders in the implementation of the team's decisions as part of the consensuality imperative—specifically those directly affected by the decision one way or another.

We now need to extend the stakeholder group further, to include anyone who needs to know about the implementation of the group's decision, whether or not they are actively involved in implementation.

In our earlier example of the team deciding to switch a major component supplier, stakeholders who we want to communicate with might, for example, include the CEO (who should clearly know about a major decision such as this); the public relations department, who will want a heads-up in case of any blowback from the decision; and the website design group, if we need to make changes to published product specs.

We develop an implementation communication plan

Having identified all those with whom we wish to communicate (the consensuality stakeholders plus those identified above), the next step is to build a clear, unambiguous communication plan.

In many cases this may be no more than a few bullet points in a memo, or a short presentation for distribution, but more complex decisions will call for a detailed, multistep communication plan. In our "switching components" example, areas requiring effective communication might include:

- The timing of the switchover: when to start sourcing from the new supplier and drop the old; how to handle the overlap period, if any.
- Production line implications: modifications to process and machinery, training for shift supervisors and production line employees.
- Changes to packaging: redesign implications and amendments to product specification.
- Information to product users: expected changes in performance, if any; replacement of old components; public relations implications of the switch, if any.

We engage in two-way communication throughout the implementation process

Everything we've looked at so far in this chapter is aimed at achieving high-quality implementation of the Synergistic team's decisions. Specifically, we've built behaviors that prevent the team from simply throwing the final decision into the wider organization and hoping it will be adopted.

It's easy, however, to make precisely the same error at this stage—to believe that developing a communication plan is enough on its own, when in fact, lobbing a communication plan at the rest of the organization is just as ineffective as lobbing them the decision itself. Communication plans involve just that—communication. They have to engender a two-way dialogue, not broadcast as a one-way monologue.

It's important to take the communication plan—structured according to the one-voice behavior, with one team member identified as the lead conduit to each of the communication plan's stakeholder groups—out to the wider organization and engage them in understanding it, rather than delivering it to them passively and hoping they get it. Ways to do this include:

- Web broadcast: Don't just email folks a presentation. Set up a short web-based presentation to walk them through it and take questions. Record the presentation for later reuse.
- Town hall: Go to where each stakeholder group works—the production line, their offices. If they're in a remote location, do a closed web chat just for them—and engage in a live Q & A.
- A dynamic FAQ: Set up a web page where stakeholders can ask questions—and don't forget to provide answers! Include the questions asked during the web broadcasts and town halls.
- Peer meetings: Don't communicate only within silos (separately with each stakeholder group). Instead, ask people at a peer level across different stakeholder groups to come together with you to discuss the implementation of the team's decision. In our earlier example, 30 minutes with the chief purchasing officer, the CFO, the senior plant supervisor, and the head of public relations together will greatly accelerate the rate of implementation, compared to a series of sequential are-on-due meetings with each individial. If necessary, hold these as virtual meetings.

We provide fast response to action-based communications

Ever been involved in an employee engagement survey that you knew pointed up serious morale issues but was never acted on? Or put something into a suggestion box and never even received an acknowledgment of your submission?

If so, you know the danger of reaching out to people then not responding when a response is expected: it has a negative effect—the opposite of what was intended.

The same principle applies here. In the Implementation stage of the 3-I pattern, the team must remain active, not passive. Even when the implementation plan has been agreed on and communication has seeded it effectively in the wider organization, it isn't yet time for the team to turn out the lights and go home.

The reason is simple: no implementation plan is perfect. Something will go wrong, or will not work in the way the team expected. And having opened up a dialogue with the key stakeholders, it won't be long before they tell you what those problems are.

The Synergistic team needs to put a response mechanism in place as part of the communication plan (we'll see some ways to do so in the next imperative, accountability). Failure to have a response mechanism not only dilutes the effectiveness of implementation by leaving problems uncorrected, but also radically reduces the likelihood of external consensus and engagement by the wider organization next time around. After all, if you spent all that time communicating with them, even in a two-way dialogue, but didn't listen or act when they gave you feedback, why should they devote time and energy helping you implement anything in the future?

ACCOUNTABILITY

The road to implementation is paved with good intentions. Most Synergistic team members I've worked with accept the need for consensuality and good communications to ensure high-quality implementation. The problem comes not with their mental assent but with physical follow-through.

Most people who work on teams are busy people. They have other responsibilities, and as the team winds toward the end of its work, it's natural for the pressure of those other responsibilities to move to the forefront. Once they've reached the Implementation stage, many team members have begun to shift their time and attention to other things, and their commitment to following through on their Implementation responsibilities is weakened.

This trend toward disengagement at the Implementation stage is heightened in project teams. With a permanent team, such as an executive committee or a board, the fact that the team will continue to meet regularly, irrespective of which stage individual decisions are at, ensures that team members *must* continue to remain engaged—although even then, the group's collective focus can shift too soon to a new agenda item, leaving the just-made decision precariously un-implemented.

With a project team, however, it's often the case that the Implementation stage presages disbandment. The team will likely not meet again, and therefore disengagement and lack of follow-through by individual team members can happen without consequence.

The issue is one of accountability. Whether it's a permanent team that wants to fully implement each decision even as it moves on to a new agenda item, or a project team that wants to complete its mandate, the Synergist will ensure that everyone on the team fulfills their implementation responsibilities, not by leaving it to each individual team member's good intent, but by making accountability an integral part of the Implementation stage.

In this context, here's the definition of the accountability imperative: *The establishment of formal structures and processes in which each team member is held accountable for the satisfactory conclusion of his or her implementation commitments.*

Table 12.4 shows the minimum behaviors the Synergist will wish to see their team display, in order to meet the accountability imperative. How does your team score?

Table 12.4   Behaviors indicating accountability

	Never→Sometimes→Always				
We set clear implementation milestones					
We allocate unambiguous responsibility for achieving those milestones					
We put in place an accountability framework for each milestone					
We react quickly when implementation milestones are not met					
We conduct an implementation postmortem					

We set clear implementation milestones

Every accountability commitment starts and ends with a milestone: What are you being asked to do, and by when will it be done?

An implementation plan consisting of to-do items is not actually a plan—it's a statement of intent, at best. Only when those to-do items have a date attached do they become actionable items, and the list becomes a true plan.

The first step to accountability in the Synergistic team is therefore a relatively simple one: to attach clear, time-based expectations around each item in the implementation plan.

Two important points here. First, this step of setting implementation milestones applies also to the consensuality and communication imperatives. Setting a date when something must be done without consulting with those who will do it is a sure way to an imposed solution, rather than a consensual one, and failing to communicate milestones adequately is one of the most common ways implementation goes awry. Second, consider carefully which milestones the team should be setting and which it should be leaving to the stakeholders. If it makes no difference to the eventual outcome of the overall implementation process, letting stakeholders set their own milestones (in consultation with the team) is always preferable to imposing milestones on them.

We allocate unambiguous responsibility for achieving those milestones

Ambiguity in delegation is as bad as no delegation at all—everyone becomes confused as to who is really responsible, and the orphaned milestone is usually unmet. To achieve successful implementation, there must be no confusion as to precisely who is responsible for each milestone.

This can be tricky in the consensual environment, where, as we've just seen, responsibility for one or more milestones may have been delegated outside of the team to one stakeholder or another. The key is to link the ultimate responsibility for every milestone—whether delegated or not—to one named team member.

We've already put in place the mechanism to do this—through the one-voice behavior under the consensuality imperative. Once the team has allocated one team member to take responsibility for the communication process for each major element in the implementation plan, it's a short step to extend that responsibility to encompass agreed implementation milestones.

Using this model, the relevant team member is responsible not only for those implementation milestones they directly control, but also for any milestones in their area of responsibility that have been delegated to outside stakeholders. Their job in such cases is to liaise with those stakeholders, to assist them where they can in the completion of their milestones, and to report back to the group accordingly.

We put in place an accountability framework for each milestone

It's not a tautology to say that accountability requires accountability. Unless the team puts an actual framework in place to exercise accountability, it will never get around to doing it. In practical terms, this usually means scheduling meetings at specific times (usually around key milestone dates) when everyone reports to the group on progress with implementation.

The main problem with such meetings is that they are so often, and so easily, rescheduled or postponed—often indefinitely. There are three reasons why this happens:

1. *They're boring.* Most people loathe accountability meetings, primarily because they have to spend most of the time listening to other people talk about stuff that has no direct relevance to them.
2. *No one's done what they should have.* Often as the date for an accountability check-in rolls around, a series of email exchanges or phone calls takes place in which a number of team members establish that, no, they haven't completed their milestone yet either—and with a complicit mea culpa the meeting is postponed.
3. *They're amorphous.* Unlike meetings to actually *decide* things, it feels like there's little or no consequence to missing a check-in—after all, if we check in next week instead, nothing much will be seriously impacted, right?

Here are a few suggestions to make the accountability framework more robust and avoid postponements and cancellations:

- Have fewer meetings. Bring the whole team together only when absolutely necessary.
- Have dyads instead. Make the core accountability process a one-on-one exercise, where the responsible individual reports in to another person on the team. (The reporting should be one-way, just one member reporting to the other, not a two-way, mutual check-in—otherwise the complicit mea culpa will cause it to be postponed, too.)
- Place the outputs on a shared document. The results of the dyad check-ins can be made available for the rest of the team to read and comment on in their own time. This bypasses the "bored out of my skull listening to stuff of no relevance to me" dynamic without depriving the team of needed information.

- Meet to work only on exceptions. The whole team can then concentrate its formal meetings on actual work—discussing and fixing exceptions where implementation milestones have not been met rather than working through a vote checklist of everything.
- Be explicit about consequence. Milestones have meaning (or they should have—if the team has set meaningless milestones, then there is little purpose in enforcing accountability in any case). In our earlier example, not placing the first order for the new component on time will lead to a production slowdown when inventory of the old component runs out. Not changing the packaging information in time means the product cannot be sent to stores, leading to a rise in inventory and loss of sales.
- Involve a higher power. A high-performing team can up the stakes for its own accountability by inviting a senior executive to sit in on their accountability meetings.

We react quickly when implementation milestones are not met

The main reason for accountability is to ensure that the implementation process remains on track. This means that the chief goal of the accountability framework must be to identify exceptions: milestones that have been—or are about to be—missed, and to correct them as soon as possible.

In the behavior above we've already identified a number of ways in which the accountability process can be fine-tuned in order to highlight those exceptions, primarily by turning down the background noise of compliant activity, thus enabling team members to concentrate on identifying exceptions.

The key question now is, how do we effectively respond to missed or potentially missed milestones?

This is one area where the V-O-P model can be exceptionally helpful, by returning to the strengths of V-O-P subcombinations. You will recall that the Visionary and Operator combination is particularly effective in crisis management—together they have the right mix of creative thinking and task focus to grab a problem and quickly fix it. They also enjoy working together and can avoid much of the V-O-P dysfunction.

The Synergistic team should consider formalizing a V+O rescue team as part of the accountability process—specifically nominated V and O team members whose job it is to take over responsibility for, and rescue, recalcitrant milestones.

This process is highly effective for three reasons:

1. As we've seen, they're good at it.
2. It provides a simple, easily invoked go-to response when a milestone is in danger of being missed—no more time is wasted in working out how to get it fixed.
3. Most powerfully, the very existence of such a "rescue team" dramatically reduces the likelihood of milestones slipping. Under normal circumstances team members may feel that they can let a milestone slip with little consequence. Now the stakes are higher, and their competitive instinct (together with concerns about how such a rescue reflects on their own ability) will make a laissez-faire approach less likely.

We conduct an implementation postmortem

Completing a project, or implementing one part of a rolling agenda, is not just a one-time event; it's also part of the development of institutional skills—specifically the ability of the organization to change, to make those constant adjustments necessary to keep the organization in Predictable Success, oscillating between Whitewater and Treadmill.

As the team completes the third, Implementation stage of the 3-I pattern, there is more to learn than just the ramifications of the implemented decision itself. Every implementation process reveals much about the organization as a whole—what we're good at and where we can improve; where we're flexible and change readily; where we're more sclerotic and resist change.

An autopsy of each major implementation is important not in order to allocate praise and blame—although often the former and sometimes the latter are valuable activities in and of themselves—but to learn about the organization itself. Specifically to learn how it learns. As with the previous behavior, this process of conducting a positive postmortem that identifies major learning opportunities for the organization overall is best conducted by a V-O-P-S subgroup, in this case a Processor and a Synergist. (Specifically, either a natural Synergist or an Operator+Synergist—placing a Processor and a Visionary+Synergist together will pull the Visionary+Synergist too far out of Synergist mode and back to their natural Visionary style.) The reason for this combination is that they share three characteristics that are essential for an effective postmortem:

1. *Objectivity.* Both the Processor and Synergist operate more out of objectivity than subjectivity.
2. *The enterprise commitment.* As we know, the Synergist is innately motivated by the enterprise commitment, and of the three natural styles, the Processor most easily embraces it.
3. *Pattern recognition.* The essence of a good implementation postmortem is to spot patterns—what and where in the organization things go right (and wrong) most often; and about what, and where the organization is more and less responsive to change. The Processor's natural proclivity to bring order to data is invaluable here, and next to the Visionary (who wouldn't work well in this mix), the Synergist is best able to see patterns in otherwise unconnected events.

Every postmortem will vary, of course, and is only necessary after enterprise-level implementation—smaller decisions needn't trigger one—but the key components should include at least:

- Which milestones were most easily achieved, and what, if anything, that says about the organization's ability to implement.
- Which milestones were *least* easily achieved (or failed entirely), and what, if anything, that says about the organization's ability to implement.
- Which implementation steps were overlooked initially (if any) and had to be added later—and why.
- Which parts of the organization most struggled with implementation, and which implemented most easily—and why in each case.
- How close the final implementation came to the projected outcomes, and any lessons that can be gleaned from comparing the two.

CHAPTER SUMMARY

The third stage of the 3-I process is the Implementation stage, when the group or team must determine what needs to happen for their decisions to be implemented.

The three imperatives during the Interpretation stage are Consensuality, Communication, and Accountability.

The consensuality imperative implies that the team will commit to early, frequent, and congruent consultation with key individuals—specifically, those holding authority, responsibility, and/or influence over the implementation or outcome of key decisions.

The communication imperative implies that the team will fully explain, to as many stakeholders as possible, as often and in as much detail as is required, the key implementation steps for all major decisions.

The accountability imperative implies that the team will establish formal structures and processes by which each team member is held accountable for the satisfactory conclusion of his or her implementation commitments.

 Scan this QR code to be taken to a web page containing case studies and examples specific to this chapter, or point your web browser to http://PredictableSuccess.com/syn-ch12.

Epilogue

EXPLORING NEW PATHWAYS

Andy, Brad, and Riya Meet Their Synergist

THE TENSION IN THE ROOM was palpable and highly focused—on an elastic band, to be precise. Andy, surrounded by his 12 top executives, was idly fingering the band around his left wrist while staring at the binder in front of him.

It was six months since I had last been in the same windowless room, and we were now two hours into a half-day session Andy had scheduled to review the previous quarter and plan the next. The meeting had gone well so far, with Andy chairing his newly trained executive team, all of whom had responded enthusiastically and energetically to their Synergist training. This was the first opportunity for everyone to come together as a Synergistic team, and it had gone well—until now.

Andy had opened the meeting with a reading of the enterprise commitment, and followed it—in full Visionary mode—with a stirring ten-minute speech about the importance of working together Synergistically. I had watched as everyone around the table nodded approval, at the same time noticing some skepticism in their body language. After all, here was Andy doing what he always did—leading the charge and inspiring everyone with the big picture. It all seemed very familiar, and if the past was anything to go by, Andy would disengage as soon as the meeting plunged into anything detailed.

Instead, for two hours Andy had stayed the course resolutely and with good grace. Turning to Joanne for a run-through of the last quarter's financials, he remained focused and involved, until the discussion turned to reviewing inventory and numbers. It was then that I noticed the elastic band around Andy's wrist.

It was obvious that Andy was using the band as a reminder to stay in Synergist mode when necessary—during the inventory discussion he had quietly snapped it a couple of times. I smiled to myself, remembering his initial dismissal of the need for anything so mechanistic.

"I've done harder things than this," he said during one of our coaching sessions. "I don't think I need to use props to help me think Synergistically." I was pleased he'd decided in the end that using the elastic band for the first meeting couldn't hurt.

Now, however, something different was happening. Brendan, the senior v-p of marketing, was sharing his previous quarter's data—information Andy already knew in detail. Becoming increasingly bored, Andy, clearly struggling not to truncate the discussion, was flushed from repeated snapping of the band.

Slowly, everyone's attention moved from Brendan to Andy. It was clear Andy was moving back into Visionary mode and was about to do something to vent his frustration. I watched as his fingers slipped from the elastic band—no snap this time—and his calves stiffened as he began to stand up.

"I think this would be a great time for a comfort break!" said Joanne, from the other side of the room. "Why don't we take 15 minutes and be back here at 10:25?" A startled Brendan looked at Joanne—he'd been too engaged in delivering his presentation to notice Andy's building frustration—but the rest of the group nodded enthusiastically and lapsed gratefully into small talk and phone-checking. Andy, stranded halfway between standing and sitting, looked at Joanne, paused, and sat down again, smiling.

"Very good call," he said, his wide grin indicating that he knew full well what had almost happened.

"I'd never have done that before," Joanne said to me during the break. "We all just accepted Andy's behavior, and the Processor in me would have plowed on, hoping to just get through the meeting. Now it seems like a simple no-brainer."

"Working Synergistically cuts both ways," I replied. "Andy can only contribute part of the input to the team. You and the others need to keep doing what you just did—make interventions when he's finding it tough."

I wandered out to the hallway and saw Andy at the far end, finishing off a call on his cell. As he pocketed the phone, he mock-swept his brow. "That was close in there," he said, still grinning. "I was just about to stand up and take a little wander."

"No biggie," I said, smiling back, "the world wouldn't have ended—it'll take time for you to build the Synergist muscle. I'm just delighted Joanne saw what to do to help."

As the group reconvened and Brendan finished his part of the agenda, I noticed Andy was back in the zone—as were the rest of the team. For the rest of the morning they swept through item after item, cycling through the 3-I pattern, stumbling occasionally when one of the team members lapsed into a too-overt V, O, or P response at the wrong time—but mostly working together, albeit with the slightly self-aware choreography of a group doing something for the first time.

"You know, I never thought I'd be able to focus for that long on that amount of detail," said Andy, as we headed off for a celebratory lunch. "And I never thought we could be that productive," said Joanne. "That was undoubtedly the most effective meeting we've had in years."

They both had puzzled expressions on their faces as if what they had just said was a surprise to them.

"I suspect there's a connection between the two," I replied. "And it's only going to get stronger."

It looked ominous even from 50 feet away.

As I walked across the open-plan area toward Brad's office, I could see through the glass wall the four-person summit that was occurring around his conference table: Brad, his assistant Max, and the two people who last time I visited had upbraided Brad for his errant ways. Brad and Max were on one side of the table, facing the others. Car-park-guy had a large stack of folders in front of him, and burst-into-the-office lady seemed to be ticking something off on a giant spreadsheet.

As I got closer to Brad's office, he glanced up at me through the glass wall. But instead of the hangdog expression I expected from someone being put through the third degree, Brad grinned and made an "I'll only be a moment" gesture.

Grinning? I knew the mental anguish Brad went through every time he returned to the office. It's the relief of seeing me, I thought—he's happy because he can use our scheduled meeting as an excuse to escape.

Before I'd had a chance to sit down on the small visitor's sofa, the door to Brad's office opened. I could hear Brad speaking: "…turned out it was Iowa, not Oahu!" he bellowed, and the two visitors burst into surprised laughter. I knew the story, one of Brad's oldest and best.

"What's going on here?" I asked.

"Oh, you mean Judy and Alonzo?" said Brad, lifting his chin toward them as they exited the other side of the open-plan area. "Great folks. We get on really well together."

"Um, Brad, last time I saw you with each of them it looked like they were trying to set you on fire."

Brad wrinkled his brow. "Oh yeah," he said, after a moment. "That's right. They were a bit teed off with me last time you were here." He grinned. "Well, I've got you to thank for that. Operator Brad doesn't get on well with them, but Synergist Brad is their new best buddy."

"So that wasn't a grilling you were getting in there?"

Max looked over from where he was clearing away the residue of the meeting. "Les!" He grinned his broad toothy smile. "Don't you know we've gone all proactive now?" He strolled over to where Brad and I were standing, both he and Brad sporting an expression of some smugness.

"So tell me about it," I said. "What's with the meeting, and what's with the endless grinning from you two?"

I'd known from our coaching sessions that Brad was struggling to learn the Synergist style—not unusual for an Operator—and that although he'd made great progress, last time we'd talked he'd been unhappy with how often he had "dropped the ball" as he put it, and slipped from Synergist into Operator mode at inappropriate moments.

"So," said Brad, "you know I've been struggling with the Operator-Synergist thing," he said, looking up at me for a confirmatory nod. "Well, strange thing. On a whim I got Max here to take your styles quiz." He looked sideways at Max and smiled—again. "Turns out the kid's a natural Synergist." Brad raised his eyebrows at me as if he was letting me work out the rest.

"I think I can work out the rest," I said. "With Max around, he's taking some of the Synergist load off you, and he helps you stay in Synergist mode more often when you need to."

"Bingo!" said Brad. "It's ten times easier when Max is around, 'cause he sees all the warning signals flashing before I do. Like these guys—Judy and Alonzo.

It was Max's idea to have this meeting every month to plan ahead—get everything in place for my sales trips rather than have me—um—improvise and apologize later."

"And we do the same with Carla and Tony," said Max, chiming in enthusiastically. "I got Brad set up for meetings with each of them every other week."

I shot a look at Brad—every two weeks? This was impressive.

"It's only 30, 40 minutes at the most," continued Max, "and Brad can do it by webcam from the road." Brad took over the storyline: "We've cut Carla and Tony's memos down to about a tenth of what they used to be, and Max conferences into the call so he can follow up with the paperwork and any other stuff that needs to be done as a result."

"Wow—that's impressive," I said. Max nodded and wandered back to finish clearing the conference table. I steered Brad out of Max's earshot. "So what about the 'Carla and Tony are driving me nuts so I'm leaving' thing. How's that going?"

Brad motioned to the sofa and we both sat down. "Turns out you were right. I was contributing to the whole thing much more than I ever imagined. I suppose the Operator in me had just gotten out of control, and I was avoiding interacting with them each so much, that they responded in the only way they knew how—Tony with his notes and memos, and Carla with her big ideas."

I nodded. "And what about the future—is this just a truce between the three of you, or have you moved past that?" Brad stood up as he replied. "Oh no, we're way past a truce. Things aren't perfect—probably never can be—but with your coaching all three of us can use the Synergist style now, and our meetings are generally great. You wanna get lunch?"

"Sure," I said. "Mexican?" "Sure," Brad echoed. "I'll go get Max."

"I think that's one of the bravest professional gambles I've ever seen anyone take. I hope this doesn't sound patronizing, but I'm really proud of you both."

I was sitting with Riya and Brianna in one corner of a vast ballroom, surrounded by the detritus of their company's just-completed annual shareholder's meeting. Behind us, audiovisual technicians were carting massive black boxes from place to place. Their schedules were such that this was the only time we had for a debriefing—one I was very anxious to have.

Just 90 days earlier we had concluded six months of Synergist coaching with Riya, Brianna, and Riya's other direct reports—and all three of us were feeling glum at the results. While every other combination of people in the group had benefited from the coaching—some immeasurably so—we'd failed to move the needle on the interaction between Riya and Brianna.

"I get the Synergist thing," Riya had told me, "and it has really made a difference for me with everyone else. But with Brianna the difference is barely noticeable. It's like nothing has changed." Brianna had said precisely the same thing in her own words, and even after I explained to them that the Visionary-Processor relationship was the hardest one to make work—even after they had transformed into a Visionary+Synergist and Processor+Synergist, it was clear that they were both enormously deflated.

"It's not just the two of us, it's undercutting the team as whole," Riya had confided in me. "With the coaching, I can tell we're on the brink of a massive breakthrough as a team—I've seen glimpses of us performing at a level we've never reached before, and it's very powerful. But then something either I or Brianna says or does sparks the Visionary or Processor in the other, and we get bounced out of Synergist mode."

I could tell that Riya in particular was not just frustrated; she was bewildered. Three people in the same post in a short time, and now she was looking at her third relational failure in a row. So when she had called me a few days later, I was half expecting the news that she'd reluctantly decided to let Brianna go. Instead, she'd shared a plan that seemed audaciously bold.

"We're going to job-swap," Riya had told me. "For a month. We'll spend the next six weeks planning for it—briefing our assistants, shadowing each other for a while, letting key people know in advance. Then we're going to do each other's job for one month and see what we discover. I've discussed it with the COO, and he's okay with it."

It had been Brianna's idea. "It seems to me there's something about what we each have to do from day to day that the other is entirely failing to understand," she had explained to me. "And I don't think—to be honest—that my Processor self really cares to understand. But the Synergist in me cares deeply. As part of the enterprise commitment—for the sake of the organization as a whole—I want to get a sense of what Riya does every day so I can better understand it, and perhaps I can then use that understanding to be a better Synergist."

Six weeks later they had started their experiment, and I hadn't heard from them since—until now, three weeks after the job-sharing had ended.

"So," I said, trying to hide the anxiety in my voice. "How'd it work out? Has it helped at all?"

The two women looked at each other, checking to see which of them would respond. I discovered I was holding my breath.

"Pretty darn good," said Riya, looking to Brianna and receiving a confirmatory nod. "We just had our second team meeting since we finished the job swap, and we made it the whole way through the agenda for the first time I can remember."

"And not just, you know—tick, tick, tick," said Brianna, miming the ticking off of agenda items. "We used the 3-I pattern the entire time and made really good decisions." She smiled over at Riya. "And no bickering."

Riya leaned over and handed me a slim file. "I know you like case studies. I made a few notes of what I think happened during the job swap, and Brianna has added her thoughts. Long story short: it was fine for us both to have learned the Synergist role—vital, in fact. But we are both in jobs that demand such a high level of our natural style from each of us that we were each bringing much more V and P into the team meetings than the other could cope with."

Brianna took over the debriefing. "We understand enough now about what the other has to do each day that it doesn't bother us so much. And we've learned not to go into team meetings directly after doing something very V or P. We've each learned to decompress first. It allows the Synergist in us to come to the fore much more easily."

"And the rest of the team?" I knew that many on Riya's team had been disconcerted by the obvious dysfunction between her and Brianna.

Riya stood up—she had warned me that their schedule was tight and we wouldn't have long to talk. "We're meeting in 45 minutes," she said. "Big decision to make about next year's marketing budget. And that shareholder meeting"—she nodded into the body of the ballroom—"had me in full V mode, so I'm going to grab a coffee and doughnut and decompress."

Brianna looked at her watch and smiled. "And I think I can fit in a quick visit to the gym."

ACKNOWLEDGMENTS

THIS BOOK COULDN'T HAVE BEEN WRITTEN without the willing (and sometimes unwilling) collaboration of the many thousands of Visionaries, Operators, Processors, and Synergists who I've had the privilege of working with during the past 35 years. To you all, my (genuinely) humble thanks. I have truly learned more from you than you ever could from me.

There are countless books on the topic of management and leadership styles and many accomplished thought leaders who have paved the way in the field of successful teamwork. I owe a debt of gratitude to all of them and stand on their shoulders.

My agent, the urbane and quietly exceptional Herb Schaffner, together with the team at Palgrave Macmillan led by my wise editor, Laurie Harting, brought the book into being.

Julie Wilson, founder and executive director of the Institute for the Future of Learning (and amazingly, somehow, my wife), found time during the launch of her own substantial enterprise to provide more support than any author deserves. I look forward to repaying her in kind as she continues her groundbreaking work in revolutionizing education.

APPENDIX

Implementing the Synergist in Your Organization or Team

If you'd like to implement the Synergist principles in your organization or team, the outline on the following page shows the sequential steps involved.

For more help in becoming a Synergist or with developing a Synergistic team, point your web browser to http://PredictableSuccess.com/syn-appendix.

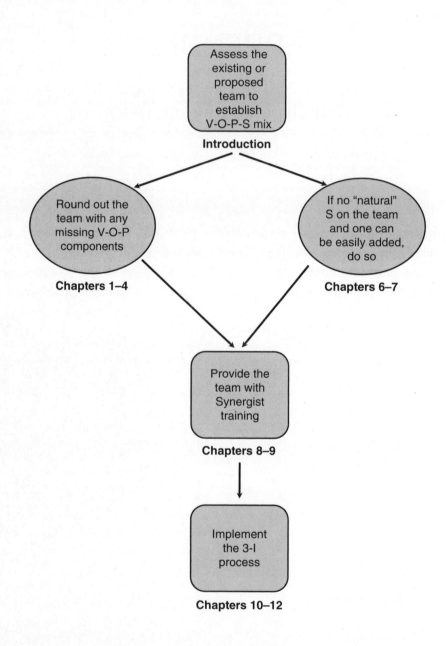

Assess the existing or proposed team to establish V-O-P-S mix
Introduction

Round out the team with any missing V-O-P components
Chapters 1–4

If no "natural" S on the team and one can be easily added, do so
Chapters 6–7

Provide the team with Synergist training
Chapters 8–9

Implement the 3-I process
Chapters 10–12

INDEX